Resource Economics

Resource Economics is a text for students with a background in calculus and intermediate microeconomics and a familiarity with the spreadsheet software Excel. The book covers basic concepts, shows how to set up spreadsheets to solve dynamic allocation problems, and presents economic models for fisheries, forestry, nonrenewable resources, stock pollutants, option value, and sustainable development. Within the text, numerical examples are posed and solved using Excel's Solver. These problems help make concepts operational, develop economic intuition, and serve as a bridge to the study of real-world problems of resource management.

Jon M. Conrad is Professor of Resource Economics at Cornell University. He taught at the University of Massachusetts, Amherst, from 1973 to 1977 before joining the Cornell faculty in 1978. His research interests focus on the use of dynamic optimization techniques to manage natural resources and environmental quality. He has published articles in *The Journal of Political Economy, The Quarterly Journal of Economics, The American Journal of Agricultural Economics, The Canadian Journal of Economics, Land Economics, Marine Resource Economics, Biomathematics, Ecological Economics,* and *The Journal of Environmental Economics and Management,* for which he served as an associate editor. He is the coauthor with Colin Clark of the text *Natural Resource Economics: Notes and Problems* (Cambridge University Press, 1987).

Resource Economics

JON M. CONRAD
Cornell University

CAMBRIDGE
UNIVERSITY PRESS

PUBLISHED BY THE PRESS SYNDICATE OF THE UNIVERSITY OF CAMBRIDGE
The Pitt Building, Trumpington Street, Cambridge, United Kingdom

CAMBRIDGE UNIVERSITY PRESS
The Edinburgh Building, Cambridge CB2 2RU, UK   www.cup.cam.ac.uk
40 West 20th Street, New York, NY 10011-4211, USA   www.cup.org
10 Stamford Road, Oakleigh, Melbourne 3166, Australia
Ruiz de Alarcón 13, 28014 Madrid, Spain

© Jon M. Conrad 1999

First published 1999

Printed in the United States of America

Typeface Times Roman 10/12 pt.   *System* QuarkXPress [BTS]

A catalog record for this book is available from the British Library.

Library of Congress Cataloging-in-Publication Data
Conrad, Jon M.

Resource economics / Jon M. Conrad.

p. cm.

Includes index.

ISBN 0-521-64012-1. – ISBN 0-521-64974-9 (pbk.)

1. Natural resources – Management – Mathematical models.
2. Resource allocation – Mathematical models.   3. Microsoft Excel
(Computer file) I. Title.
HC59. 15. C656   1999   98–49529
333.7 – dc21   CIP

ISBN 0 521 64012 1 hardback
ISBN 0 521 64974 9 paperback

Contents

For Janice, Andrew, and Ben

Preface

This book was written for students seeking an intermediate-level text in resource economics. It presumes that students have had differential calculus and intermediate microeconomics. It is designed to bridge the gap between texts which require only introductory economics and those which require graduate microeconomics and advanced methods of dynamic optimization such as the maximum principle and dynamic programming.

This text employs first-order difference equations to describe the change in a resource as it is harvested or extracted. Resource management is cast as a problem of optimal allocation over time, or dynamic optimization. The method of Lagrange multipliers is introduced to pose such problems conceptually and to examine the conditions that optimal management must satisfy. The unique and ideally appealing feature of this text is the use of Microsoft Excel Spreadsheet and Solver, a nonlinear programming algorithm within Excel, to solve numerical problems. Numerical problems help students see the dynamic trade-offs inherent in resource management and serve as a bridge from a general model to an empirical study of a real-world resource management problem. A familiarity with Excel is helpful but not essential. Chapter 2 introduces the student to Excel and shows how spreadsheets might be set up so that Solver can determine the optimal extraction of a nonrenewable resource or the optimal harvest of a renewable resource. By working through the examples in the text and the exercises at the end of each chapter the student will develop a feel and economic intuition for dynamic allocation problems along with an ability to solve and interpret numerical optimization problems.

The introductory chapter on basic concepts and Chapter 2 on solving numerical problems are followed by four chapters which develop economic models for the management of fisheries, forests, nonrenewable resources, and stock pollutants. Chapter 7 reviews the basic concepts in cost–benefit analysis on the way to a discussion of option value and the evaluation of decisions that are risky and irreversible. Chapter 8 explores the concept of sustainable development from several perspectives.

Following Chapter 8 is an annotated Bibliography of the topics covered in Chapters 1–8.

Policies which might improve the management of real-world resources are also examined. These policies include the use of individual transferable quotas in fisheries, the public acquisition of old-growth forest, emission taxes, and pollution permits. By working through the optimization problems first, the student will have a firm understanding of the role shadow prices play in optimal allocation. It is then easier to understand how policies which can introduce shadow prices into markets where they are absent are more likely to improve resource allocation than policies which ignore the motives and behavior of firms or individuals who harvest natural resources or generate residual wastes.

I would like to thank Jon Erickson and Chris Cole for their thorough reading of an earlier draft, checking the spreadsheets in the text and the answers to the numerical exercises at the end of each chapter.

CHAPTER 1

Basic Concepts

1.0   Renewable, Nonrenewable, and Environmental Resources

Economics might be defined as the study of how society allocates scarce resources. The field of resource economics would then be the study of how society allocates scarce natural resources such as stocks of fish, stands of trees, fresh water, oil, and other naturally occurring resources. A distinction is sometimes made between resource and environmental economics, where the latter field is concerned with the way wastes are disposed of and the resulting quality of air, water, and soil serving as waste receptors. In addition, environmental economics is concerned with the conservation of natural environments and biodiversity.

Natural resources are often categorized as being renewable or nonrenewable. A renewable resource must display a significant rate of growth or renewal on a relevant economic time scale. An economic time scale is a time interval for which planning and management are meaningful. The notion of an economic time scale can make the classification of natural resources a bit tricky. For example, how should we classify a stand of old-growth coast redwood or an aquifer with an insignificant rate of recharge? Whereas the redwood tree is a plant, and can be grown commercially, old-growth redwoods may be 800 to 1,000 years old, and their remaining stands might be more appropriately viewed as a nonrenewable resource. Whereas the water cycle provides precipitation that will replenish lakes and streams, the water contained in an aquifer with little or no recharge might be more economically similar to a pool of oil (a nonrenewable resource) than to a lake or reservoir that receives significant recharge from rain or melting snow.

A critical question in the allocation of natural resources is "How much of the resource should be harvested (extracted) today?" Finding the "best" allocation of natural resources over time can be regarded as a dynamic optimization problem. In such problems it is common to try to maximize some measure of net economic value, over some future horizon, subject to the dynamics of the harvested resource and any other relevant constraints. The solution to the dynamic optimization of a natural resource would be a schedule or "time path" indicating the optimal amount to be harvested (extracted) in each period. The optimal rate of harvest or extraction in a particular period may be zero. For example, if a fish stock has been historically mismanaged, and the current stock is below what is deemed optimal, then zero harvest (a moratorium on fishing) may be best until the stock recovers to a size at which a positive level of harvest is optimal.

Aspects of natural resource allocation are depicted in Figure 1.1. On the right-hand side (RHS) of this figure we depict an ocean containing a stock of fish. The fish stock at the beginning of period t is denoted by the variable X_t, measured in metric tons. In each period the level of net growth depends on the size of the fish stock and is given by the function $F(X_t)$. We will postpone a detailed discussion of the properties of $F(X_t)$ until Chapter 3. For now, simply assume that if the fish stock is bounded by some "environmental carrying capacity," denoted K, so that $K \geq X_t \geq 0$, then $F(X_t)$ might be increasing as X_t goes from a low level to where $F(X_t)$ reaches a maximum sustainable yield (MSY) at X_{MSY}, and then $F(X_t)$ declines as X_t goes from X_{MSY} to K. Let Y_t denote the rate of harvest, also measured in metric tons, and assume that net growth occurs before harvest. Then, the change in the fish stock, going from period t to period $t + 1$, is the difference $X_{t+1} - X_t$ and is given by the difference equation

$$X_{t+1} - X_t = F(X_t) - Y_t \tag{1.1}$$

Note, if harvest exceeds net growth [$Y_t > F(X_t)$], the fish stock declines ($X_{t+1} - X_t < 0$), and if harvest is less than net growth [$Y_t < F(X_t)$], the fish stock increases ($X_{t+1} - X_t > 0$).

During period t, harvest, Y_t, flows to the economy, where it yields a net benefit to various firms and individuals. The stock left in the ocean forms the inventory at the beginning of the next period: i.e., X_{t+1}. This future stock also conveys a benefit to the economy, because it provides the basis for future growth, and it is often the case that larger stocks will lower the cost of future harvest. Thus, implicit in the harvest decision is a balancing of current net benefit from Y_t and future benefit that a slightly larger X_{t+1} would provide the economy.

On the left-hand side (LHS) of Figure 1.1 we show an equation describing the dynamics of a nonrenewable resource. The stock of extractable ore in period t is denoted by R_t and the current rate of extraction by q_t. With no growth or renewal the stock in period $t + 1$ is simply the stock in period t less the amount extracted in period t, so $R_{t+1} = R_t - q_t$. The amount extracted also flows into the economy, where it generates net benefits, but in contrast to harvest from the fish stock, consumption of the nonrenewable resource generates a residual waste, αq_t, propor-

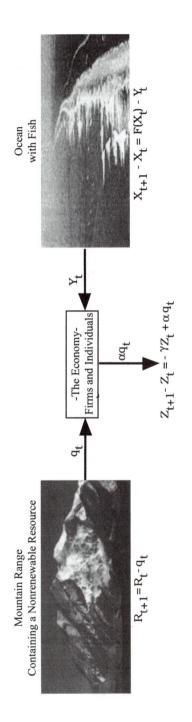

Mountain Range
Containing a Nonrenewable Resource

$R_{t+1} = R_t - q_t$

q_t

-The Economy-
Firms and Individuals

αq_t

$Z_{t+1} - Z_t = -\gamma Z_t + \alpha q_t$

Y_t

Ocean
with Fish

$X_{t+1} - X_t = F(X_t) - Y_t$

X_t = stock of fish in year t
Y_t = harvest of fish in year t
$F(X_t)$ = a net growth function

Key

R_t = the stock of the nonrenewable resource in year t
q_t = the rate of production from nonrenewable resource in year t
αq_t = the flow of waste from q_t, $1 > \alpha > 0$
Z_t = the stock of accumulated waste
γZ_t = the rate of waste decomposition, $1 > \gamma > 0$

Figure 1.1. Renewable, Nonrenewable, and Environmental Resources

tional to the rate of extraction ($1 > \alpha > 0$). For example, if R_t were a deposit of coal (measured in metric tons) and q_t were the number of tons extracted and burned in period t, then αq_t might be the tons of CO_2 or SO_2 emerging from the smokestacks of utilities or foundries.

This residual waste can accumulate as a stock pollutant, denoted Z_t. If the rate at which the pollutant is generated, αq_t, exceeds the rate at which it is assimilated (or decomposed), $-\gamma Z_t$, the stock pollutant will increase, ($Z_{t+1} - Z_t > 0$), whereas if the rate of generation is less than assimilation, then the stock will decrease. The parameter γ is called the assimilation or degradation coefficient, where $1 > \gamma > 0$. Not shown in Figure 1.1 are the consequences of different levels of Z_t. Presumably there would be some social or external cost imposed on the economy (society). This is sometimes represented through a damage function, $D(Z_t)$. Damage functions will be discussed in greater detail in Chapter 6.

If the economy is represented by the box in Figure 1.1, then the natural environment, surrounding the economy, can be thought of as providing a flow of renewable and nonrenewable resources, and also various media for the disposal of unwanted (negatively valued) wastes. Missing from Figure 1.1, however, is one additional service, usually referred to as *amenity value*. A wilderness, a pristine stretch of beach, or a lake with "swimmable" water quality provides individuals in the economy with places for observation of flora and fauna, relaxation, and recreation that are fundamentally different from comparable services provided at a city zoo, an exclusive beach hotel, or a backyard swimming pool. The amenity value provided by various natural environments may critically depend on the location and rate of resource extraction and waste disposal. Thus, the optimal rates of harvest, extraction, and disposal should take into account any reduction in amenity values. In general, current net benefit from, say, Y_t or q_t, must be balanced with the discounted future costs from reduced resource stocks, X_{t+1} and R_{t+1}, and any reduction in amenity values caused by harvest, extraction, or disposal of associated wastes.

1.1   Discounting

When attempting to determine the optimal allocation of natural resources over time one immediately confronts the issue of "time preference." Most individuals exhibit a preference for receiving benefits now, as opposed to receiving the same level of benefits at a later date. Such individuals are said to have a positive time preference. In order to induce these individuals to save (thus providing funds for investment), an interest payment or premium, over and above the amount borrowed, must be offered. A society composed of individuals with positive time prefer-ences will typically develop "markets for loanable funds" (capital markets) where the interest rates which emerge are like prices and reflect, in part, society's underlying time preference.

An individual with a positive time preference will discount the value of a note or contract which promises to pay a fixed amount of money at some future date. For example, a bond which promises to pay $10,000 10 years from now is not worth $10,000 today in a society of individuals with positive time preferences. Suppose you own such a bond. What could you get for it if you wished to sell it today? The answer will depend on the credit rating (trustworthiness) of the government or corporation promis-ing to make the payment, the expectation of inflation, and the taxes that would be paid on the interest income. Suppose the payment will be made with certainty, there is no expectation of inflation, and there is no tax on earned interest. Then, the bond payment would be discounted by a rate that would approximate society's "pure" rate of time preference. We will denote this rate by the symbol δ, and simply refer to it as the *discount rate*. The risk of default (nonpayment), the expectation of inflation, or the presence of taxes on earned interest would raise private market rates of interest above the discount rate. (Why?)

If the discount rate were 3%, so $\delta = 0.03$, then the "discount factor" is defined as $\rho = 1/(1 + \delta) = 1/(1 + 0.03) \approx 0.97$. The present value of a $10,000 payment made 10 years from now would be $10,000/(1 + \delta)^{10} = \$10,000\rho^{10} \approx \$7,441$. This should be the amount of money you would get for your bond if you wished to sell it today. Note that the amount $7,441 is also the amount you would need to invest at a rate of 3%, compounded annu-ally, to have $10,000 10 years from now.

The present-value calculation for a single payment can be generalized to a future stream of payments in a straightforward fashion. Let N_t denote a payment made in year t. Suppose these payments are made over the horizon $t = 0, 1, 2, \ldots, T$, where $t = 0$ is the current year (period) and $t = T$ is the last year (or terminal period). The present value of this stream of payments can be calculated by adding up the present value of each individual payment. We can represent this calculation mathematically as

$$N = \sum_{t=0}^{t=T} \rho^t N_t \tag{1.2}$$

Suppose that $N_0 = 0$ and $N_t = A$ for $t = 1, 2, \ldots, \infty$. In this case we have a bond which promises to pay A dollars every year, from next year until the end of time. Such a bond is called a perpetuity, and with $1 > \rho > 0$, when $\delta > 0$, equation (1.2) becomes an infinite geometric progression which converges to $N = A/\delta$. This special result might be used to approximate the value of certain long-lived projects or the decision to preserve a natural environment for all future generations. For example, if a proposed park were estimated to provide $A = \$10$ million in annual net benefits into the indefinite future, it would have a present value of \$500 million at $\delta = 0.02$.

The preceding examples presume that time can be partitioned into discrete periods (for example, years). In some resource allocation problems, it is useful to treat time as a continuous variable, where the future horizon becomes the interval $T \geq t \geq 0$. Recall the formula for compound interest. It says that if A dollars is put in the bank at interest rate δ, and compounded m times over a horizon of length T, then the value at the end of the horizon will be given by

$$V(T) = A(1+\delta/m)^{mT} = A\left[(1+\delta/m)^{m/\delta}\right]^{\delta T} = A\left[(1+1/n)^{n}\right]^{\delta T} \quad (1.3)$$

where $n = m/\delta$. If interest is compounded continuously, both m and n tend to infinity and $[1 + 1/n]^{n}$ tends to e, the base of the natural logarithm. This implies $V(T) = A\ e^{\delta T}$. Note that $A = V(T)e^{-\delta T}$ becomes the present value of a promise to pay $V(T)$ at $t = T$ (from the perspective of $t = 0$). Thus, the continuous-time discount factor for a payment at instant t is $e^{-\delta t}$, and the present value of a continuous stream of payments $N(t)$ is calculated as

$$N = \int_0^T N(t)e^{-\delta t}\,dt \quad (1.4)$$

If $N(t) = A$ (a constant) and if $T \to \infty$, equation (1.4) can be integrated directly to yield $N = A/\delta$, which is interpreted as the present value of an asset which pays A dollars in each and every instant into the indefinite future.

Our discussion of discounting and present value has focused on the mathematics of making present-value calculations. The practice of discounting has an important ethical dimension, particularly with regard to the way resources are harvested over time, the evaluation of investments or policies to protect the environment, and more generally the way the current generation weights the welfare and options of future generations.

In financial markets the practice of discounting might be justified by society's positive time preference and by the economy's need to allocate scarce investment funds to firms which have expected returns that equal or exceed the appropriate rate of discount. To ignore the time preferences of individuals and to replace competitive capital markets by the decisions of some savings/investment czar would likely lead to inefficiencies, a reduction in the output and wealth generated by the economy, and the oppression of what many individuals regard as a fundamental economic right. The commodity prices and interest rates which emerge from competitive markets are highly efficient in allocating resources toward those economic activities which are demanded by the individuals with purchasing power.

Although the efficiency of competitive markets in determining the allocation of labor and capital is widely accepted, there remain questions about discounting and the appropriate rate of discount when allocating natural resources over time or investing in environmental quality. Basically the interest rates that emerge from capital markets reflect society's underlying rate of discount, the riskiness of a particular asset or portfolio, and the prospect of general inflation. These factors, as already noted, tend to raise market rates of interest above the discount rate.

Estimates of the discount rate in the United States have ranged between 2% and 5%. This rate will vary across cultures at a point in time and within a culture over time. A society's discount rate would in theory reflect its collective "sense of immediacy" and its general level of development. A society where time is of the essence or where a large fraction of the populace is on the brink of starvation would presumably have a higher rate of discount.

As we will see in subsequent chapters, higher discount rates tend to favor more rapid depletion of nonrenewable resources and lower stock levels for renewable resources. High discount rates can make investments to improve or protect environmental quality unattractive when compared to alternative investments in the private sector. High rates of discount will greatly reduce the value of harvesting decisions or investments that have a preponderance of their benefits in the distant future. Recall that a single payment of $10,000 in 10 years had a present value of $7,441 at $\delta = 0.03$. If the discount rate increases to $\delta = 0.10$, its present value drops to $3,855. If the payment of $10,000 would not be made until 100 years into the future, it would have a present value of only $520 at $\delta = 0.03$ and the minuscule value of $0.72 (72 cents) if $\delta = 0.10$.

The exponential nature of discounting has the effect of weighting near-term benefits much more heavily than benefits in the distant future. If 75 years were the life span of a single generation, and if that generation had absolute discretion over resource use and a discount rate of $\delta = 0.10$, then the weight attached to the welfare of the next generation would be similarly minuscule. Such a situation could lead the current generation to throw one long, extravagant, resource-depleting party that left subsequent generations with an impoverished inventory of natural resources, a polluted environment, and very few options to change their economic destiny.

There are some who would view the current mélange of resource and environmental problems as being precisely the result of tyrannical and selfish decisions by recent generations. Such a characterization would not be fair or accurate. Although many renewable resources have been mismanaged (such as marine fisheries and tropical rain forest), and various nonrenewable resources may have been depleted too rapidly (oil reserves in the United States), the process, though nonoptimal, has generated both physical and human capital in the form of buildings, a housing stock, highways and public infrastructure, modern agriculture, and the advancement of science and technology. These also benefit and have expanded the choices open to future generations. Further, any single generation is usually closely "linked" to the two generations which preceded it and the two generations which will follow. The current generation has historically made sacrifices in their immediate well-being to provide for parents, children, and grandchildren. Although intergenerational altruism may not be obvious in the functioning of financial markets, it is more obvious in the way we have collectively tried to regulate the use of natural resources and the quality of the environment. Our policies have not always been effective, but their motivation seems to derive from a sincere concern for future generations.

Determining the "best" endowment of human and natural capital to leave future generations is made difficult because we do not know what they will need or want. Some recommend that if we err, we should err on the side of leaving more natural resources and undisturbed natural environments. By saving them now we derive certain amenity benefits and preserve the options to harvest or develop in the future.

The process of discounting, to the extent that it reflects a stable time preference across a succession of generations is probably appropriate when managing natural resources and environmental quality for the maximum benefit of an ongoing society. Improving the well-being of the current generation is a part of an ongoing process seeking to improve the human condition. And when measured in terms of infant mortality, caloric intake, and life expectancy, successive generations have been made better off.

Nothing in the preceeding discussion helps us in determining the precise rate of discount which should be used for a particular natural resource or environmental project. In the analysis in future chapters we will explore the sensitivity of harvest and extraction rates, forest rotations, and rates of waste disposal to different rates of discount. This will enable us to get a numerical feel for the significance of discounting.

1.2 A Discrete-Time Extension of the Method of Lagrange Multipliers

In subsequent chapters we will encounter many problems where we wish to maximize some measure of economic value subject to resource dynamics. Such problems can often be viewed as special cases of a more general dynamic optimization problem. The method of Lagrange multipliers is a technique for solving constrained optimization problems. It is regularly used to solve static allocation problems, but it can be extended to solve dynamic problems as well. We will work through the mathematics of a general problem in this section. In Chapter 2 we will show how numerical problems can be posed and solved using Excel's Solver. Chapters 3–8 will examine how these problems arise when seeking to maximize the net value from renewable and nonrenewable resources, the control of stock pollutants, risky investment, and the selection of activities which might promote sustainable development.

Let X_t denote a physical measure of the size or amount of some resource in period t. In a fishery X_t might represent the number of metric tons of some (commercially valued) species. In a forest it may represent the volume of standing (merchantable) timber.

Let Y_t denote the level of harvest, measured in the same units as X_t. For renewable resources we will frequently assume that resource dynamics can be represented by the first-order difference equation (1.1). In that equation $X_{t+1} - X_t = F(X_t) - Y_t$, where $F(X_t)$ was the net growth function for the resource. It assumed that the net growth from period t to period $t + 1$ was a function of resource abundance in period t. We will assume that the net growth function has continuous first- and second-order derivatives. The current resource stock is represented by the initial condition, X_0, denoting the stock at $t = 0$.

The net benefits from resource abundance and harvest in period t are denoted by π_t and given by the function $\pi_t = \pi(X_t, Y_t)$, which is also assumed to have continuous first- and second-order derivatives. Higher levels of harvest of the resource stock will normally yield higher net benefits. The resource stock, X_t, may enter the net benefit function because a larger stock conveys cost savings during search and harvest, or because an intrinsic value is placed on the resource itself.

It is common practice to compare different harvest strategies, say $Y_{1,t}$ to $Y_{2,t}$, by computing the present value of the net benefits that they produce. Note from equation (1.1) that different harvest strategies will result in different time-paths for the resource stock, X_t. Suppose $Y_{1,t}$ results in $X_{1,t}$ and $Y_{2,t}$ results in $X_{2,t}$, and we wish to calculate present value over the horizon $t = 0, 1, 2, \ldots, T$. As in the previous section we will denote the discount factor by $\rho = 1/(1 + \delta)$, where δ is called the periodic rate of discount. In this problem we will assume a constant, time-invariant rate of discount, which implies that the discount factor is also time-invariant. It is not difficult to allow for changes in the discount rate over time. You would, however, need to be able to predict the future values for this rate.

The present value comparison for the preceding two harvest strategies would require a comparison of

$$\sum_{t=0}^{T} \rho^t \pi(X_{1,t}, Y_{1,t}) \quad \text{with} \quad \sum_{t=0}^{T} \rho^t \pi(X_{2,t}, Y_{2,t})$$

In the first summation we are calculating the present value of the harvest schedule $Y_{1,t}$ and the resulting biomass levels, $X_{1,t}$. We would want to know if this summation is greater than, less than, or equal to the present value calculation for the second harvest schedule, $Y_{2,t}$, which results in $X_{2,t}$.

Frequently we will seek the "best" harvest policy: that is, a harvest strategy that maximizes the present value of net benefits. Candidate harvest strategies must also satisfy equation (1.1) describing resource dynamics. Mathematically we wish to find the harvest schedule, Y_t, which will

$$\text{Maximize} \quad \pi = \sum_{t=0}^{T} \rho^t \pi(X_t, Y_t)$$

$$\text{Subject to} \quad X_{t+1} - X_t = F(X_t) - Y_t$$

$$X_0 \text{ Given}$$

Thus, the objective is to maximize π, the present value of net benefits, subject to the equation describing resource dynamics and the initial condition, X_0.

There are likely to be an infinite number of feasible harvest strategies. How can we find the optimal Y_t? Will it be unique? If $T \rightarrow \infty$, will it ever be the case, after some transition period, that the level of harvest and the resource stock are unchanging through time and the system attains a "steady state"? These are difficult but important questions. Let's take them one at a time.

Recall from calculus that when seeking the extremum (maximum, minimum, or inflection point) of a single variable function, a necessary condition requires that the first derivative of the function, when evaluated at a candidate extremum, be equal to zero. Our optimization problem is more complex because we have to determine the $T + 1$ values for Y_t which maximize π, and we have constraints in the form of our first-order difference equation and the initial condition X_0. We can, however, follow a similar procedure after forming the appropriate Lagrangian expression for our problem. This is done by introducing a set of new variables, denoted λ_t, called Lagrange multipliers. In general, every variable defined by a difference equation will have an associated Lagrange multiplier. This means that X_t will be associated with λ_t, X_{t+1} will be associated with λ_{t+1}, and so on. It will turn out that the new variables, λ_t, will have an important economic interpretation. They are also called "shadow prices" because their value indicates the marginal value of an incremental increase in X_t in period t.

We form the Lagrangian expression by writing the difference equation in implicit form, $X_t + F(X_t) - Y_t - X_{t+1} = 0$, premultiplying it by ρ^{t+1} λ_{t+1}, and then adding all such products to the objective function. The Lagrangian expression for our problem takes the form

$$L = \sum_{t=0}^{T} \rho^t \{\pi(X_t, Y_t) + \rho\lambda_{t+1}[X_t + F(X_t) - Y_t - X_{t+1}]\} \tag{1.5}$$

The rationale behind writing the Lagrangian this way is as follows: Since the Lagrange multipliers are interpreted as shadow prices which measure the value of an additional unit of the resource, we can think of the difference equation, written implicitly, as defining the level of X_{t+1} that will be available in period $t + 1$. The value of an additional (marginal) unit of X_{t+1} in period $t + 1$ is λ_{t+1}. This value is discounted one period, by ρ, to put it on the same present-value basis as the net benefits in period t. Thus, the expression in the curly brackets, $\{\bullet\}$, is the sum of net benefits in period t and the discounted value of the resource stock (biomass) in period $t + 1$. This sum is then discounted back to the present by ρ^t and similar expressions are summed over all periods.

After forming the Lagrangian expression we proceed to take a series of first-order partial derivatives and set them equal to zero. Collectively they define the first-order necessary conditions, analogous to the first-order condition for a single-variable function. They will be used in solving for the optimal levels of Y_t, X_t, and λ_t in transition and, if $T \to \infty$, at a steady state, if one exists. For our problem the necessary conditions require

$$\frac{\partial L}{\partial Y_t} = \rho^t \{\partial\pi(\bullet)/\partial Y_t - \rho\lambda_{t+1}\} = 0 \tag{1.6}$$

$$\frac{\partial L}{\partial X_t} = \rho^t \{\partial\pi(\bullet)/\partial X_t + \rho\lambda_{t+1}[1 + F'(\bullet)]\} - \rho^t\lambda_t = 0 \tag{1.7}$$

$$\frac{\partial L}{\partial[\rho\lambda_{t+1}]} = \rho^t \{X_t + F(X_t) - Y_t - X_{t+1}\} = 0 \tag{1.8}$$

The partial of the Lagrangian with respect to X_t may seem a bit puzzling. When we examine the Lagrangian and the representative term in period t, we observe X_t as an argument of the net benefit function $\pi(X_t, Y_t)$, by itself, and as the sole argument in the net growth function, $F(X_t)$. These partials appear in the brackets $\{\bullet\}$ in equation (1.7). Where did the last term, $-\rho'\lambda_t$, come from? If we think of the Lagrangian as a long sum of expressions, and if we wish to take the partial with respect to X_t, we need to find all the terms involving X_t. When we back up one period, from t to $t - 1$, most of the terms are subscripted $t - 1$, with the notable exception of the last term, which becomes $-\rho'\lambda_t X_t$, with partial derivative $-\rho'\lambda_t$.

In addition to equations (1.6)–(1.8), which hold for $t = 0, 1, \ldots, T$, there are two boundary conditions. The first is simply the initial condition that X_0 is known and given. To make things more concrete, suppose $X_0 = A$, where A is a known, positive constant. The second boundary condition for this problem is a condition on λ_{T+1}. Recall that the Lagrange multipliers were to be interpreted as shadow prices. Thus, λ_{T+1} would be the marginal value of one more unit of X_{T+1}. Let's suppose we are free to choose λ_{T+1} as some nonnegative number B, so that $\lambda_{T+1} = B \geq 0$. Then, along with $X_0 = A$ and $\lambda_{T+1} = B$, equations (1.6)–(1.8) can be thought of as a system of $(3T + 5)$ equations in $(3T + 5)$ unknowns. The unknowns are the optimal values for $Y_t, t = 0, 1, \ldots, T, X_t, t = 0, 1, \ldots, T + 1$, and $\lambda_t, t = 0, 1, \ldots, T + 1$.

Equations (1.6)–(1.8) are likely to be nonlinear; this means there could be more than one solution. It is also possible that there could be no solution in the sense that there is no set of values Y_t, X_t, λ_t which simultaneously solve (1.6)–(1.8) and the boundary conditions. It is possible to impose some curvature assumptions on $\pi(\bullet)$ and $F(\bullet)$ which will guarantee a unique solution for $A > 0$ and $B \geq 0$. The details of these conditions are a bit technical and need not concern us here. Of concern is the economic interpretation of equations (1.6)–(1.8).

We can simplify and rewrite the first-order conditions to facilitate their interpretation.

$$\partial\pi(\bullet)/\partial Y_t = \rho\lambda_{t+1} \tag{1.9}$$

$$\lambda_t = \partial\pi(\bullet)/\partial X_t + \rho\lambda_{t+1}[1 + F'(\bullet)] \tag{1.10}$$

$$X_{t+1} = X_t + F(X_t) - Y_t \tag{1.11}$$

The LHS of equation (1.9) is the marginal net benefit of an additional unit of the resource harvested in period t. For a harvest strategy to be optimal this marginal net benefit must equal the opportunity cost, also called *user cost*. User cost is represented by the term $\rho\lambda_{t+1}$, equal to the discounted value of an additional unit of the resource in period $t + 1$.

Thus equation (1.9) requires that we account for two types of costs, the standard marginal cost of harvest in the current period (which has already been accounted for in $\partial\pi(\bullet)/\partial Y_t$) and the future cost that results from the decision to harvest an additional unit of the resource today, which is $\rho\lambda_{t+1}$. In some problems we may see this condition written $p = \partial C(\bullet)/\partial Y_t + \rho\lambda_{t+1}$, implying that price today should equal marginal cost ($\partial C(\bullet)/\partial Y_t$) plus user cost, $\rho\lambda_{t+1}$,

On the LHS of equation (1.10) we have λ_t, the value of an additional unit of the resource, in situ, in period t. When a resource is optimally managed, the marginal value of an additional unit of the resource in period t equals the current period marginal net benefit, $\partial\pi(\bullet)/\partial X_t$, plus the marginal benefit that an unharvested unit will convey in the next period, $\rho\lambda_{t+1}[1 + F'(\bullet)]$. Note that this last term is the discounted value of the marginal unit itself plus its marginal growth.

Equation (1.11) is simply a rewrite of equation (1.1), but now obtained from the partial of the Lagrangian with respect to $\rho\lambda_{t+1}$. This should occur in general: that is, the partial of the Lagrangian with respect to a discounted multiplier should yield the difference equation for the associated state variable, in this case the resource stock.

What if $T \to \infty$? In this case we have an infinite-horizon problem. Equations (1.6)–(1.8) become an infinitely large system of equations in an infinite number of unknowns, a potentially daunting problem. Under certain conditions such problems will have a transitional period, say for $\tau \geq t \geq 0$, where Y_t, X_t, and λ_t are changing, followed by a period $\infty > t > \tau$, where Y_t, X_t, and λ_t are unchanging. In this infinitely long latter period the variables or "system" is said to have reached a steady state because $X_{t+1} = X_t = X^*$, $Y_{t+1} = Y_t = Y^*$, and $\lambda_{t+1} = \lambda_t = \lambda^*$. The triple $[X^*, Y^*, \lambda^*]$ is called a steady-state optimum.

It is often possible to solve for the steady-state optimum by evaluating the first-order necessary conditions when X_t, Y_t, and λ_t are unchanging. In steady state we can dispense with all the time subscripts in equations (1.6)–(1.8), which simply become three equations in three unknowns, X^*, Y^*, and λ^*, and may be written as

$$\rho\lambda = \partial\pi(\bullet)/\partial Y \tag{1.12}$$

$$\rho\lambda[1 + F'(X) - (1 + \delta)] = -\partial\pi(\bullet)/\partial X \tag{1.13}$$

$$Y = F(X) \tag{1.14}$$

Equation (1.13) requires a little bit of algebra and use of the definition $\rho = 1/(1 + \delta)$. It can be further manipulated to yield

$$-\rho\lambda[\delta - F'(X)] = -\partial\pi(\bullet)/\partial X \tag{1.15}$$

Multiplying both sides by −1, substituting (1.12) into (1.15), and isolating δ on the RHS yields

$$F'(X) + \frac{\partial \pi(\bullet)/\partial X}{\partial \pi(\bullet)/\partial Y} = \delta \qquad (1.16)$$

Equation (1.16) has been called the "fundamental equation of renewable resources." Along with equation (1.14) it will define the optimal steady-state values for X and Y.

Equation (1.16) has an interesting economic interpretation. On the LHS, the term $F'(X)$ my be interpreted as the marginal net growth rate. The second term, called the "marginal stock effect," measures the marginal value of the stock relative to the marginal value of harvest. The two terms on the LHS sum to what might be interpreted as the resource's internal rate of return. Equation (1.16) thus requires that the optimal steady-state values of X and Y cause the resource's internal rate of return to equal the rate of discount, δ, which presumably equals the rate of return on investments elsewhere in the economy. From this capital-theoretic point of view, the renewable resource is viewed as an asset, which under optimal management will yield a rate of return comparable to that of other capital assets. Are all renewable resources capable of yielding an internal rate of return equal to the rate of discount? We will revisit this question in Chapter 3.

Equation (1.14) results when equation (1.1) is evaluated at steady state. It has an obvious and compelling logic. At the bioeconomic optimum, and in fact at any sustainable equilibrium, harvest must equal net growth. If this were not the case, if net growth exceeded harvest or if harvest exceeded net growth, the resource stock would be changing and we could not, by definition, be at a steady-state equilibrium. Thus $Y = F(X)$ at any sustainable equilibrium, including the bioeconomic optimum.

Equation (1.16), by the implicit function theorem, will imply a curve in $X - Y$ space. Under a plausible set of curvature assumptions for $F(X)$ and $\pi(X,Y)$, the slope of this curve will be positive. Its exact shape and placement in $X - Y$ space will depend on all the bioeconomic parameters in the functions $F(X)$ and $\pi(X,Y)$, and on the discount rate δ.

Several possible curves (for different underlying parameters) are labeled ϕ_1, ϕ_2, and ϕ_3 in Figure 1.2. The net growth function is assumed to take a logistic form where $Y = F(X) = rX(1 - X/K)$. The intersection of $F(X)$ and a particular $\phi(X)$ would represent the solution of equations

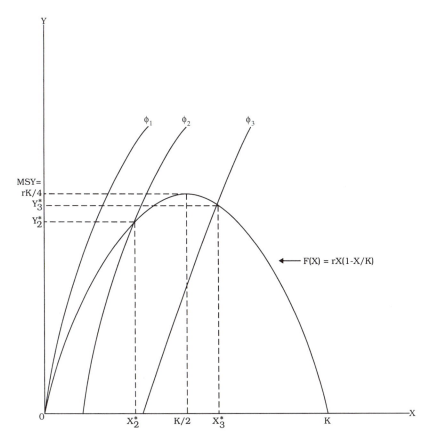

Figure 1.2. Maximum Sustainable Yield (MSY) and Three Bioeconomic Optima

(1.14) and (1.16) and therefore depict the steady-state bioeconomic optimum.

Figure 1.2 shows four equilibria: three bioeconomic optima and maximum sustainable yield (MSY). The bioeconomic optimum at the intersection of ϕ_1 and $F(X)$ would imply that extinction is optimal! Such an equilibrium might result if a slow-growing resource were confronted by a high rate of discount and if harvesting costs for the last members of the species were less than their market price.

The intersection of $F(X)$ and ϕ_2 implies an optimal resource stock of X_2^*, positive, but less than $K/2$, which supports $MSY = rK/4$. This would be the case if the marginal stock effect is less than the discount rate. (Look at equation [1.16] and see if you can figure out why this is true.)

The curve ϕ_3 implies a large marginal stock effect, greater in magnitude than the discount rate, δ. This would occur if smaller fishable stocks significantly increased cost. In such a case it is optimal to maintain a large stock at the bioeconomic optimum, even greater than the maximum sustainable yield stock, $K/2$. The conclusion to be drawn from Figure 1.2 is that the optimal stock, from a bioeconomic perspective, may be less than or greater than the stock level supporting maximum sustainable yield. Its precise location will depend on the forms for $\pi(X,Y)$ and $F(X)$ and the relevant bioeconomic parameters.

In our discussion of the infinite-horizon problem we mentioned that for certain problems the dynamics of the system has two stages, a transitional stage, where the variables are changing, and a steady state, where the variables are unchanging. Equations (1.14) and (1.16), when plotted in $X - Y$ space, would define the steady-state values X^* and Y^*. A possible transition (approach) to X^* from $X_0 < X^*$ is shown in Figure 1.3. This might be the approach and steady state in a single-species fishery where open access or mismanagement allowed the stock to be overfished to a suboptimal level. By restricting harvest to a level less than net growth $[Y_t < F(X_t)]$, the fish stock would grow, reaching X^* at $t = \tau$.

Although the general problem has the virtue of providing some broad and important insights into resource management from an economic perspective, its presentation has been tedious and abstract. In the next chapter we will solve some numerical problems using Excel's Solver. These numerical problems, and the problems found elsewhere in this book, will, it is hoped, make the basic concepts and the economic approach introduced in this chapter more operational, and thus more meaningful.

1.3   Questions and Exercises

Q1.1 What is the central subject in the field of resource economics?

Q1.2 What is the economic distinction between renewable and nonrenewable resources?

Q1.3 What is meant by the term user cost? If user cost increases, what happens to the level of harvest or extraction today?

E1.1 Suppose the dynamics of a fish stock are given by the difference equation (written in "iterative" form) $X_{t+1} = X_t + rX_t(1 - X_t/K) - Y_t$, where

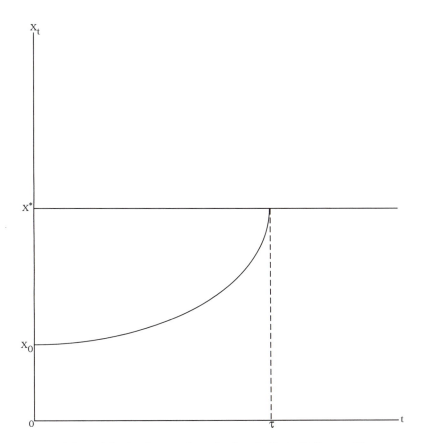

Figure 1.3. An Approach to the Steady-State Optimum X^*

$X_0 = 0.1$, $r = 0.5$, and $K = 1$. Management authorities regard the stock as being dangerously depleted and have imposed a 10-year moratorium on harvesting ($Y_t = 0$ for $t = 0, 1, 2, \ldots, 9$). What happens to X_t during the moratorium? Plot the time path for X_t ($t = 0, 1, 2, \ldots, 9$) in $t - X$ space. (Hint: Set up an Excel Spreadsheet.)

E1.2 After the moratorium the management authorities are planning to allow fishing for 10 years at a harvest rate of $Y_t = 0.125$ (for $t = 10, 11, \ldots, 19$). Suppose the net benefit from harvest is given by $\pi_t = pY_t - cY_t/X_t$, where $p = 2$, $c = 0.5$, and $\delta = 0.05$. What is the present value of net benefits of the 10-year moratorium followed by 10 years of fishing at $Y_t = 0.125$? (Hint: Modify the Excel Spreadsheet of **E1.1**.)

E1.3 In steady state the fishery will yield $Y = F(X) = rX(1 - X/K)$ and an annual net benefit of $\pi(X,Y) = (p - c/X)Y$. Take the derivatives $F'(X)$, $\partial\pi(\bullet)/\partial X$, and $\partial\pi(\bullet)/\partial Y$, substitute them and $Y = rX(1 - X/K)$ into equation (1.16), and simplify the LHS. We will make use of the result in Chapter 3.

CHAPTER 2

Solving Numerical Allocation Problems

2.0   Introduction and Overview

Numerical allocation problems can serve at least two functions. First, they can make theory and methods less abstract and more meaningful. Second, they can serve as a useful bridge from theory and general models to the actual analysis of "real-world" allocation problems.

By a numerical problem we mean a problem in which functional forms have been specified and all relevant parameters and initial conditions have been estimated or calibrated. Recall in Section **1.2** that the general net benefit function took the form $\pi_t = \pi(X_t, Y_t)$. The specific functional form adopted in **E1.2** was $\pi_t = pY_t - cY_t/X_t$, where $p > 0$ was a parameter denoting the per unit price for fish at the dock, Y_t was the level of harvest in period t, $c > 0$ was a cost parameter reflecting the cost of effort for a particular fishing technology, and X_t was the fishable stock in period t. In a numerical problem we would need values for p and c which might be econometrically estimated from cross-sectional or time-series data, or calibrated on the basis of knowledge of a particular vessel or fleet of vessels.

Numerical analysis might involve both the simulation and the optimization of a dynamic system. By simulation we will usually mean the forward iteration of one or more difference equations. For example, in **E1.1**, you were told that a fish stock evolved according to the equation $X_{t+1} - X_t = rX_t(1 - X_t/K) - Y_t$, or in iterative form $X_{t+1} = X_t + rX_t(1 - X_t/K) - Y_t$. With numerical values for r, K, and X_0, it is relatively simple to use spreadsheet software on a personal computer to determine the dynamic implications for the fish stock from a particular (numerical) schedule of harvests, Y_t, over some future horizon $t = 0, 1, \ldots, T$. Simulation analysis is frequently referred to as a "what if" analysis. *If* we allow this level of harvest over the next 10 years, *what* will happen to the fish stock?

Optimization asks the question "What's best?" Economists are always wondering what's best. What is the best mix of inputs for a firm seeking to produce a particular level of output? What is the best allocation of a consumer's limited budget? What conditions describe an optimal allocation of resources and distribution of output for an economy? What is the

19

optimal level for a public good? What is the optimal harvest schedule for a fish stock?

Of course, what's best depends on (1) your objectives, (2) current resource abundance, (3) available technology, and (4) the dynamic response of the resource to harvesting. There are typically a number of possible objectives for resource management, but for a well-defined optimization problem, a single objective or a weighted sum of multiple objectives will need to be specified. Selection of a particular objective or a set of weights for the relevant multiple objectives is a value judgment. One can argue for the compelling nature of a particular objective, but it will still amount to a normative or subjective decision. Thus, optimization, whether conducted by economic agents or by a social planner, is said to be a normative exercise.

Showing students how to pose and solve dynamic allocation problems has been difficult until recently, when the developers of spreadsheet software started to include nonlinear programming algorithms in their menu of spreadsheet options. Within the context of a spreadsheet (which can be thought of as a large matrix) the nonlinear programming algorithm can seek to maximize or minimize the value in a particular cell, by changing the values in one or more related cells, while trying to satisfy constraints on the values or relationships between other cells. Consider the stylized spreadsheet in Spreadsheet 2.1.

This spreadsheet (or worksheet) is a matrix with 19 rows and 4 columns (A–D). In organizing our worksheets we will typically list the parameters to the problem in column A and assign them values in column B. In this hypothetical worksheet we have three parameters and a Lagrange multiplier, or shadow price, λ_{10}. In column B the entries #1, #2, #3, and #4 indicate that we would be assigning numerical values to the three parameters and to λ_{10}.

Leaving row 5 empty allows us to separate the set of parameters from the body of the worksheet. In cell A6 we introduce the heading "t" and enter below it the numbers 0, 1, ..., 10, indicating our optimization horizon will have $T = 9$, and that we are including $T + 1 = 10$, in order to assign a weight (shadow price) to the resource stock in period 10 (X_{10}). In cell B6 we place the heading "Y_t" above the 10 numerical values (#5, #6, ..., #14), which will be the harvest schedule we wish to simulate or the initial guess for the optimal harvest schedule we wish to find.

In cell C6 we introduce the heading "X_t." The initial condition, X_0, will be a known, given number indicated by #15 in cell C7. The other values of X_t are determined by formulas based on net growth and harvest in the previous period. For example, $X_1 = X_0 + rX_0(1 - X_0/K) - Y_0$ might be a formula we would want to enter in cell C8, where r might be "parame-

	A	B	C	D
1	parameter 1 =	#1		
2	parameter 2 =	#2		
3	parameter 3 =	#3		
4	$\lambda 10 =$	#4		
5				
6	t	Yt	Xt	PVNBt
7	0	#5	#15	formula 11
8	1	#6	formula 1	formula 12
9	2	#7	formula 2	formula 13
10	3	#8	formula 3	formula 14
11	4	#9	formula 4	formula 15
12	5	#10	formula 5	formula 16
13	6	#11	formula 6	formula 17
14	7	#12	formula 7	formula 18
15	8	#13	formula 8	formula 19
16	9	#14	formula 9	formula 20
17	10	0	formula 10	formula 21
18				
19			Sum PVNB =	formula 22

Spreadsheet 2.1

ter 1" and K might be "parameter 2." If this were the case, then in cell C8 we would type

$$=C7+\$B\$1*C7*(1-C7/\$B\$2)-B7 \tag{2.1}$$

Equation (2.1) makes use of the worksheet language used in Microsoft's Excel. Other spreadsheet softwares use a similar language. Excel is available for MS Windows and Macintosh operating systems. In writing worksheet formulas, cells may be referenced with or without dollar signs (\$) prefacing the column and row address. We will often wish to keep parameter values unchanged when using certain worksheet commands, like the useful "Fill Down" command. If the value of parameter 1 is to be the same regardless of where it appears in the worksheet, we will preface the cell that contains its numerical value with dollar signs before the column and row address. Thus, the value for parameter 1 becomes \$B\$1. When a cell address is written without dollar signs and a Fill Down command is used, Excel will assume we wish to iterate the formula, incrementing the row number by 1 for each cell below the highlighted cell at the top of the Fill Down command. This is a useful convention and will save you the time it would take to write each formula in an iteration.

In equation (2.1) addition, subtraction, multiplication, and division are accomplished by the operators $+$, $-$, $*$, and $/$. Note also that C7 is the address for our initial condition, X_0; \$B\$2 is the cell containing the value of parameter 2 (K); and B7 contains the harvest level in period zero (Y_0). If you pressed the mouse while pointing at cell C8 and dragged the cursor down to cell C17 before releasing, you would be selecting cells C8 through C17. By pressing on the edit menu, dragging, and releasing on the Fill Down command, Excel will enter all the correct formulas for X_2, $X_3, \ldots, X_{10}$. The formula in cell C17 (calculating the value for X_{10}) should read

$$=C16+\$B\$1*C16*(1-C16/\$B\$2)-B16 \qquad (2.2)$$

In cell D6 we introduce the column heading "*PVNBt*" to indicate that the formulas below the heading will calculate the present value of net benefits in period t. We will see in the next sections how discounting can be appropriately coded and how the Fill Down command can be used to avoid having to write equations which iterate in a recursive fashion. Note that in cell B17 we have arbitrarily imposed a zero level of harvest in t $= 10$. We could have left this cell blank, as it will not typically enter present-value calculations for the horizon $t = 0, 1, \ldots, 9$. We do calculate the value for X_{10} in cell C17 and leave open the option of calculating its present value according to the expression $\rho^{10}\lambda_{10}X_{10}$ in cell D17. Recall that for this problem we are treating λ_{10} as a parameter which allows us subjectively to weight the value of the marginal fish, in the water, in period 10. This approach will be useful in moderating the "end of the world" effect which is typically encountered in finite-horizon optimization problems. This aspect will also be discussed in greater detail in the next two sections.

Finally, in cell C19 we indicate that in cell D19 we will be calculating the present value of all net benefits (*PVNB*). This will typically be the sum of the calculations under *PVNBt*, D7 through D17 in this hypothetical worksheet. Recall that the numbers we entered under Y_t represented a candidate harvest schedule. Those values determined, in part, the values for X_t and the present values $\rho^t\pi(X_t,Y_t)$ under the heading *PVNBt*. The present-value calculation which would appear in cell D19 would tell us the present value of the particular harvest schedule with the numbers #5, #6, $\ldots$, #14. The resulting spreadsheet would depict the simulation of this particular harvest schedule. If we wish to find the optimal harvest schedule, we may tell Excel's Solver to maximize the value in cell D19 by changing the harvest values in cells B7 through B16, subject to certain constraints. At this point we are ready to work through the details of two numerical problems.

	A	B	C	D
1	$\delta =$	0.05		
2	$\rho =$	0.95238095		
3	$\lambda 10 =$	0		
4				
5	t	qt	Rt	PVNBt
6	0	0.1	1	0.09531018
7	1	0.1	0.9	0.0907716
8	2	0.1	0.8	0.08644914
9	3	0.1	0.7	0.08233252
10	4	0.1	0.6	0.07841192
11	5	0.1	0.5	0.07467802
12	6	0.1	0.4	0.07112192
13	7	0.1	0.3	0.06773517
14	8	0.1	0.2	0.06450968
15	9	0.1	0.1	0.06143779
16	10	0	1.3878E-16	0
17				
18			PVNB=	0.77275794

Spreadsheet 2.2

2.1 An Optimal Depletion Problem

Our first numerical example will be a simple depletion problem. Suppose you own a mine where the initial reserves have been normalized to $R_0 = 1$. You wish to determine the extraction rates, q_t, which will maximize the present value of net benefits over the 10-year horizon $t = 0, 1, \ldots, 9$. The net benefit function is $\pi_t = \ln(1 + q_t)$, where $\ln(\bullet)$ is the natural log operator. The discount rate is $\delta = 0.05$, and, for starters, we will assume that any reserves left over in period 10 have a value of zero, so that $\lambda_{10} = 0$. Our initial worksheet is shown in Spreadsheet 2.2.

In Column A, rows 1–3, we list the parameters delta (δ), rho (ρ), and lambda 10 (λ_{10}). With δ assigned the value of 0.05 in cell B1 we write the formula =1/(1+$B$1) in cell B2 to define the parameter value for the discount factor, ρ. The value of zero for λ_{10} appears in cell B3.

In the body of the spreadsheet we define the headings t, qt, Rt, and *PVNBt* in row 5. Under the period heading, t, we can enter zero in A6 and then use the "Series Option" to generate period indices $1, 2, \ldots, 10$ in cells A7–A16. Under the heading qt we enter the value 0.1 in cell B6 and then use the Fill Down command under the Edit Menu to enter 0.1 in cells B7–B15. We enter a zero in B16 implying $q_{10} = 0$. You could also leave B16 empty. Under the heading Rt we enter 1 in cell C6 to indicate our initial condition is $R_0 = 1$. In cell C7 we enter the formula =C6-B6 and then after pressing the mouse while pointing at C7, dragging, and releasing on C16, we can use Fill Down to enter all the recursive formulas for $R_2, R_3, \ldots, R_{10}$. If you've done it correctly you should get reserves declining linearly in increments of 0.1 and you should be able to click on cell C16 and in the formula bar see =C15-B15.

Under the heading *PVNBt* we will enter the formulas calculating the present value of net benefits from q_t and any leftover X_{10}. In cell D6 we enter the formula =($B$2^A6)*LN(1+B6) Note: The exponent operator is the "^". Use the Fill Down command to enter this formula recursively in cells D7 through D15. Did you get the same numbers as in Spreadsheet 2.2?

In cell D16 enter the formula =($B$2^A16)*$B$3*$C$16. This is the spreadsheet equivalent of $\rho^{10}\lambda_{10}X_{10}$, which, with $\lambda_{10} = 0$, yields a value of 0 in cell D16. We will change λ_{10} to a positive parameter value momentarily.

Finally, in cell C18 enter PVNB=, and in cell D18 enter the formula =SUM($D$6:$D$16). This formula tells Excel to sum the present value calculations in cells D6 through D16. Your spreadsheet should now be identical to Spreadsheet 2.2 and we are ready to maximize *PVNB*.

Click and release on cell D18, which gives the *PVNB* for an extraction schedule of $q_t = 0.1, t = 0, 1, \ldots, 9$. Now load Solver by clicking and dragging on the menu which contains Solver, and releasing when Solver is highlighted. (The exact location of Solver will depend on what version of Excel you are running.)

It will take Excel a few seconds to load Solver. When loading is completed, a dialogue box entitled "Solver Parameters" will appear. At the top left Solver will indicate that $D$18 has been designated as the Set Cell and that the preset operation is to maximize the value in this cell (the Max option is active by default). You now need to tell Solver what cells it can change while seeking to maximize $D$18. Click in the box below the label "By Changing Cells" and enter $B$6:$B$15. This tells Solver that it can change our candidate values of q_t, currently set at 0.1. The remaining box permits you to enter any additional constraints. Click and release the Add button and in the constraint box enter $B$6:$B$15, choose >=, and enter 0. This constrains the q_t to be nonnegative. Click and release the Add button again and this time enter $C$16, choose >=, and enter 0. This constrains the remaining reserves in $T + 1 = 10$ to be nonnegative, thus preventing Solver from extracting more ore than was initially available to extract.

To summarize, we are maximizing the value in $D$18 by changing the values in cells $B$6 through $B$15 and constraining those values (corresponding to q_t) and $C$16 (corresponding to X_{10}) to be nonnegative. Click and release on the Solve button and Solver's nonlinear program-

	A	B	C	D
1	δ =	0.05		
2	ρ =	0.95238095		
3	λ10 =	0		
4				
5	t	qt	Rt	PVNBt
6	0	0.31342631	1	0.27263922
7	1	0.25093658	0.68657369	0.21323099
8	2	0.19143511	0.43563711	0.15887397
9	3	0.13457016	0.244202	0.10906283
10	4	0.08046111	0.10963185	0.06366722
11	5	0.02917072	0.02917074	0.02252901
12	6	0	1.4862E-08	0
13	7	0	1.4862E-08	0
14	8	0	1.4862E-08	0
15	9	0	1.4862E-08	0
16	10	0	1.4862E-08	0
17				
18			PVNB=	0.84000324

Spreadsheet 2.3

ming algorithm swings into action. After 10 trials (iterations) Solver announces that it has found a solution and that all constraints and optimality conditions are satisfied. The solution is shown in Spreadsheet 2.3.

The first thing to note is that the value in cell D18 has been increased from approximately 0.773 in Spreadsheet 2.2 to approximately 0.840 in Spreadsheet 2.3. The second thing to note is that initial values of $q_t = 0.1$ for $t = 0, 1, \ldots, 9$ have been changed to $q_0 = 0.313$, $q_1 = 0.251$, $q_2 = 0.191$, $q_3 = 0.135$, $q_4 = 0.080$, $q_5 = 0.029$, and $q_6 = q_7 = q_8 = q_9 = 0$. Thus, Solver says if you are maximizing the present value of net benefits, when the discount rate is $\delta = 0.05$, you have high rates of extraction early on, and exhaustion by period 6 ($R_6 = 0$).

Zero values for q_6, q_7, q_8, and q_9 are sometimes called "corner solutions," and they necessitate a modification of the first-order necessary condition discussed in Chapter 1. The Lagrangian for this problem may be written

$$L = \sum_{t=0}^{9} \rho^t \{\ln(1+q_t) + \rho\lambda_{t+1}[R_t - q_t - R_{t+1}]\} \qquad (2.3)$$

and if $q_t > 0$ the $\partial L/\partial q_t = 0$ implies $1/(1 + q_t) = \rho\lambda_{t+1}$. When $R_t > 0$, the $\partial L/\partial R_t = 0$ implies $\rho\lambda_{t+1} = \lambda_t$, so $1/(1 + q_0) = \rho\lambda_1 = \lambda_0 = 0.761$. If it is optimal to set a particular $q_t = 0$, the first-order condition becomes what is called a Kuhn–Tucker condition and takes the form $[1/(1 + q_t) - \rho\lambda_{t+1}]q_t = 0$. For this example, if the marginal net benefit, equal to $1/(1 + q_t)$, is less than

	A	B	C	D
1	δ =	0.05		
2	ρ =	0.95238095		
3	λ10 =	1.4		
4				
5	t	qt	Rt	PVNBt
6	0	0.16349595	1	0.15142922
7	1	0.10809171	0.83650405	0.09775177
8	2	0.05532554	0.72841234	0.04884289
9	3	0.00507381	0.6730868	0.00437186
10	4	0	0.668013	0
11	5	0	0.668013	0
12	6	0	0.668013	0
13	7	0	0.668013	0
14	8	0	0.668013	0
15	9	0	0.668013	0
16	10	0	0.668013	0.57414284
17				
18			PVNB=	0.87653859

Spreadsheet 2.4

user cost, $\rho\lambda_{t+1}$, then extraction in period t should be zero! Thus, the first-order conditions presented in Chapter 1 are only correct if all Y_t and X_t (harvests and fish stocks) are optimally positive.

The calculation that $\lambda_0 = 0.761$ has an interesting interpretation. It is the value of having slightly larger initial reserves, R_0. Knowing λ_0 we can calculate λ_t when the optimal $R_t > 0$, since $\partial L/\partial R_t = 0$ implies $\rho\lambda_{t+1} = \lambda_t$, which in turn implies $\lambda_t = (1 + \delta)^t\lambda_0$. This says that the shadow price on remaining reserves is increasing at the rate of discount when the resource is being optimally extracted. We will return to this result in Chapter 5.

The solution in Spreadsheet 2.3 assumes $\lambda_{10} = 0$ and there is no weight attached to reserves in $t = 10$. A zero weight on remaining resources in $t = 10$ is akin to saying that the world ends after $t = 9$. This result provides a strong incentive to use up anything of value before the end of the world. In setting up our problems thus far, we have allowed for the possibility of assigning a weight to resources at the end of the optimization horizon. In Chapter 1 we allowed for the possibility of setting $\lambda_{T+1} = B \geq 0$. Increases in B will place greater weight on retaining resources for use (optimization) after the current horizon.

In Spreadsheet 2.4 we show the results when $\lambda_{10} = 1.4$, and Solver is initiated from $q_t = 0.1$ for $t = 0, 1, \ldots, 9$. Remaining reserves in $t = 10$ (R_{10}) are weighted (multiplied) by λ_{10}, discounted by ρ^{10}, and added to the discounted net benefits from earlier periods. The constraints are unchanged.

After 22 iterations Solver announces it has found a solution that satisfies all constraints and optimality conditions. By assigning a weight of $\lambda_{10} = 1.4$ to R_{10} initial extraction rates are reduced, falling to zero in periods 4 through 9, thus maintaining reserves of 0.668 for the next optimization horizon. Although a positive weight on the resource stock in period $T + 1$ has the anticipated conservation effect, it must be remembered that this weight has an implicit opportunity cost in the form of forgone discounted net benefits in the current optimization problem. Now $\lambda_0 = 1/(1 + q_0) = 0.859$, which is the marginal value (shadow price) of a positive increment in R_0.

2.2   An Optimal Harvest Problem

In our second example we will consider a fishery where population dynamics are given by the difference equation $X_{t+1} - X_t = F(X_t) - Y_t$. We have seen that treating λ_{T+1} as a choice variable allows us to place a subjective weight on the resource stock in period $T + 1$. Larger values of λ_{T+1} will normally lead to higher stock levels at the beginning of period $T + 1$, and thus a higher inventory from which to start the next round of resource management (optimization). Higher resource inventories will usually have an opportunity cost in the form of lower extraction or harvest benefits during the current management (optimization) problem. The expression $\rho^{T+1}\lambda_{T+1}X_{T+1}$ can be thought of as a type of *final function*.

There is another final function which might be used to approximate the solution of an infinite-horizon, renewable resource problem. Suppose in periods $t \geq T + 1$ we required sustainability in the harvest of the renewable resource. Specifically, suppose that the harvest in periods $t \geq T + 1$ had to equal net growth: i.e., $Y_t = \overline{Y} = F(X_{T+1})$, where the stock X_{T+1} supports the sustainable harvest $\overline{Y}$, and both are constant.

If the net benefit function is $\pi_t = \pi(X_t, Y_t)$, then in each period net benefit is $\overline{\pi} = \pi(X_{T+1}, F(X_{T+1}))$, also a constant. What is the present value, in period $T + 1$, of sustainably harvesting X_{T+1}? It will be given by the following expression.

$$\sum_{t=T+1}^{\infty} \rho^{t-T-1}\overline{\pi} = \overline{\pi}\sum_{t=0}^{\infty}\rho^t = \overline{\pi}[1+\rho+\rho^2+\ldots] = \overline{\pi}\left[\frac{1}{1-\rho}\right] = \overline{\pi}\left[\frac{1+\delta}{\delta}\right]$$

Note: Because $\overline{\pi} = \pi(X_{T+1}, F(X_{T+1}))$ is a constant we can take it outside the first summation, and because we have an infinite horizon we can reindex the summation from $t = T + 1$ to ∞ to $t = 0$ to ∞ and get the same convergent series $[1 + \rho + \rho^2 + \ldots] = (1 + \delta)/\delta$ since $\rho = 1/(1 + \delta)$.

Now suppose a resource manager were told to maximize the present value of net benefits over the finite horizon, $t = 0, 1, \ldots, T$, but with the final function $\rho^{T+1}\bar{\pi}(X_{T+1}F(X_{T+1}))\left[\dfrac{1+\delta}{\delta}\right] = \rho^{T}\bar{\pi}(X_{T+1}F(X_{T+1}))\Big/\delta$. The optimization problem may be formally stated as

$$\text{Maximize } \sum_{t=0}^{T}\rho^{t}\pi(X_{t},Y_{t})+\rho^{T}\bar{\pi}(X_{T+1}F(X_{T+1}))/\delta$$

$$\text{Subject to } X_{t+1} - X_{t} = F(X_{t}) - Y_{t}, \ X_{0} \text{ given}$$

In essence we're telling the resource manager that she is free to choose the harvest levels $Y_{t}, t = 0, 1, \ldots, T$, but that whatever the resulting value of X_{T+1}, that stock level must be sustainably harvested forever. Such a final function should give some weight to X_{T+1}, and in some cases the values chosen for $Y_{t}, t = 0, 1, \ldots, T$ will approximate the optimal approach from X_{0} to the bioeconomic optimum (X^*,Y^*,λ^*). To see how this might work, consider the following numerical example.

Suppose our net benefit function is a quadratic in Y_{t}, taking the form $\pi(Y_{t}) = aY_{t} - (b/2)Y_{t}^{2}$, where $a > b > 0$. We saw in Chapter 1 that the steady-state optimal stock was given by the fundamental equation of renewable resources, equation (1.16). With net benefits only a function of harvest, the marginal stock effect vanishes, and we are left with $F'(X) = \delta$ as the expression defining the steady-state optimal stock. Suppose we assume that net growth is given by $F(X) = rX(1 - X/K)$. Then $F'(X) = r(1 - 2X/K) = \delta$. Solving for X yields the explicit expression

$$X^* = \frac{K(r-\delta)}{2r} \tag{2.4}$$

With $Y^* = rX^*(1 - X^*/K)$ some algebra will show

$$Y^* = \frac{K(r^{2}-\delta^{2})}{4r} \tag{2.5}$$

With $\rho\lambda = \pi'(Y)$ (see equation [1.12]) we get $\lambda = (1 + \delta)(a - bY^*)$ or

$$\lambda^* = (1+\delta)[a-bK(r^{2}-\delta^{2})/(4r)] \tag{2.6}$$

Suppose $a = 10$, $b = 1$, $r = 0.5$, $K = 1$, and $\delta = 0.05$. The preceding formulas yield the numerical values $X^* = 0.45$, $Y^* = 0.12375$, and $\lambda^* = 10.37$. What if we set up a spreadsheet and ask Solver to maximize

$$\sum_{t=0}^{9}\rho^{t}\left(aY_{t} - (b/2)Y_{t}^{2}\right)$$

$$+\rho^{9}\left[a(rX_{10}(1-X_{10}/K))-(b/2)(rX_{10}(1-X_{10}/K))^{2}\right]\Big/\delta$$

	A	B	C	D
1	a=	10		
2	b=	1		
3	r=	0.5		
4	K=	1		
5	δ=	0.05		
6	ρ=	0.95238095		
7				
8	t	Yt	Xt	PVNBt
9	0	0.05	0.2	0.49875
10	1	0.05	0.23	0.475
11	2	0.05	0.26855	0.45238095
12	3	0.05	0.31676545	0.430839
13	4	0.05	0.374978	0.41032286
14	5	0.05	0.44216275	0.39078368
15	6	0.05	0.51549017	0.37217493
16	7	0.05	0.5903702	0.35445231
17	8	0.05	0.66128681	0.33757363
18	9	0.05	0.7232801	0.3214987
19	10		0.7733531	11.2490718
20				
21			PVNB=	15.2928479

Spreadsheet 2.5

Will Solver select harvest levels for Y_t, $t = 0, 1, \ldots, 9$, that will cause X_t to go from X_0 to $X_{10} \approx X^*$?

Consider Spreadsheet 2.5. The parameter values are found in cells $B$1 through $B$6. In cells $A$9 through $A$19 we define the period index. In cells $B$9 through $B$18 we provide an initial guess (0.05) for the optimal harvest levels $Y_t^*, t = 0, 1, \ldots, 9$. These will be the values that Solver will be allowed to change.

In cell $C$9 we specify the initial condition (also a parameter) $X_0 = 0.2$. In cell $C$10 we type =C9+$B$3*C9*(1-C9/$B$4)-B9, which is the Excel equation for X_1. We fill down to $C$19, where the formula is =C18+$B$3*C18*(1-C18/$B$4)-B18, which is Excel's expression for X_{10}.

In cell $D$9 we type =($B$6^A9)*($B$1*B9-($B$2/2)*B9^2), which is the expression for $\rho^0 \pi(Y_0)$, the present value of harvest in period $t = 0$. We fill down this expression to cell $D$18, where it becomes =($B$6^A18)*($B$1*B18-($B$2/2)*B18^2). The final function is programmed in cell $D$19 as the Excel equation

	A	B	C	D
1	a=	10		
2	b=	1		
3	r=	0.5		
4	K=	1		
5	δ=	0.05		
6	ρ=	0.95238095		
7				
8	t	Yt	Xt	PVNBt
9	0	0	0.2	0
10	1	0	0.28	0
11	2	0.05532824	0.3808	0.50045512
12	3	0.11724753	0.44336744	1.00689067
13	4	0.12353095	0.44951629	1.01001498
14	5	0.12333454	0.44971104	0.96039913
15	6	0.12371539	0.45011201	0.91747271
16	7	0.12402237	0.45015221	0.87593812
17	8	0.12377992	0.44988744	0.8326061
18	9	0.12358891	0.44985189	0.79174218
19	10		0.45000557	15.8553903
20				
21			PVNB=	22.7509093

Spreadsheet 2.6

$$=(\$B\$6^\wedge A18)*(\$B\$1*\$B\$3*\$C\$19*(1-\$C\$19/\$B\$4)-$$
$$(\$B\$2/2)*(\$B\$3*\$C\$19*(1-\$C\$19/\$B\$4))^\wedge 2)/\$B\$5$$

Finally, in cell $D$21 we type =SUM($D$9:$D$19), which sums the present values from the harvest levels Y_t^*, $t = 0, 1, \ldots, 9$, plus the final function. If you've entered everything correctly your spreadsheet should be identical to Spreadsheet 2.5.

Now call up Solver. The set cell to be maximized is $D$21. The changing cells are $B$9:$B$18. The constraints are $B$9:$B$18 >= 0 and $C$19 >= 0. Tell Solver to "Solve" and in 22 trials (iterations) it should announce that it has found a solution and that all constraints and optimality conditions are satisfied. This solution should be identical to Spreadsheet 2.6. Note that the optimal harvest schedule involves zero harvest in periods $t = 0$ and $t = 1$. In periods $t = 2$ through $t = 9$ harvest is slowly increased toward $Y^* = 0.12375$ as X_t approaches $X^* = 0.45$.

Pretty cool! We will make use of this type of final function again in Chapter 6. We will make use of equations (2.4)–(2.5) when we talk about sustainability in the context of a renewable resource–based economy in Chapter 8.

2.3   Questions and Exercises

Q2.1 What is the difference between simulation and optimization?

Q2.2 What is meant when it is said that "λ_{T+1} is a subjective weight assigned to X_{T+1}"? What is likely to happen to the optimal value of X_{T+1} if we set λ_{T+1} at a higher value?

Q2.3 In the optimal depletion problem, what is the interpretation of λ_0?

E2.1 A mine has initial reserves of $R_0 = 1$ and may be operated over the horizon $t = 0, 1, \ldots, 9$. In $t = 10$ the mine will be expropriated. Current owners set $\lambda_{10} = 0$. The net revenue in period t is given by $\pi_t = (p - cq_t/R_t)q_t$, where q_t is the extraction rate, R_t are remaining reserves, $p > 0$ is the unit price for ore at the mill, and $c > 0$ is a cost parameter. Suppose $p = 1, c = 0.5$, and $\delta = 0.05$. What is the optimal extraction rate, q_t, for $t = 0, 1, \ldots, 9$? Use Solver from an initial guess of $q_t = 0.1$ for $t = 0, 1, \ldots, 9$.

E2.2 Consider a fishery where $X_{t+1} = X_t + rX_t(1 - X_t/K) - Y_t$. The net benefits from harvest are given by $\pi_t = \ln(1 + Y_t)$, where $\ln(\bullet)$ is the natural log operator. With the discount factor given by $\rho = 1/(1 + \delta)$, and with $r = 0.5, K = 100$, and $\delta = 0.05$ you wish to

$$\text{Maximize} \quad \pi = \sum_{t=0}^{9} \rho^t \ln(1 + Y_t)$$

$$\text{Subject to} \quad X_{t+1} = X_t + rX_t(1 - X_t/K) - Y_t$$

$$X_0 = 100 \quad \text{and} \quad \lambda_{10} = 0$$

(a) Use Solver to find the optimal harvest schedule from an initial guess of $Y_t = 10$ for $t = 0, 1, \ldots, 9$. In the constraint box, specify $Y_t \geq 0$, for $t = 0, 1, \ldots, 9$ and $X_{10} \geq 0$.

(b) Now set $\lambda_{10} = 0.075$ and solve for the optimal harvest schedule, again from an initial guess of $Y_t = 10$, for $t = 0, 1, \ldots, 9$, with the same constraints.

CHAPTER 3

The Economics of Fisheries

3.0   Introduction and Overview

In this chapter we will explore in greater detail the general renewable resource model used to introduce the method of Lagrange multipliers in Chapter 1. This model will serve as a vehicle to examine traditional and "bioeconomic" management policies. Before embarking on this more detailed excursion we will construct some models that provide insight into why fisheries are chronically overfished. Overfishing results in depleted stocks that can support only a fraction of what might be harvested if stocks were maintained at higher levels. These models are referred to as *open access models*, and they show, graphically, what happens when there are unregulated access and harvesting of a common property resource. By a *common property resource* we mean a resource that is not recognized as "private property" until it is captured. The *inability* of traditional management policies to avert the tragedy of overfishing has recently led to a willingness among coastal nations to experiment with bioeconomic or "incentive-based" policies, such as Individual Transferable Quotas (ITQs). Although the jury is still out on the effectiveness of ITQs the initial results seem promising. A discussion of the experience with these policies in New Zealand, Australia, Canada, and the United States will close out this chapter.

3.1   Net Growth

In equation (1.1) we introduced a difference equation to describe the change in a renewable resource from period t to period $t + 1$. The function $F(X_t)$ was referred to as a net growth function. This function indicates the net amount of new biomass or additional numbers of fish as a function of the current biomass or current number of fish, X_t. It indicates net biological growth. There are numerous functional forms which might be used to describe (model) net biological growth. We have already employed one function, $F(X_t) = rX_t(1 - X_t/K)$, which we will call the logistic growth function, where $r > 0$ is referred to as the intrinsic growth rate and $K > 0$ is called the environmental carrying capacity. Three other possible functional forms are given in equations (3.1a)–(3.1c).

$$F(X_t) = X_t \left[e^{r(1-X_t/K)} - 1 \right] \tag{3.1a}$$

$$F(X_t) = rX_t \ln (K/X_t) \tag{3.1b}$$

$$F(X_t) = rX_t (X_t/K_0 - 1)(1 - X_t/K) \tag{3.1c}$$

A plot of $X_{t+1} - X_t = \Delta X = F(X)$ provides some insight into the dynamics implied by these different net growth functions. The logistic and functions (3.1a)–(3.1c) are plotted in Figure 3.1 for $r = K = 1$ and $K_0 = 0.25$. Points where $F(X) = 0$ will correspond to steady-state equilibria in the unharvested or "pristine" fishery. Points where $F(X) > 0$ correspond to positive growth, and for function (3.1c), points where $F(X) < 0$ (for $K_0 > X > 0$) correspond to negative net growth, where rates of natural mortality are greater than the rates of birth and survival.

Figure 3.1 reveals that all four growth functions have steady states at $X = 0$ and $X = K$. For the logistic and the functions (3.1a) and (3.1b), these are the only steady states. Since net growth for $K > X > 0$ is positive, the unharvested population, starting from X_0, where $K > X_0 > 0$, would, for "small" values of r, tend to the steady state at $X = K$.

For the function (3.1c) $X = K_0$ is also a steady state, but it is said to be unstable. If the stock were displaced slightly to the left of K_0, net growth would be negative $(F(X) < 0)$ and a process leading to extinction would result. Alternatively, if the stock were displaced slightly to the right of K_0, net growth would be positive and the stock would grow toward K. The value K_0 is sometimes referred to as the *minimum viable population size*.

With our logistic form, or any of the forms in (3.1a)–(3.1c), we have a nonlinear difference equation which might converge to $X = K$, but which also has the potential for cyclical and chaotic behavior when the parameter r increases above a critical level. By cyclical behavior we mean that after a transition, X_t takes on only a finite number of values. The number of values will be an even number and the cycles might be 2-point, 4-point, 8-point, or 2^n-point cycles. If r increases above the critical value, $n \to \infty$, and the dynamic behavior becomes chaotic, with X_t appearing to fluctuate randomly between upper and lower bounds.

Classifying the stability of steady states and determining the onset of cyclical behavior in the dynamics of a single species are relatively straightforward. For a candidate $F(X_t)$ (1) solve for the steady-state equilibria by solving $F(X) = 0$ (implying $X_{t+1} = X_t = X$), (2) write the equation for population dynamics in iterative form as $X_{t+1} = X_t + F(X_t) = \phi(X_t)$, and (3) take the first derivative of $\phi(\bullet)$, denoting it as $\phi'(\bullet)$. Then, a particular steady state, X, will be stable if $|\phi'(X)| < 1$, where $|\bullet|$ is the absolute-value operator.

The Logistic F(X)=rX(1-X/K)

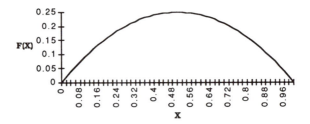

Equation (3.1a) F(X)=X(exp(r(1-X/K))-1)

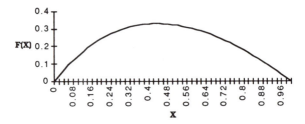

Equation (3.1b) F(X)=rXln(K/X)

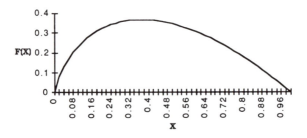

Equation (3.1c) F(X)=rX(X/K₀-1)(1-X/K)

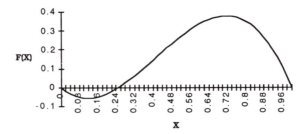

Figure 3.1. Net Growth Functions for $r = K = 1$, $K_0 = 0.25$

Consider our logistic $F(X_t) = rX_t(1 - X_t/K)$, where we set $K = 1$. In this case we obtain $\phi(X_t) = (1 + r)X_t - rX_t^2$ and $\phi'(X_t) = 1 + r - 2rX_t$. If the steady state of interest is $X = K = 1$, then $\phi'(1) = 1 - r$, and for $K = 1$ to be stable $|1 - r| < 1$, which for r positive requires $2 > r > 0$. In other words, for $2 > r > 0$ we would expect the population ultimately to converge to $K = 1$, but for $r > 2$ we could get 2^n-point cycles or chaos.

Spreadsheet 3.1 shows the population dynamics for our logistic form when $r = 1.9$, $K = 1$, and $X_0 = 0.4$. The initial simulation, for $t = 0,1,$ . . . ,30, is plotted as the uppermost time path. The other three time paths show the resulting values of X_t when r is increased to 2.2, 2.55, and 2.9. When $r = 2.2$ we get a two-point cycle, when $r = 2.55$ we get a four-point cycle, and when $r = 2.9$ we get chaos, where X_t appears to be fluctuating randomly.

3.2   Fishery Production Functions

In this chapter a fishery production function will relate harvest in period t to the fish stock and fishing effort, also in period t. Harvest is regarded as the output and the fish stock and effort are regarded as inputs. In general, the production function will be written as $Y_t = H(X_t, E_t)$. One normally expects such production functions to be concave, with positive first partial derivatives $(\partial H(\bullet)/\partial X_t > 0, \partial H(\bullet)/\partial E_t > 0)$; a nonnegative mixed, second partial $(\partial^2 H(\bullet)/\partial X_t \partial E_t = \partial^2 H(\bullet)/\partial E_t \partial X_t \geq 0)$; and nonpositive, pure second partials $(\partial^2 H(\bullet)/\partial X_t^2 \leq 0, \partial^2 H(\bullet)/\partial E_t^2 \leq 0)$. Two frequently encountered functional forms are

$$Y_t = qX_t E_t \tag{3.2a}$$

$$Y_t = X_t\left(1 - e^{-qE_t}\right) \tag{3.2b}$$

where $q > 0$ is sometimes called a "catchability coefficient." Production function (3.2a) is a special case of the Cobb–Douglas form $Y_t = qX_t^\alpha E_t^\beta$, where $\alpha = \beta = 1$. It is often referred to as the *catch-per-unit-effort* (CPUE) production function because it was originally the result of the assumption that catch per unit effort (Y_t/E_t) was proportional to the fishable stock, qX_t.

We will refer to (3.2b) as the exponential production function. Note that as $E_t \to \infty$, $Y_t \to \infty$ in (3.2a) and $Y_t \to X_t$ in (3.2b). The latter limit is more realistic, but either function (or the more general Cobb–Douglas) is best viewed as an approximation of a harvest technology, with the choice among (3.2a), (3.2b), or other functional forms to be decided by the available data.

r =	1.9
K =	1

t	Xt
0	0.4
1	0.856
2	1.0902016
3	0.90335954
4	1.0692316
5	0.92858484
6	1.05458341
7	0.94521417
8	1.04360442
9	0.95714346
10	1.03508119
11	0.96608862
12	1.02833527
13	0.97297277
14	1.02293661
15	0.97835748
16	1.01858831
17	0.98261402
18	1.01507306
19	0.98600257
20	1.01222543
21	0.98871314
22	1.00991613
23	0.99088866
24	1.00804247
25	0.99263888
26	1.00652206
27	0.99404933
28	1.00528832
29	0.99518737
30	1.00428736

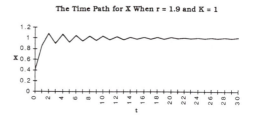

The Time Path for X When r = 1.9 and K = 1

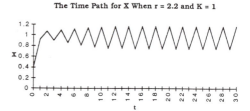

The Time Path for X When r = 2.2 and K = 1

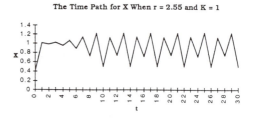

The Time Path for X When r = 2.55 and K = 1

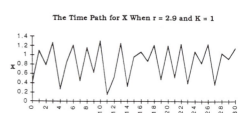

The Time Path for X When r = 2.9 and K = 1

Spreadsheet 3.1

3.3   The Yield–Effort Function

Consider a single-species fishery where the amount harvested in period t is given by the general production function $Y_t = H(X_t, E_t)$, With harvest, the resource stock changes according to $X_{t+1} - X_t = F(X_t) - Y_t$. If we substitute the production function into this equation and evaluate it at a steady state (where $X_{t+1} = X_t = X$) we conclude that $F(X) = H(X,E)$. This is nothing more than a restatement of our earlier observation that harvest must equal net growth in a steady state. Suppose we can solve this last equation for X as a function of E, say, $X = G(E)$. If we take this function and substitute it into the production function we have $Y = H(G(E),E) = Y(E)$, where $Y(E)$ is called the *yield* or *yield–effort function*. It gives the steady-state relationship between harvest (or yield) and fishing effort. This function might be useful in the "long-run" management of a fishery, and it has the potential to be estimated with appropriate time-series data on effort and harvest.

Suppose we adopt the logistic form $F(X) = rX(1 - X/K)$ and the *CPUE* production function $Y = H(X,E) = qXE$. Then, the steady-state condition $H(X,E) = F(X)$ implies $X = K[1 - (q/r)E]$ and $Y = Y(E) = qKE[1 - (q/r)E]$. The logistic net growth function and the yield–effort function are plotted in Figure 3.2. Although they appear the same (they are both quadratics, and both have a maximum at $Y_{MSY} = rK/4$), the net growth function shows the steady-state relationship between X and Y, and the yield–effort function shows the steady-state relationship between E and Y.

Measuring fishing effort, E_t, is problematic. In a fishery where similar vessels pull identical nets through the water (a trawl fishery), one might ideally measure effort as the total number of hours nets were deployed and actively fishing during the year or season. In a troll or longline fishery, one might measure effort as the total number of "hook hours" by a fleet, again in a season or year. In fixed gear fisheries (gill net, lobster, and crab), effort might be measured as the total number of units deployed (nets, traps, or pots) assuming that they are fishing continuously throughout the season or year. Unfortunately, there is typically some vessel diversity within a fleet, records are not required or kept on the number of hours a particular gear was actively fishing, and snags or improper deployment may reduce the effectiveness of a particular set. Often fishery scientists have to settle for the data available, which might be days from port or simply the number of vessels in a fleet (with no record of the number or length of trips during a season or year). Fishers are typically reluctant to reveal information on the time, location, and extent of their fishing effort, making time-series data on the ideal measure of effort unavailable. Even with less than ideal data there seems to be conclusive evidence as to what happens when a fishery is harvested under open access conditions.

3.4　The Static Model of Open Access

With the yield–effort function, $Y = Y(E)$, we can analyze the long-run equilibrium in an open access fishery. Suppose the per unit dockside price

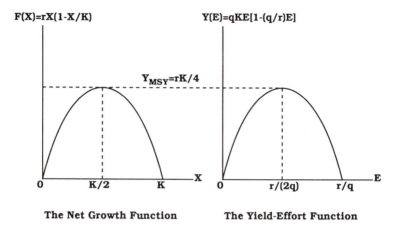

Figure 3.2. The Net Growth and Yield–Effort Functions

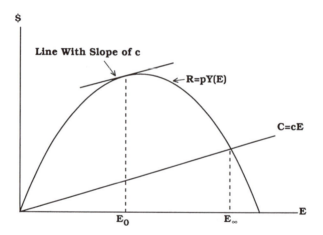

Figure 3.3. The Open Access (E_∞) and Rent Maximizing (E_0) Levels of Effort

is $p > 0$. Then, the steady-state revenue from yield $Y(E)$ is simply $R = pY(E)$. This revenue function will look identical to the yield–effort function, but the vertical axis will now measure dollars ($\$$), or whatever is the appropriate "coin of the realm." Suppose further that the cost of fishing is given by the simple linear equation $C = cE$, where $c > 0$ is the unit cost of effort. Both the revenue and the cost equations are plotted in Figure 3.3. They intersect at $E = E_\infty$, which is referred to as the *open access equilibrium level of effort*. At E_∞ revenue equals cost and net revenue or profit is zero ($\pi = R - C = 0$). The "zero-profit" condition is, in theory, encountered in all competitive industries, where it is viewed as the healthy outcome of socially desirable competitive forces. This is not the case in an open access fishery.

At E_∞ the cost of effort (including compensation to vessel owners and crew) is being covered, but there is nothing left to pay the other important factor, the fish stock! Because access is free, the fish stock is reduced until it is worthless, in the sense that at X_∞ effort cannot be expanded without incurring a net financial loss. The open access equilibrium $(X_\infty, Y_\infty, E_\infty)$ is frequently described as having "too many vessels chasing too few fish." From society's point of view, there is too much effort and the stock is so small that it can only support a small sustainable yield. The open access equilibrium is also nonoptimal in that, if effort could be reduced, the positive net revenues that would result could more than financially compensate those fishers who reduced effort or left the fishery entirely.

This simple static model would seem consistent with the observed outcome of many open access regimes throughout history and across cultures. In addition to fish stocks, case studies describing the depletion of wildlife, forests, groundwater, and grassland could be documented. What the static model does not do is describe the dynamics of the resource and the harvesting industry from an initial condition, where the resource is often abundant. It will turn out that the open access equilibrium, described by the static model, may not be reached, and that the resource might be driven to extinction along an "approach path."

3.5   The Dynamic Model of Open Access

The dynamic model of open access will consist of two difference equations, one describing the change in the resource when harvested, the other describing the change in fishing effort. Substituting the fishery production function into equation (1.1) will give us $X_{t+1} - X_t = F(X_t) - H(X_t, E_t)$, which we will use as the first equation. The second equation, describing effort dynamics, is more speculative because it seeks to explain the economic behavior of fishers. There are many possible models, but perhaps the simplest and most compelling would hypothesize that effort is adjusted in response to last year's profitability. If the per unit price is $p > 0$ and the per unit cost of effort is $c > 0$, then profit or net revenue in period t may be written as $\pi_t = pH(X_t, E_t) - cE_t$. If profit in period t is positive we would think that effort in period $t + 1$ would be expanded, and if that response were linear we could write $E_{t+1} - E_t = \eta[pH(X_t, E_t) - cE_t]$, where $\eta > 0$ is called an adjustment or "stiffness" parameter. We could write our two difference equations in iterative form as a "dynamical system."

$$X_{t+1} = X_t + F(X_t) - H(X_t, E_t)$$
$$E_{t+1} = E_t + \eta[pH(X_t, E_t) - cE_t] \tag{3.3}$$

With functional forms for $F(\bullet)$ and $H(\bullet)$; parameter values for η, p, and c; and initial values for X_0 and E_0 we could simulate (iterate) system (3.3) forward in time and observe the dynamics of X_t and E_t. System (3.3) is likely to be nonlinear and thus has the potential for periodic and chaotic behavior. This raises the question of whether the system will ever reach the equilibrium identified in the static open access model.

To illustrate the potential behavior of the dynamic open access system, let's specify logistic growth and the CPUE production function so that system (3.3) can be written as

$$X_{t+1} = [1 + r(1 - X_t/K) - qE_t]X_t$$
$$E_{t+1} = [1 + \eta(pqX_t - c)]E_t \tag{3.4}$$

With parameter values for r, K, q, η, p, and c, and with initial values X_0 and E_0 we could iterate this system forward in time and observe the behavior of X_t and E_t. Before presenting the results of some numerical simulations of system (3.4), it will be helpful to derive analytical expressions for the open access equilibrium.

In steady state $\pi = pqXE - cE = 0$ implies $X_\infty = c/(pq) > 0$ and using the yield–effort function $pqKE[1 - (q/r)E] = cE$. Solving this last expression for E yields $E_\infty = r(pqK - c)/(pq^2K)$, which is positive provided $pqK > c$. In a numerical analysis of (3.4) we can calculate X_∞ and E_∞, which will provide a reference by which to judge convergence. The point $X_\infty = 0, E_\infty = 0$, is also an equilibrium, one in which both the resource and harvesters go extinct. Barring species reintroduction, this equilibrium is stable and may be the ultimate destination of (X_t, E_t) if other equilibria are unstable. We will examine this possibility numerically.

In Figure 3.4 we show the results of three open access simulations. The base-case parameter set is $c = 1, \eta = 0.3, K = 1, p = 200, q = 0.01$, and $r = 0.1$. The initial values are $X_0 = E_0 = 1$, and the time path for X_t and phase-plane diagram (X_t, E_t) are plotted for $t = 0, 1, \ldots, 100$. The base-case results are shown in Figure 3.4a and reveal a slow spiral convergence to $X_\infty = 0.5$ and $E_\infty = 5$.

In Figure 3.4b, η has been increased to 1, while all other parameter values are unchanged. The values of X_∞ and E_∞ are unchanged, but instead of convergence, X_∞ and E_∞ would appear to be the focus of a limit cycle. A stable limit cycle would be approached from outside or inside the closed orbit defining the cycle. A limit cycle is conditionally stable if it is approached from the outside or inside but not both. With $\eta = 1$, try starting this open access system from $X_0 = 0.5$ and $E_0 = 20$. It would appear that this limit cycle is stable.

In Figure 3.4c η has been returned to its base-case value of 0.3, and r has been increased to 2.9. Recall that $r = 2.9$ induced chaos in the pristine ($Y_t = 0$) fishery, as was shown at the bottom of Spreadsheet 3.1. After a chaotic transition, X_t and E_t lock onto the open access equilibrium at $X_\infty = 0.5$ and $E_\infty = 145$. In this last case, the presence of open access harvesting caused a qualitative change in the dynamics of the resource from that found in the pristine system.

3.6   Static Rent Maximization by a Sole Owner

The economic inefficiency of open access was recognized by the mid-1950s. The policy prescription which was proposed at that time was either "sole ownership" (privatization) of the resource or the limitation of effort to the level which would be adopted by a sole owner seeking to maximize static profit or rent. The rent-maximizing level of effort is also shown in Figure 3.3, where the revenue function $R = pY(E)$ and cost equation $C = cE$ were used to identify the open access equilibrium.

A sole owner, with the exclusive right to harvest the fish stock, would invest in a fleet or hire vessels so that effort maximized rent (profit) $\pi = pY(E) - cE$. The simple first-order condition $d\pi/dE = 0$ implies $pY'(E) = c$, where $Y'(E)$ is the first derivative of the yield–effort function and $pY'(E)$ is marginal revenue. Thus, the level of effort which maximizes rent satisfies the familiar economic dictum that marginal revenue should equal marginal cost. Graphically, the rent-maximizing level of effort is identified by finding the point where the revenue curve has a slope of c, the marginal cost of effort, and dropping a vertical to the E-axis. This occurs at E_0 in Figure 3.3. At E_0 the vertical distance between $R = pY(E)$ and $C = cE$ *is* maximized.

Auctioning off the permanent access to a fishery to the highest-bidding sole owner was not a politically acceptable solution to the problem of open access. A more feasible, although still controversial, policy that emerged from the analysis of the rent-maximizing sole owner was "limited entry." If fishery managers could somehow remove excess vessels so that effort was reduced from E_∞ to E_0, they would maximize the static net value of the fishery, and then, if they could auction off licenses granting seasonal or permanent access to the resource, they would be able to capture all or a portion of the discounted static rent.

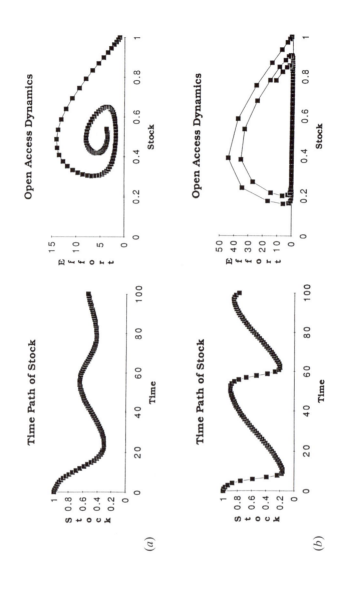

Open Access Dynamics

Time Path of Stock

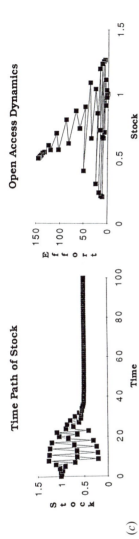

(c)

Figure 3.4. Open Access Dynamics: (a) The Base Case: Spiral Convergence to (X_∞, E_∞); (b) With $\eta = 1$, (X_∞, E_∞) Appears to Be the Focus of a Limit Cycle; (c) With $r = 2.9$, Initial Chaos, Then Convergence to (X_∞, E_∞)

Such revenues might be earmarked for enforcement, management, research, or habitat improvement.

The problem became how to encourage the appropriate number of vessels to leave the fishery and how to prevent the remaining vessels from investing in vessel improvements which would increase "fishing power" or de facto effort. Several countries, including Canada, instituted vessel buy-out programs, whereby federal or provincial funds were used to buy vessels from owners participating in "overcapitalized" fisheries. After purchase the government might sell the vessel for scrap metal or resell it, with the restriction that it could never participate in the fishery it was paid to leave.

The vessels remaining were usually given a license and only licensed vessels were allowed access to the resource. Provisions frequently allowed a license holder to sell his or her license upon retiring from the fishery. If the buy-out program was successful, and remaining vessels were making profits, the market price for a license will reflect the expected present value of profits. In the limited entry salmon fisheries of British Columbia and Alaska these licenses have sold at prices exceeding \$200,000.

The problem of restricting effort to E_0 is not trivial. Even with a fixed number of vessels, the effective level of effort might increase if vessels refit to higher-horsepower engines or add new electronics, including sonar to locate schools of fish and satellite-based navigational systems to pinpoint the location of fishing effort. These sorts of vessel improvements, referred to as *capital stuffing*, can, over time, lead to stock depletion in the limited entry fishery. This has often caused fishery managers to impose input restrictions on hull length, storage capacity, engine horsepower, or net size. These sorts of gear restrictions are likely to create inefficiencies themselves and to start a regulatory "game" in which rent-seeking fishers are trying to find new ways to increase the effectiveness of their vessel in hopes of increasing their share of the total catch. Limited entry by itself is unlikely to achieve optimal management over the long run.

3.7   Present Value Maximization

Is static revenue maximization, with effort set at E_0, optimal in terms of the present value or wealth that might be generated by a fishery? It will turn out that static rent maximization is not optimal if your objective is the maximization of present value. It also turns out that the abstract exercise of present value maximization reveals an important management concept which does not even arise in a static model. So, from both a theoretical and a practical perspective, it is important to revisit the dynamic optimization problem posed in Chapter 1 to illustrate the method of Lagrange multipliers. We have done quite a bit of the tedious spade work and in this section we can concentrate on the economic and management implications.

Recall from Chapter 1 that $\pi_t = \pi(X_t, Y_t)$ represented the net benefits in period t of harvest Y_t from a stock of size X_t. The harvested resource changed according to $X_{t+1} - X_t = F(X_t) - Y_t$, and the stock was initially given by X_0. Maximizing the present value of net benefits, now over an infinite horizon, leads to the problem

$$\text{Maximize} \quad \pi = \sum_{t=0}^{\infty} \rho^t \pi(X_t, Y_t)$$

$$\text{Subject to} \quad X_{t+1} - X_t = F(X_t) - Y_t$$

$$X_0 \text{ given}$$

The modification of the Lagrangian in equation (1.5) to an infinite horizon does not alter the first-order necessary conditions given by equations (1.6)–(1.8), and with the infinite horizon the prospect of reaching a steady-state optimum is more valid than in a finite-horizon problem. (Recall in that Section 2.2 we were able to derive a final function that resulted in a harvest schedule that established the optimal steady-state stock in period $T + 1$, and that the harvest schedule would approximate the infinite-horizon approach.)

In steady state the first-order conditions collapse to three equations, (1.12)–(1.14), in three unknowns, X, Y, and λ. It was possible to eliminate the term $\rho\lambda$ and, after some algebra, we obtained the two-equation system which we rewrite for convenient reference here as

$$F'(X) + \frac{\partial \pi(\bullet)/\partial X}{\partial \pi(\bullet)/\partial Y} = \delta \tag{3.5}$$

$$Y = F(X) \tag{3.6}$$

We referred to (3.5) as the *fundamental equation of renewable resources* and noted that it required the steady-state levels of X and Y to equate the "resource's own rate of return," (the LHS) to the rate of discount, δ. By the implicit function theorem equation (3.5) implied a curve $Y = \phi(X)$, which we could plot along with $Y = F(X)$ to identify the optimal levels X^* and Y^* (see Figure 1.2).

For the case where $F(X_t) = rX_t(1 - X_t/K)$, $Y_t = H(X_t, E_t) = qX_tE_t$, and $C_t = cE_t$, we can solve the production function for $E_t = Y_t/(qX_t)$ and substitute into the cost equation to obtain the *cost function* $C_t = cY_t/(qX_t)$.

This permits us to write $\pi_t = pY_t - cY_t/(qX_t) = [p - c/(qX_t)]Y_t$, which has the partials $\partial\pi(\bullet)/\partial X_t = c/(qX_t^2)$ and $\partial\pi(\bullet)/\partial Y_t = (p - c/(qX_t))$. The derivative of the net growth function is $F'(X_t) = r(1 - 2X_t/K)$. Evaluating these partials at steady state and then substituting into (3.5) will yield

$$r(1 - 2X/K) + \frac{cY}{X(pqX - c)} = \delta \tag{3.7}$$

Solving for (3.7) for Y we obtain

$$Y = \phi(X) = \frac{X(pqX - c)[\delta - r(1 - 2X/K)]}{c} \tag{3.8}$$

We see that $\phi(X)$ depends on the entire set of bioeconomic parameters: c, δ, K, p, q, and r. Changes in any of the parameters will cause $Y = \phi(X)$ to shift in $X - Y$ space, as was implied by the curves $\phi_i(X), i = 1,2,3$, drawn in Figure 1.2.

Recall that one of the conclusions drawn from Figure 1.2 was that the intersection of $\phi(X)$ and $F(X)$ could result in the optimal stock's lying above or below $X_{MSY} = K/2$. We should have expected this. Maximum sustainable yield and X_{MSY} only depend on the parameters r and K and if we have an objective that maximizes the present value of net benefit (in this case, net revenue), then the optimal stock should depend on the economic parameters, c, δ, p, and q as well.

By substituting $Y = rX(1 - X/K)$ on the LHS of equation (3.8) we end up with a single equation in X which has an explicit solution

$$X^* = \frac{K}{4}\left[\left(\frac{c}{pqK} + 1 - \frac{\delta}{r}\right) + \sqrt{\left(\frac{c}{pqK} + 1 - \frac{\delta}{r}\right)^2 + \frac{8c\delta}{pqKr}}\right] \tag{3.9}$$

This is the positive root of a quadratic expression (the negative root, not making any economic sense, is discarded). Although notationally cumbersome it has the advantage, when programmed on a spreadsheet, of permitting the numerical calculation of the optimal stock, based on the six bioeconomic parameters. Numerically, one could change any of the parameters and observe how X^* changes (thus performing numerical "comparative statics"). Knowing X^*, one could calculate $Y^* = rX^*(1 - X^*/K)$, $E^* = Y^*/(qX^*)$, and $\lambda^* = (1 + \delta)[p - c/(qX^*)]$, thus obtaining values for all the variables (unknowns) at the optimal steady state.

If one took the appropriate derivatives of (3.9) or entered a numerical example on a spreadsheet, one would conclude $dX^*/dr > 0$, $dX^*/dK > 0$, $dX^*/dc > 0$, $dX^*/dp < 0$, $dX^*/dq < 0$, and $dX^*/d\delta < 0$. In words, if r, K, or c increases, the optimal stock increases. If p, q, or δ increases, the optimal stock decreases.

We are now in a position to explain the logic behind the subscripts used in identifying the open access and rent-maximizing levels of effort in Figure 3.3. For $\infty > \delta > 0$, $E_\infty > E^* > E_0$. In words, the open access level of effort will exceed the optimal level of effort, which will exceed the rent-maximizing level of effort, for a finite and positive rate of discount. Further, as $\delta \to \infty$, $E^* \to E_\infty$, and as $\delta \to 0$, $E^* \to E_0$, hence the subscripts.

That E^* approaches E_∞ as the discount rate goes to infinity has an interesting interpretation. In open access, individual fishers are caught in something of a dilemma. Collectively, they know that by harvesting less today they would leave a larger fish stock, which would support larger sustainable yields in the future, but unless they could trust all fishers to cooperate in such a conservation strategy they would only be leaving fish that another fisher would harvest, and their individual effort at building the stock would be for naught. The game-strategic aspects of conservation make stock maintenance above X_∞ an unlikely and unstable outcome in open access, with the result that individual fishers appear to behave as if "there were no tomorrow," or more precisely, that they employ an infinite discount rate to evaluate the benefit of conservation.

At the other extreme, if $\delta \to 0$, then a dollar's worth of net benefit is valued the same regardless of when it occurs, and it is optimal to maximize sustainable rent. Note that in steady state $X_0 > X^*$ when $\delta > 0$. Present value can always be increased by harvesting $(X_0 - X^*)$, thus increasing present value in the near term to an extent that will more than offset the small reduction in sustainable net benefits once you reach X^*.

The preceding discussion has been an attempt to compare three steady-state equilibria: open access, static rent maximizing, and the present value or "bioeconomic" optimum. For a positive but finite rate of discount, it will be the case that $E_\infty > E^* > E_0$ and $X_0 > X^* > X_\infty$. The relationship of Y_∞ to Y_0 and Y^* is ambiguous because of the nonlinear net growth function, which will usually have a single maximum at X_{MSY}. It is possible that $Y_\infty > Y_0$. For example, when $F(X) = rX(1 - X/K)$, $H(X,E) = qXE$, and $C = cE$, some algebra will reveal that

$$X_\infty = c/(pq) \tag{3.10}$$

$$E_\infty = r(pqK - c)/(pq^2 K) \tag{3.11}$$

$$Y_\infty = cr(pqK - c)/(p^2 q^2 K) \tag{3.12}$$

$$E_0 = r(pqK - c)/(2pq^2 K) = E_\infty/2 \tag{3.13}$$

$$Y_0 = r(pqK - c)(pqK + c)/(4p^2 q^2 K) = (pqK + c)Y_\infty/(4c) \tag{3.14}$$

$$X_0 = (pqK + c)/(2pq) = (K + X_\infty)/2 \tag{3.15}$$

r=	0.1		r=	0.1		r=	0.1
K=	1		K=	1		K=	1
q=	0.01		q=	0.01		q=	0.01
p=	200		p=	200		p=	200
c=	1		c=	1		c=	1
δ =	0.05		δ =	0		δ =	500
X_∞=	0.5		X_∞=	0.5		X_∞=	0.5
E_∞=	5		E_∞=	5		E_∞=	5
Y_∞=	0.025		Y_∞=	0.025		Y_∞=	0.025
E_0=	2.5		E_0=	2.5		E_0=	2.5
Y_0=	0.01875		Y_0=	0.01875		Y_0=	0.01875
X_0=	0.75		X_0=	0.75		X_0=	0.75
X^*=	0.6830127		X^*=	0.75		X^*=	0.50004999
Y^*=	0.02165064		Y^*=	0.01875		Y^*=	0.025
E^*=	3.16987298		E^*=	2.5		E^*=	4.99950005

Spreadsheet 3.2

In Spreadsheet 3.2 we calculate $(X_\infty, E_\infty, Y_\infty)$, (E_0, Y_0, X_0), and (X^*, Y^*, E^*) for the base-case parameter set $r = 0.1$, $K = 1$, $q = 0.01$, $p = 200$, $c = 1$, and $\delta = 0.05$. Only the bioeconomic optimum depends on δ, and we see that the bioeconomic optimum is identical with the rent-maximizing optimum when $\delta = 0$ and essentially identical to the open access equilibrium when $\delta = 500$.

With a comparative sense of the open access, rent-maximizing (sole owner), and bioeconomic (present value–maximizing) equilibria, we now return to the concept of "user cost" to see the crucial role it plays in moving from open access to a bioeconomic optimum. In Chapter 1, equation (1.9) required $\partial\pi(\bullet)/\partial Y_t = \rho\lambda_{t+1}$. This equation was interpreted as equating the marginal net benefit from harvest in period t to the discounted value of an additional unit of fish in the water in period $t + 1$, where the latter term was referred to as user cost. From the recursive structure of the first-order conditions, it can be shown that λ_{t+1} reflects the discounted value that the additional unit contributes over the entire (possibly infinite) future horizon. Thus user cost reflects the entire future benefit given that an increment in the stock in period $t + 1$ will provide additional biological growth and cost savings into the indefinite future.

Individual fishers, although perhaps aware of the potential benefit of a positive increment to the fish stock, may feel helpless to increase the stock effectively in the face of harvesting by other competitive fishers. Each fisher is presumably adopting a level of effort which equates the marginal value product of effort to marginal cost, and no weight is given to user cost. We will see that the success of actual management policies in avoiding the excesses of open access may critically depend on their ability to introduce user cost into the decision calculus of individual fishers. We now turn to a review of traditional management policies and then bioeconomically based policies.

3.8 Traditional Management Policies

There are at least four policies which have been used to avoid stock depletion under open access and which collectively might be regarded as the traditional approach to fishery management. They are (i) closed seasons, (ii) gear restrictions, (iii) total allowable catch (TAC), and (iv) limited entry. These policies have been employed singly and in various combinations.

A closed season specifies a period of time when harvest of the resource is illegal. The closed season may correspond to a critical stage in the life cycle of the species, when harvest might be particularly disruptive to spawning or survival. For example, the commercial harvest of Pacific salmon is prohibited when the fish enter the rivers and streams leading to their spawning grounds. The harvest of shellfish is often closed during the spring months, when warming waters induce spawning, which will determine, in part, the set, survival, and size of future harvestable cohorts. It is also the case that a closed season may reduce effort below the level, E_∞, which would have occurred with no closed season. This is not a certainty because rent-seeking behavior by fishers may simply result in a redistribution of the same amount of effort, with greater effort expended during the open season when harvest is legal.

Gear restrictions are often imposed deliberately to reduce the efficiency of fishers or to prevent adverse impacts on the supporting ecosystem. In the groundfishery (cod, haddock, flounder) off the coast of New England in the United States, the regional management council has imposed a minimum mesh size of 5.25 inches for nets pulled by trawlers. It was hoped that by keeping the mesh size at or above this minimum juveniles in this "multispecies fishery" would be able to escape through the net as it was being pulled along the sandy and relatively shallow bottom on Georges Bank. In Maryland, watermen harvesting oysters from Chesapeake Bay are restricted to pulling dredges using only sail-powered boats called skipjacks. In the bays of southern Long Island, the harvest of hard clams is restricted to hand pulled rakes or tongs. In the latter two shellfisheries, the restrictions are thought to preclude diesel powered vessels pulling larger dredges with vacuum pumps which might destroy the benthic ecosystem, and thus the ability to grow future "crops" of oysters and clams.

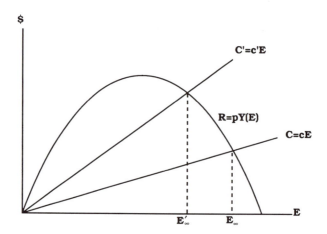

Figure 3.5. The Effect of Gear Restrictions That Raise the Cost of Effort

Gear restrictions might be viewed as raising the unit cost of effort from, say, c to c', as shown in Figure 3.5. This causes the cost equation to rotate upward, establishing a new steady-state equilibrium at $E'_\infty < E_\infty$. Thus, gear restrictions may reduce effort, but do nothing about the underlying problem of economic inefficiency and a resource harvested to the point where it has a zero marginal value.

A *total allowable catch* (TAC) is an aggregate quota which fishery managers regard as the "appropriate" harvest for the current year or season. The appropriate harvest is often ill defined and may be based on advice from biologists, economists, and industry representatives. Biologists and economists may develop "adaptive models" whereby the TAC in period t, denoted TAC_t, is a function of the current stock estimate, X_t. Mathematically we might write $TAC_t = \phi(X_t)$, where the function $\phi(\bullet)$ might be derived from the solution of a dynamic optimization problem.

Once determined, a TAC is announced along with a starting date for the season. On the day the season opens employees of the fishery management agency will monitor harvest by the participating vessels, and when the harvest is estimated to have reached the TAC, the season is closed and further fishing prohibited. This creates what has been referred to as "a race for the fish," the marine equivalent of the Oklahoma land rush.

Management by a TAC has at least three shortcomings. First, it encourages a frenzied and often reckless expenditure of effort as fishers compete to obtain as large a share of the TAC as possible for themselves before the season is closed. Second, over time, the season often becomes "compressed," with a large volume of fish entering the market in a short period, causing prices to plummet, and fresh fish to be processed, frozen, and sold at prices considerably lower than what they will fetch on the fresh market. The compressed season often leaves boats idle or, after regearing, contributing to excess capacity in other fisheries.

The problems with management via a TAC were well illustrated by the Alaskan halibut fishery prior to 1995. In 1991, the season was reduced to two days, during which 4,000 commercial fishermen lowered over 25,000 miles of baited hooks to harvest a fish which might weigh up to 400 pounds and sell for $2.00 per pound on the dock. A lucky boat might gross over $100,000 worth of fish in a single day. But with fatigue, overloading, and the harsh and unpredictable weather of the north Pacific, hooked hands, broken ribs, and capsized vessels were not uncommon. Ten years earlier the season lasted a leisurely 160 days, and consumers had fresh fish for almost six months out of the year. (In 1995, a management system based on Individual Transferable Quotas [ITQs] replaced the frenzy of the "halibut derby." This change in management policy has resulted in a dramatic change in the conduct of the fishery and the price and availability of fresh halibut. We will discuss ITQs in greater detail in the last section of this chapter.)

The fourth traditional policy is limited entry. Under a limited entry program only licensed vessels are allowed to harvest fish. These vessels are often selected on the basis of their historical participation in a fishery. They are issued licenses which they might sell to another vessel owner should they decide to retire or leave the fishery.

When a limited entry program is initially established the management agency is often forced to admit almost all vessels that have previously participated in the fishery. This typically causes an excessive number of licenses to be issued as a result of the overcapitalization chronic to open access. Fishery managers may then institute a buy-out program, as discussed earlier in this chapter. If the limited entry program is successful, it will generate positive rents (profit) for the vessels holding licenses, and if a license holder wishes to sell his or her license, the price received will reflect the expected discounted value of future rents.

The generation of positive rents can cause problems for fishery managers. If the limited entry fishery is also managed using a TAC, then each vessel owner may have an incentive, and now the money, to invest in a larger-horsepower engine, more sophisticated electronics, or simply a larger vessel, in hopes of increasing his or her share of the TAC. Although vessel numbers may have declined, if "upgrades" are made in the remaining vessels, then effective effort (or "fishing power") may actually increase, and any recovery of the stock may be halted or reversed. To prevent the more obvious effort-enhancing investments (for example, a new or larger vessel), fishery managers will sometimes impose gear restrictions. You quickly end up with a complex regulatory situation, where a limited entry fishery is managed using a TAC and vessels are subject to hull length, hold capacity, or other gear restrictions. As noted earlier, matters can degenerate into a regulatory "game," in which regulators impose a restriction and fishers reoptimize inputs hoping to improve their position in the race for the fish.

The continued decline in commercial fish stocks worldwide has raised serious questions about the long-run effectiveness of any combination of the traditional policies. None of them seems capable of introducing user cost into the decision calculus of individual fishers. There are two policies which have the potential to approximate user cost, landings taxes and the previously mentioned Individual Transferable Quotas.

3.9   Bioeconomic Management Policies

To introduce user cost into the harvest decisions of rent-seeking fishers, one needs to introduce an opportunity cost to the decision to harvest an additional unit of the resource today. The first suggestion by economists was to impose a "landings tax," a per unit tax on fish brought to the dock.

Suppose that $\tau > 0$ is the tax rate, say, in dollars/pound. If fishers face a constant expected price, p, then $(p - \tau)$ becomes the relevant aftertax price. Confronted with a landings tax fishers would presumably harvest where the after tax price equaled marginal cost. If we denote $C_t = C(X_t, Y_t)$ as a general stock-dependent cost function, a fisher would choose Y_t so $p - \tau = \partial C(\bullet)/\partial Y_t$, or $p - \partial C(\bullet)/\partial Y_t = \tau$. In this last expression, if managers had the knowledge and ability to set $\tau = \rho \lambda_{t+1}$, they would have achieved the desired first-order condition requiring $\partial \pi(\bullet)/\partial Y_t = \rho \lambda_{t+1}$. With the stock changing over time, the tax would, in theory, need to be changed, increasing as the stock increases. If $X_0 < X^*$, and if $\pi_t = [p - c/(qX_t)]$ before the landings tax, then setting the tax at the steady-state rate, $\tau^* = \rho \lambda^*$, would, in theory, induce a moratorium until the stock recovers to X^*, at which time fishing is resumed with $Y^* = F(X^*)$. Thus, in theory, a landings tax could be used both to establish and to maintain a fishery at the bioeconomic optimum.

In the mid-1970s, when the United States was considering the extension of its territorial waters, it was also trying to revise the way it managed coastal fish stocks, which had been depleted by both domestic and foreign harvests. The suggestion of a landings tax had already appeared in the academic literature, and representatives of the fishing industry were vehemently opposed to the use of taxes to manage fisheries in the United States. They were successful in introducing language which specifically forbids the use of taxes in the Fisheries Conservation and Management Act (FCMA) of 1976, which extended territorial waters to 200 miles and created the fishery conservation zone (FCZ) and eight regional management councils to develop plans for the management of the stocks within their regions.

Although the use of landings taxes was forbidden, economists struck upon another approach, which had not been ruled out, and which might also introduce user cost into the calculus of fishers. The concept was subsequently dubbed Individual Transferable Quotas (ITQs) and had also been proposed as a way to control emissions which reduced environmental quality. Basically, the idea was to allocate shares of a TAC to a limited set of fishers, who would have the choice of either harvesting their share or selling it or a portion of it to another licensed fisher. The option of sale (transfer) can be shown to create an opportunity cost to harvest which might be manipulated, through the TAC, to reflect user cost.

In Figure 3.6 we show the relationship among the demand for ITQs, their supply, and the market clearing quota price. The inverse demand for quota is presumed to be downward sloping so that $P_t^Q = D(TAC_t, X_t)$, where P_t^Q is the price in the quota (ITQ) market, TAC_t is the total allowable catch, and X_t is the fish stock, all in period t. It is assumed that the TAC can be denominated into relatively small units so that a quota holder can buy and sell units which could incrementally increase or decrease the holder's initial allocation. An increase in the fish stock would cause the inverse demand curve to shift upward, since a larger fish stock would reduce harvest cost and increase the rent associated with each unit of ITQ.

Suppose that initially $X_0 < X^*$ and the total allowable catch is set at TAC_0. The price for a unit of quota in the quota market would be P_0^Q, which becomes the opportunity cost of exercising the option to harvest remaining quota. Suppose TAC_0 and subsequent TACs are set which allow for an increase in X_t until the optimal stock, X^*, is reached. At that time the management council will want to set the total allowable catch at $TAC^* = Y^* = F(X^*)$ and demand for quota will have shifted to $D(TAC, X^*)$.

The market clearing quota price is now P^{Q*}, and in theory $P^{Q*} = \rho\lambda^*$. Thus, by appropriately choosing the TAC_t and allowing the ITQs to be transferable, the management council could guide a suboptimal stock to the optimal level and sustain it.

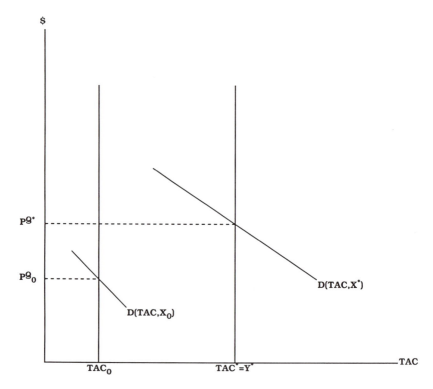

Figure 3.6. The Price for ITQ in the Quota Market When $X = X_0 < X^*$ and When $X = X^*$

3.10   ITQ Programs in New Zealand, Australia, and Canada

Much of our experience with ITQ programs comes from their adoption in New Zealand, Australia, and Canada. Iceland was actually the first country to introduce an ITQ program, but restrictions on transferability and firmly held fishing traditions within coastal communities apparently have not led to dramatic changes in the size or efficiency of the Icelandic industry. In the United States, ITQs are being used to manage the Alaskan halibut and the surf clam in the mid-Atlantic.

In Canada ITQs have been used to manage herring, groundfish, scallop, lobster, perch (in Lake Erie), and sablefish. Effort, measured by the number of participating vessels, was reduced by 36% in the sablefish fishery (from 47 to 30 vessels), 21% across two areas in the herring fishery (65 to 51 vessels), 16% across two scallop areas (73 to 61 vessels), and 26% in Lake Erie (248 to 182 vessels). There was no reduction in effort in two areas of the Canadian lobster fishery. (Lobster fisheries in North America have not experienced the typical stock depletion associated with open access because access to inshore areas is often regulated by informal, community-based sanctions.) The preceding are percentage reductions which occurred during the first two to four years of a program, and we would predict that the removal of excess capital from a fishery may take several years.

A more dramatic reduction has taken place in Australia's southern bluefin tuna fishery, where the number of quota holders declined from 143 in 1984 (when ITQs were introduced) to 63 in 1988. There was also a significant regional redistribution of bluefin ITQs among Western Australia, South Australia, and New South Wales, with the latter state's quota dropping from 1,872 metric tons in 1984–1985 to 0 in 1985–1986. This probably reflects the ability of vessels in Western Australia and South Australia to fish quota at a lower cost, thus permitting them to purchase quota from the higher-cost vessels in New South Wales. Although this might result in some painful adjustments to a local fishing economy, it represents an improvement in efficiency which will lead to higher net revenues for the fishery as a whole.

The New Zealand ITQ program began in 1986. The government announced that the initial ITQs would be based on the average of the two highest annual harvests during the last three years. Further, the quota was initially issued in actual pounds instead of a share of a changing TAC. This resulted in a de facto TAC which was too high and necessitated a government buy-back program to reduce catch and effort. In 1986 and 1987 the New Zealand government spent approximately $30 million (U.S.) to buy back quota. The ITQ program was subsequently changed to a "share of TAC" program whereby the TAC was set adaptively each year.

The New Zealand program is extensive, covering 31 species in 10 management areas. Because of the announcement that quota would be initially awarded on the two best years of the last three, the resulting TAC and number of vessels actually increased in the first year. The subsequent buy-back program and the switch to a share of TAC program have resulted in a decrease in vessel numbers, particularly of smaller vessels, and a slight increase in the amount of quota held by the largest fishing consortia. New Zealand limits the amount of quota which can be held by an individual or company to 20% for an inshore fishery and 35% for an offshore fishery.

The TACs in New Zealand, like those elsewhere, are often based on the analysis and advice of fishery scientists and representatives of the industry. The fishing industry has frequently lobbied for larger TACs than those proposed by biologists, and for certain species, like the orange roughy, the stocks have actually declined since the initiation of the ITQ program. Often there was not a lot of good analysis on which to estimate stock size or models to simulate future population dynamics. New Zealand has increased its scientific capability in these areas and the TACs for many of the 31 species have been reduced. Perhaps most importantly, the fishing industry now views the ITQ program as a valid approach to management and appears willing to support a reduction in the current TACs if solid analysis exists to justify it: specifically, that it will allow greater harvests tomorrow.

In the Alaskan halibut fishery the ITQ program has delivered many of the benefits that economists had promised. Fresh halibut is available eight months of the year. The ex-vessel price in early 1997 was about $2.50/lb., an increase of about $0.58/lb. from the price received in Alaska in 1994. The price increase for fresh halibut has occurred despite the fact that total landings of Pacific halibut increased from 54.7 million pounds in 1994 to 65 million pounds in 1997. Search-and-rescue calls have declined by 80% from 1994 to 1996, as vessels can choose to fish their quota under safer weather conditions. Thus, the limited experience in the Alaskan halibut fishery has been quite positive, and it is likely to lead to more ITQ experiments in other U.S. fisheries.

Two potential problems with management via ITQs are high-grading and nonselective gear in multispecies fisheries. If a vessel has an ITQ in a fishery where there is a premium paid for larger fish, the vessel has an incentive to try to maximize the number of large fish in its catch. This can lead a vessel to throw back smaller, usually younger fish in hopes that the next set will yield more valuable, larger fish. Often the smaller discards will not survive, and through the process of high-grading the catch to larger fish, de facto fishing mortality is increased well above what the landed catch would indicate.

In a multispecies fishery several species might be harvested simultaneously by a nonselective gear, a situation that can lead to the "by-catch problem." For example, in the previously described groundfishery off the coast of New England, cod, haddock, and flounder are harvested simultaneously by trawlers fishing on Georges Bank. If a vessel has a large quota for cod, but a small quota for haddock, it may have to discard haddock (a by-catch species) to avoid violation. Discards are again subject to a high mortality rate and a dying fish thrown back into the water won't satisfy a consumer or a marine biologist. It would make better sense for the vessel to keep the excess haddock and buy haddock ITQ when it returns to port. Thus, regulations in a multispecies fishery may need to allow for ITQ acquisition after the fact. A vessel might acquire ITQ to make its harvest "legal" by purchasing additional quota from a reserve held back by fishery managers in anticipation of the by-catch problem. Such reserves, however, may start a "race for the reserve," a sort of smaller and species-selective version of the race for the fish under a TAC. Multispecies fisheries, harvested with nonselective gear, have always posed a major problem for fishery managers, and although ITQs might help, they do not seem be the sought-after silver bullet (solution).

3.11 Questions and Exercises

Q3.1 Is the rent-maximizing harvest, Y_0, always greater than the open access equilibrium harvest, Y_∞?

Q3.2 In the dynamic open access system will (X_∞, E_∞) always be reached by a convergent spiral?

Q3.3 Will an increase in the discount rate result in a decrease in the optimal harvest in a single-species fishery?

Q3.4 In the simple bioeconomic model, if the marginal stock effect is greater than the discount rate, what is the relationship between X^* and X_{MSY}?

E3.1 Consider a fishery where $F(X_t) = rX_t(X_t/K_1 - 1)(1 - X_t/K_2)$, $Y_t = qX_tE_t$, and $C_t = cE_t$, where $K_2 > K_1 > 0$ and r, q, and c are also positive parameters.

(a) What are the analytic expressions defining X_∞ and E_∞?

(b) If $p > 0$ is the unit price for fish on the dock and $\eta > 0$ is the adjustment (stiffness) parameter for effort, what is the system which might be used to simulate open access dynamics?

(c) If $r = 0.1$, $K_1 = 0.1$, $K_2 = 1$, $q = 0.1$, $p = 1$, and $c = 0.01$, what are the numerical values for X_∞ and E_∞? If $\eta = 5$, $X_0 = 0.6$, and $E_0 = 1$, simulate the system for $t = 0, \ldots, 1,000$, and describe, in words, the dynamics and the stability of X_∞ and E_∞.

(d) If c increases to $c = 0.05$, what are the new numerical values for X_∞ and E_∞? With $\eta = 5$, $X_0 = 0.6$, and $E_0 = 1$, simulate the system for $t = 0, \ldots, 1,000$, and describe, in words, the dynamics and the stability of X_∞ and E_∞.

E3.2 Suppose the fishery in **E3.1** were to be managed so as to maximize the present value of net revenue where $\rho = 1/(1 + \delta)$ is the discount factor.

(a) What is the expression for $F'(X)$?

(b) What is the expression for the "marginal stock effect"? (Hint: It should be a function of X, c, r, K_1, K_2, p, and q.)

(c) For the initial parameter set in **E3.1** ($r = 0.1$, $K_1 = 0.1$, $K_2 = 1$, $q = 0.1$, $p = 1$, and $c = 0.01$), and with $\delta = 0.05$, solve for the numerical values for the bioeconomic optimum, (X^*,Y^*,E^*). Start Solver from a guess of $X^* = 0.5$.

(d) Suppose that the resource stock were estimated to be $X_0 = 0.3$ and that fishery managers decided to maximize the present value of net revenues for $t = 0, 1, 2, \ldots, 9$, subject to $X_{10} = X^*$ (from part **c** of this question). What are the optimal values for $Y_t \geq 0$ for $t = 0, 1, 2, \ldots, 9$?

(e) What is the shadow price on fish in the water at the bioeconomic optimum?

CHAPTER 4

The Economics of Forestry

4.0   Introduction and Overview

In this chapter we will examine the economics of even-aged forestry and the optimal inventory of old-growth forest. By an even-aged forest we mean a forest that contains trees of the same species and age. Such a forest might be established by a lightning-induced fire or by clear-cutting of a stand of trees. The first non-native settlers in western Washington and Oregon encountered vast stretches of even-aged forest (predominantly Douglas fir) which had been established by natural ("volunteer") reseeding following a fire. Today, silvicultural practices by forest firms are specifically designed to establish an age-structured forest inventory or "synchronized forest," where tracts of land contain cohorts ranging in age from seedlings to "financially mature" trees, that provide the forest firm with a more or less steady flow of timber to their mills.

In western Washington and Oregon in the mid-1800s most forest stands contained trees over 200 years old with diameters in excess of five feet. Collectively, these forests constituted a huge inventory of old-growth timber, which was used in the construction of houses and commercial buildings, the building of ships, and the manufacture of railroad ties, telegraph poles, furniture, musical instruments, and a plethora of other items. In the 1850s the old-growth forests of the Pacific Northwest must have seemed limitless and inexhaustible, but by the 1920s foresters were already contemplating the end of this period of "old-growth mining" and the establishment of a forest economy based on the sustainable harvest of timber from even-aged forest "plantations." An obvious question would be "When should we cease the cutting of old-growth forest and preserve what's left?"

This question has become a controversial policy issue in the Pacific Northwest and Alaska, where most of the remaining old-growth forest is on land owned by the federal government. The remaining inventory of old-growth forest provides a valuable flow of "amenity services," as a result of its ability to provide (1) sites for hiking and camping, (2) habitat for wildlife, (3) watershed protection, and (4) what we will later refer to as option value.

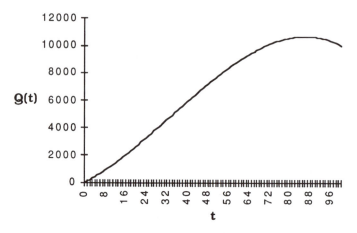

Figure 4.1. The Volume of Merchantable Timber, $Q(t)$

In determining the optimal age at which to cut an even-aged stand of trees we will take the perspective of a private present-value maximizing individual or firm. When trying to determine the optimal inventory of old-growth forest to preserve we will take the perspective of a social forester or planner who seeks to balance the flow of nontimber amenity value with the desire for net revenue and jobs in the forest economy. Many of these same issues arise in the management of the mixed hard-wood forests of the north central and northeastern United States and in the tropical forests found in developing countries. The administration of these forests is more complex because it involves multispecies manage-ment with interspecific competition for light, water, and nutrients in the case of temperate forests, or the potential instability of soils in the case of tropical forests.

4.1   The Volume Function and Mean Annual Increment

Consider a parcel of land which has recently been cleared of trees by fire or cutting. Suppose the parcel is reseeded (restocked) by windblown seed from neighboring trees or by seedlings planted by a forest firm. Taking the date of reseeding as $t = 0$ and treating time as a continuous variable, let $Q = Q(t)$ denote volume of merchantable timber at instant $t > 0$. Mer-chantable volume is the volume of wood which has commercial value. A plausible shape for this volume function is shown in Figure 4.1.

Figure 4.1 shows the volume of merchantable timber increasing until about $t = 86$, after which volume decreases as a result of disease and decay (senescence). In reality, merchantable volume may not become positive until five or more years after reseeding. The functional form used in drawing Figure 4.1 is a cubic, given by

$$Q(t) = at + bt^2 - dt^3 \tag{4.1}$$

where $a = 100$, $b = 2$, and $d = 0.02$. Another functional form which is frequently used to approximate merchantable volume is the exponential

$$Q(t) = e^{a-b/t} \tag{4.2}$$

where $b > a > 0$. As $t \to \infty$, $Q(t) \to e^a$, and there is no decline in the volume of merchantable timber when using this functional form.

Foresters have long been interested in the appropriate time to wait before a recently replanted parcel should be cut and replanted again. The interval between cuttings is called the *rotation length*. Foresters were also aware that it might be desirable to arrange a more or less steady annual timber harvest from a large forest. This would presumably permit more or less steady annual employment for loggers and mill workers. It might be possible to organize a large forest into some number of smaller parcels ranging in age from zero (just replanted) to age T (about to be cut), where T is rotation length.

Suppose one wished to maximize the average annual yield from a rotation of length T. This means that every T years you would cut the representative parcel, obtaining an average annual volume $Q(T)/T$. Early foresters called this average annual volume the *mean annual increment* (MAI) and sought the rotation which would maximize it. Taking the first derivative and setting it equal to zero results in the expression $Q(T)/T = Q'(T)$. This says that the rotation which maximizes MAI must equate the average product from waiting $[Q(T)/T]$ with the marginal product from waiting $[Q'(T)]$. Graphically, this rotation can be identified by finding where a ray from the origin is just tangent to the volume function. For the cubic growth function given in equation (4.1) the rotation maximizing mean annual increment will be $T = b/(2d)$. For the exponential function in equation (4.2) this rotation is simply $T = b$. In Figure 4.2 we plot equation (4.2) for $a = 10$ and $b = 70$ and draw in the ray from the origin, which is tangent at $T = 70$.

The rotation which maximizes average annual volume is analogous to the stock level which maximizes sustainable yield in the fishery. Although at first blush it may seem a desirable rotation (it maximizes the volume harvested over an infinite horizon), it similarly ignores any economic considerations, like the net price for timber, the cost of replanting, or the discount rate.

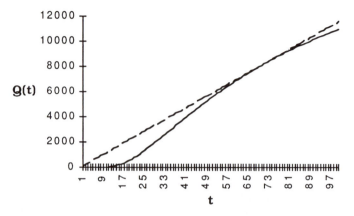

Figure 4.2. The Volume Function $Q(t) = e^{a-b/t}$

4.2   The Optimal Single Rotation

Suppose a parcel of land has recently been reseeded and you are to maximize the net present value of this single stand. After this stand is cut, the land will be converted to some other use in which you have no financial stake. How long should you wait before harvesting this single stand?

Let p denote the net price per unit volume at harvest, which is assumed known and constant. With time a continuous variable, we will use $e^{-\delta t}$ as the appropriate discount factor for calculating the present value of a financial outcome at instant $t > 0$ (see Chapter 1). With no replanting the net present value of a single rotation of length T is given by $\pi_s = pQ(T)e^{-\delta T}$. The optimal single rotation can be found by solving $d\pi_s/dT = pQ(T)e^{-\delta T}(-\delta) + pQ'(T)e^{-\delta T} = 0$ and implies

$$pQ'(T) = \delta pQ(T) \tag{4.3}$$

This equation has an important economic interpretation. On the LHS the term $pQ'(T)$ is the marginal value of allowing the stand to grow an increment $(dT > 0)$ longer. On the RHS, the term $\delta pQ(T)$ is the marginal cost of allowing the stand to grow an increment longer. It represents the forgone interest payment on not cutting the stand now. Thus, the optimal single rotation will balance the *marginal value of waiting* with the *marginal cost of waiting*.

We could have canceled p from both sides of equation (4.3) and written the first-order condition as $Q'(T)/Q(T) = \delta$. The interpretation of this equivalent equation is that the optimal single rotation equates the

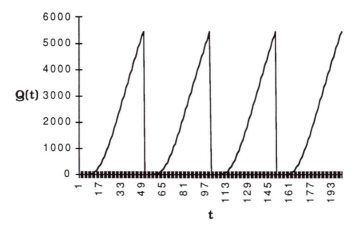

Figure 4.3. Volume with Cutting and Reseeding Every $T = 50$ Years

percentage rate of increase in volume $[Q'(T)/Q(T)]$ to the rate of discount. For the exponential volume function in equation (4.2), the optimal single rotation has an analytical (explicit) expression given by $T = \sqrt{b/\delta}$. It will normally be the case that the optimal single rotation is shorter than the rotation which maximizes mean annual increment.

4.3   The Faustmann Rotation

Suppose now that the parcel of land has just been reseeded and you are asked to determine the optimal rotation if the parcel is to be devoted to rotational (even-aged) forestry in perpetuity. Suppose c is the cost of replanting the parcel and that p, c, δ, and $Q(t)$ are unchanging over all future rotations. In this unlikely stationary environment the optimal rotation is constant and the pattern of cutting and replanting leads to the "sawtoothed" time profile for $Q(t)$ shown in Figure 4.3.

Figure 4.3 was drawn by using the exponential volume function with $a = 10$ and $b = 70$ and arbitrarily imposing a rotation of 50 years. From an economic perspective we may ask, What is the optimal rotation?

Recall we are assuming that the parcel has recently been reseeded and that cost has been "sunk." What is the expression for the present value of net revenues from an infinite series of rotations, all of length T? At the end of each rotation we would receive the same net revenue of $[pQ(T) - c]$. This would be obtained at $T, 2T, 3T, \ldots$, and so on, ad infinitum. The present value of this infinite series will equal

$$\pi = [pQ(T)-c]e^{-\delta T}\left\{1+e^{-\delta T}+e^{-2\delta T}+e^{-3\delta T}+\ldots\right\}$$

$$= \frac{[pQ(T)-c]e^{-\delta T}}{(1-e^{-\delta T})}$$

$$\pi = \frac{[pQ(T)-c]}{[e^{\delta T}-1]} \tag{4.4}$$

Note that the infinite series $\{1 + e^{-\delta T} + e^{-2\delta T} + e^{-3\delta T} + \ldots\}$ converges to $1/(1 - e^{-\delta T})$ when $1 > e^{-\delta T} > 0$, and the last expression is obtained by multiplying the top and bottom of the previous expression by $e^{\delta T}$. The Faustmann rotation is the value of T which maximizes π. It is named after a German civil servant, Martin Faustmann, who correctly formulated this problem way back in 1849. The problem was correctly solved by another German, Max Robert Pressler, in 1860. The optimal rotation must satisfy $d\pi/dT = 0$. The derivative and subsequent algebra are tedious, but ultimately lead to a logical expression with a nice economic interpretation. First, note that

$$d\pi/dT = [pQ(T)-c](-1)[e^{\delta T}-1]^{-2}e^{\delta T}\delta + [e^{\delta T}-1]^{-1}pQ'(T) = 0$$

implies

$$pQ'(T) = \frac{\delta[pQ(T)-c]e^{\delta T}}{[e^{\delta T}-1]} = \frac{\delta[pQ(T)-c]}{[1-e^{-\delta T}]}$$

Multiplying both sides by $[1 - e^{-\delta T}]$ and transposing yields

$$pQ'(T) = \delta[pQ(T)-c] + pQ'(T)e^{-\delta T}$$

Now we make use of a critical observation. The second term on the RHS is equal to $\delta\pi$ because

$$pQ'(T)e^{-\delta T} = \frac{\delta[pQ(T)-c]e^{\delta T}e^{-\delta T}}{[e^{\delta T}-1]} = \frac{\delta[pQ(T)-c]}{[e^{\delta T}-1]} = \delta\pi$$

This permits us finally to write

$$pQ'(T) = \delta[pQ(T)-c] + \delta\pi \tag{4.5}$$

On the LHS, $pQ'(T)$ is once again the marginal value of waiting. It is the incremental return from delaying the cutting of the current stand by dT. On the RHS, $\delta[pQ(T) - c]$ is the forgone interest payment if the current stand were *not* cut at instant T. This is not the only opportunity cost of delaying the cutting of the current stand. The term $\delta\pi$ is the cost of incrementally delaying all future stands. Alternatively, if the land were reseeded after cutting the current stand, $\delta\pi$ would be the forgone rental payment which the landowner could charge a forester for renting her land to grow trees. The sum of these two terms becomes the marginal cost of waiting.

How does the Faustmann rotation, which must satisfy equation (4.5), compare to the optimal single rotation of the previous section? Intuitively, delay in the infinite rotation problem incurs an additional cost ($\delta\pi$). Thus, it is typically the case that the Faustmann rotation will be *shorter* than the optimal single rotation. For high rates of discount, the Faustmann rotation may only be slightly less than the optimal single rotation. Why? What happens to $\delta\pi$ as δ increases? Remember that π depends on δ!

Another interesting concept is given by the term $[\pi(T^*) - c]$, where T^* is the Faustmann rotation. Recall that π was the present value of all future rotations given that the cost of planting the current stand had been paid (sunk). We know that T^* maximizes π. The term $[\pi(T^*) - c]$ is called the *land expectation or site value.* It is the value of bare land devoted to forestry. After cutting the current stand, but before replanting, $[\pi(T^*) - c]$ must be positive to make replanting worthwhile. In other words, the expected value of land with freshly planted seedlings, $[\pi(T^*)]$, must exceed the cost of those seedlings to make reseeding a worthwhile thing to do. If $[\pi(T^*) - c] < 0$ the landowner would probably get out of forestry and devote the land to its "next highest use."

4.4 An Example

To illustrate the concepts encountered thus far, let's consider a numerical example. Table 4.1 reports the volume of merchantable timber (in board feet) from even-aged stands of Douglas fir grown on 14 different site classes in the Pacific Northwest. The site class index runs from 80 (a low-quality site) to 210 (a high-quality site). Volume for each site class is reported in 10-year increments for stands ranging in age from 30 to 160 years.

Consider Site Class 140. Suppose we wish to fit the exponential volume function to the merchantable volume for this site class. Taking the natural log of both sides of equation (4.2) we obtain $\ln Q = a - b/t$. Taking the natural log of the volume data under Site Class 140 in Table 4.1 and regressing it on $1/t$ result in the following ordinary least squares (OLS) equation:

$$\ln Q = 12.96 - 196.11\,(1/t)$$
$$(71.51)\,(-16.72) \qquad \text{Adjusted } R^2 = 0.96 \qquad (4.6)$$

Table 4.1. *Merchantable Volume per Acre (in Board Feet) for Douglas Fir by Age and Site Class*

Age	Site Class Index													
	80	90	100	110	120	130	140	150	160	170	180	190	200	210
30	0	0	0	0	0	0	300	900	1500	2,600	4,000	6,000	8,000	10,500
40	0	0	0	200	1,200	2,600	4,500	6,500	9,000	11,900	15,500	19,600	24,400	29,400
50	30	200	1,600	3,300	5,500	8,400	12,400	17,000	22,200	27,400	32,700	38,400	44,100	50,000
60	1,100	2,600	4,800	8,100	12,500	18,000	23,800	29,600	36,200	42,800	49,300	55,900	62,000	68,300
70	2,400	5,300	9,000	14,000	20,600	27,900	35,200	42,500	50,000	57,200	64,600	71,500	78,200	85,000
80	4,400	8,600	13,900	20,100	28,600	37,000	45,700	54,300	62,100	70,000	78,000	85,400	92,500	99,800
90	6,900	12,000	18,600	26,000	35,700	45,200	55,000	64,000	72,900	81,000	89,200	97,200	104,800	112,300
100	9,600	15,400	22,800	31,400	42,000	52,400	62,800	72,400	81,800	90,400	98,900	107,100	115,100	122,900
110	12,200	18,900	26,700	36,300	47,500	58,500	69,400	79,400	89,200	98,300	107,000	115,200	123,700	131,200
120	14,700	21,800	30,400	40,700	52,400	63,900	75,000	85,500	95,500	105,100	114,100	122,500	131,100	139,000
130	17,000	24,600	33,800	44,700	56,700	68,700	80,000	91,000	101,100	111,000	120,000	128,900	137,700	146,100
140	19,200	27,200	36,800	48,300	60,600	72,900	84,500	95,900	106,200	116,300	125,500	134,500	143,500	152,000
150	21,300	29,600	39,700	51,600	64,000	76,600	88,600	100,300	111,000	121,200	130,700	139,500	148,700	157,200
160	23,300	31,900	42,200	54,600	67,100	80,100	92,400	104,400	115,400	125,700	135,400	144,400	153,500	162,000

	A	B	C	D	E	F	G
1	Site Class 140 Estimation of Exponential Volume Function						
2							
3	t	Q	lnQ	1 / t			
4	30	300	5.70378247	0.03333333			
5	40	4500	8.41183268	0.025			
6	50	12400	9.42545175	0.02			
7	60	23800	10.0774409	0.01666667			
8	70	35200	10.4688014	0.01428571			
9	80	45700	10.7298536	0.0125			
10	90	55000	10.9150885	0.01111111			
11	100	62800	11.0477104	0.01			
12	110	69400	11.1476421	0.00909091			
13	120	75000	11.2252434	0.00833333			
14	130	80000	11.2897819	0.00769231			
15	140	84500	11.3445068	0.00714286			
16	150	88600	11.3918871	0.00666667			
17	160	92400	11.4338823	0.00625			
18							
19	Regression of lnQ on 1/t						
20	Multiple R	0.97919725					
21	R Square	0.95882725					
22	Adjusted R Squ	0.95539618					
23	Standard Error	0.33529622					
24	Observations	14					
25							
26	Analysis of Variance						
27		df	Sum of Squares	Mean Square	F	Significance F	
28	Regression	1	31.4173123	31.4173123	279.454883	1.1189E-09	
29	Residual	12	1.3490827	0.11242356			
30	Total	13	32.766395				
31							
32		Coefficients	Standard Error	t Statistic	P-value	Lower 95%	Upper 95%
33							
34	a	12.963936	0.18128803	71.5101596	2.9093E-18	12.5689433	13.3589287
35	minus b	-196.105868	11.730992	-16.7169041	3.6009E-10	-221.665503	-170.546232
36							
37	a=	12.96					
38	b=	196.11					
39	c=	180					
40	p=	0.65					
41	δ=	0.05					
42							
43	T*=	61.6609933					
44	π=	542.841615					

Spreadsheet 4.1

where the *t*-statistics are given in parentheses. The transformed data and the regression results are reported in greater detail in Spreadsheet 4.1.

For the exponential volume function, we saw that the rotation maximizing average annual volume (or MAI) was simply $T = b = 196.11$ years. We also determined that the rotation maximizing the present value of a single rotation was $T_s = \sqrt{b/\delta}$. If the discount rate is $\delta = 0.05$, then the optimal single rotation is $T_s = 62.63$.

At the bottom of Spreadsheet 4.1 we entered an initial guess for the Faustmann rotation ($T^* = 50$, no longer shown) in cell $B$43. The expression for π, as given in equation (4.4), was programmed into cell $B$44. The cost of replanting was set at $c = \$180$/acre, the price per board foot for timber was $p = \$0.65$, and the discount rate was kept at $\delta = 0.05$. Excel's Solver was summoned to maximize π by changing the initial guess for T^*. The optimal (Faustmann) rotation, to which Solver quickly converged, was $T^* = 61.66$ (now in cell $B$43), which is only slightly less than the optimal single rotation of $T_s = 62.63$. The maximized value of π is \$542.84 per acre, which exceeds the cost of replanting, $c = \$180$ per acre, implying that rotational forestry is viable on Site Class 140 land.

4.5   Timber Supply

The Faustmann model can be used to analyze the supply response of a forest company to changes in p, c, and δ. We will define the *short-run supply response* to be the change in the volume of timber cut as the result of a change in the rotation length. The *long-run supply response* will be the result of a change in (i) the average annual volume, $Q(T)/T$, and (ii) the amount of land devoted to forestry. Because the long-run supply response depends on two factors, the net *qualitative* effect of a change in p or c will be ambiguous.

To determine whether the timber supply will increase or decrease in either the short run or the long run, we need to know the comparative statics of the rotation length, T, and the rent on forest land, $\delta\pi$, for changes in p, c, and δ. In deriving equation (4.5) we saw that

$$pQ'(T) = \frac{\delta[pQ(T)-c]}{[1-e^{-\delta T}]}$$

Dividing both sides by p yields

$$Q'(T) = \frac{\delta[pQ(T)-c/p]}{[1-e^{-\delta T}]}$$

or

$$\frac{Q'(T)}{[Q(T)-c/p]} = \frac{\delta}{[1-e^{-\delta T}]} \tag{4.7}$$

The comparative static results we derive assume that $Q'(T) > 0$, $Q''(T) < 0$, and that all Faustmann rotations before and after a change in p, c, or δ are less than the rotation that maximizes average annual volume. This last assumption is important in determining the long-run supply response.

Carefully examine equation (4.7), which must be satisfied by the Faustmann rotation. Suppose that p increases. How will the Faustmann rotation change in order to reestablish the equality of equation (4.7)? An increase in p will *increase* the denominator of the LHS and thus reduce the LHS overall. To reestablish equation (4.7), we must increase $Q'(T)$, which, given our assumptions, can only be done by *shortening* the Faustmann rotation from its previous value. Thus, if price increases from p_1 to p_2 ($p_2 > p_1$), the Faustmann rotation will decrease from T_1 to T_2 ($T_2 < T_1$). Since the Faustmann rotation *decreases* with an *increase* in price we write $dT/dp < 0$.

A change in c will have the opposite effect on rotation length. In fact, it is legitimate simply to regard (c/p) as a single parameter, the cost–price ratio. Increases in p decrease the cost–price ratio, and increases in c increase its value. By similar reasoning, if c increases, the denominator of the LHS of (4.7) decreases, and we need to decrease $Q'(T)$ to reestablish equality. To decrease $Q'(T)$ we would move to a *longer* rotation. Since an increase in c lengthens the rotation we write $dT/dc > 0$.

Finally, consider an increase in the discount rate, δ, which only appears on the RHS of equation (4.7). As the discount rate increases, the RHS will increase, since the numerator is increasing linearly in δ, while the denominator is asymptotically increasing to unity. To reestablish the equality of (4.7), we need to increase $Q'(T)$ on the LHS of (4.7), which can only be done by *decreasing T*. This implies $dT/d\delta < 0$.

The short-run supply response of forest firms can be inferred from these comparative results. In particular, if p, c, or δ changes so that the new rotation is shorter than the old (pre-change) rotation, then forest firms will find themselves with "over-mature" timber, which they will cut, increasing the volume (and thus supply) of timber flowing to the market. Increases in p or δ will result in a short-run *increase* in timber supply, whereas an increase in c *reduces* short-run supply, since the new, longer, rotation will necessitate a delay in cutting stands that were almost financially mature under a lower-c rotation.

In the long run, timber supply will depend on the average annual volume per acre, $Q(T)/T$, and on the number of acres devoted to forestry. The number of acres in forestry is thought to depend on $\delta\pi$, the rental value of forest land. Any change in p, c, or δ which increases $\delta\pi$ will, in theory, serve to attract more land to forestry. We can write $\delta\pi = \delta[pQ(T) - c]/[e^{\delta T} - 1]$. By inspection, an increase in p will increase $\delta\pi$, whereas an increase in c will lower $\delta\pi$. Thus, an increase in p makes it more attractive to devote land to forestry, and an increase in c makes existing forest land less profitable and some will be converted to other land uses.

An increase in δ will *reduce* $\delta\pi$! This occurs because π depends on δ

and will decrease *exponentially* with increases in δ. Since an increase in δ will lower $\delta\pi$, land devoted to forestry becomes less valuable and more susceptible to conversion.

So, what are the long-run supply implications of a change in $p, c,$ or δ? An increase in p leads to a shorter rotation and a lower average annual volume, $Q(T)/T$. This would tend to reduce long-run supply. However, an increase in p will increase $\delta\pi$ and make forest land financially more attractive. The net effect will depend on the relative strength of these two effects, which is *an empirical question*. Qualitatively, the long-run supply effect of an increase in p is said to be ambiguous.

The long-run supply implications of an increase in c (replanting cost) are also ambiguous. Why? An increase in c causes forest firms to adopt a longer rotation. This will increase $Q(T)/T$, which would tend to increase long-run supply. However, an increase in c will reduce $\delta\pi$, making forest land less profitable and reducing the amount of land devoted to forestry. Again, the average annual volume effect and the forest land value effect work at cross-purposes and the net effect cannot be determined by a qualitative analysis using comparative statics.

Finally, an increase in the discount rate, δ, will have an *unambiguous* long-run supply effect. An increase in δ will shorten the rotation of forest firms and will reduce average annual volume, $Q(T)/T$. An increase in δ will also reduce $\delta\pi$ and make land devoted to forestry less valuable. Both effects work to reduce the long-run supply of timber.

The changes in rotation length, T; short-run timber supply, $Q(T)/T$; $\delta\pi$; and long-run timber supply are summarized in Table 4.2. A plus sign indicates that an increase in the parameter will increase the variable in question, a negative sign indicates that an increase in the parameter will reduce the variable in question, and a question mark indicates that the effect is qualitatively ambiguous. For example, a negative sign in the T row under p means $dT/dp < 0$, the plus sign in the row Short-run Supply below p means that an increase in p will increase the short-run supply of timber, and so on. Study Table 4.2 to make sure the entries are consistent with your understanding of the Faustmann model.

4.6   The Optimal Stock of Old-Growth Forest

When the first white settlers arrived in the Pacific Northwest in the mid-1800s they found vast tracts of even-aged forest, the result of lightning-induced forest fires and natural reseeding. Most of these tracts contained trees in excess of 200 years in age. Western Washington and Oregon and Northern California were seen as a huge inventory of old-growth timber. At the time, there was not much concern for conservation. One hundred

Table 4.2. *The Effect of Changes in p, c, and δ on the Faustmann Rotation, Short-Run Supply, Q(T)/T, δπ, and Long-Run Supply*

	p	c	δ
T	-	+	-
Short-Run Supply	+	-	+
Q(T)/T	-	+	-
δπ	+	-	-
Long-Run Supply	?	?	-

and fifty years later less than 15% of that inventory remains. Old-growth forest is thought to convey a variety of nontimber benefits, or *amenity flows*, in the form of habitat for wildlife, watershed protection, and desirable sites for hiking and camping. Let's consider a model which addresses the question "When should we stop cutting old-growth forest and preserve what's left?"

Suppose that the flow of nontimber amenities in period t is a function of the remaining stock of old-growth forest as given by the function $A_t = A(X_t)$, where A_t is the value (\$) of the amenity flows from an old-growth stock, X_t, measured in hectares. We will assume $A'(\bullet) > 0$ and $A''(\bullet) < 0$. Suppose further that it is not possible to recreate old-growth forest, in the sense that the evolutionary processes which created the current "old-growth ecosystem" would not be operable after cutting. In other words, although it may be possible to regrow a stand of 200-year-old trees, the forest ecosystem 200 years after cutting would have a different composition of species (flora and fauna) than if the current old-growth stand were preserved. If this perspective is legitimate, the stock of old-growth forest becomes a *nonrenewable resource*, with dynamics given by $X_{t+1} = X_t - h_t$, where h_t is the number of hectares of old-growth forest cut in period t.

What is gained by cutting a hectare of old-growth forest? Suppose each hectare contains timber which has a net revenue of $N > 0$ after logging. After the old-growth timber is harvested, assume that the hectare is replanted and becomes a *permanent* part of the "new-growth" forest inventory, which is optimally managed under a Faustmann rotation with a present value of π per hectare. If X_0 is the initial stock of old-growth forest and Y_0 the initial stock of new-growth forest, then the stock of new-growth forest in period t is simply $Y_t = (Y_0 + X_0 - X_t)$.

Suppose the welfare flow in the forest economy in period t is given by

$$W_t = A(X_t) + Nh_t + \delta\pi(Y_0 + X_0 - X_t) \tag{4.8}$$

Note that the welfare flow consists of the amenity flow, $A(X_t)$; the one-time net revenue (stumpage) flow from old-growth timber if $h_t > 0$; and the rental flow from the accumulated stock of new-growth forest, where $\delta\pi$ is given at the beginning of period t, since the new-growth forest is optimized via a Faustmann rotation for a discount rate of δ.

At some point the forest economy will cease the harvesting of old-growth forest because (i) none is left or (ii) what's left is more valuable preserved. When that happens the forest economy has reached a steady state with $h_t = 0$ and $X_t = X^* \geq 0$. Let's assume that the forest economy does decide to preserve some old-growth forest ($X^* > 0$). How many hectares should they preserve? Consider the problem seeking to maximize the present value of welfare subject to old-growth dynamics.

Maximize $\displaystyle\sum_{t=0}^{\infty}\rho^t\{A(X_t) + Nh_t + \delta\pi(Y_0 + X_0 - X_t)\}$

Subject to $X_{t+1} = X_t - h_t$,   Given $X_0 > 0$ and $Y_0 \geq 0$

This problem has the associated Lagrangian

$$L = \sum_{t=0}^{\infty}\rho^t\{A(X_t) + Nh_t + \delta\pi(Y_0 + X_0 - X_t) + \rho\lambda_{t+1}[X_t - h_t - X_{t+1}]\}$$

The first-order necessary conditions include

$$\frac{\partial L}{\partial h_t}h_t = \rho^t(N - \rho\lambda_{t+1})h_t = 0, \quad h_t \geq 0$$

$$\frac{\partial L}{\partial X_t} = \rho^t\{A'(X_t) - \delta\pi + \rho\lambda_{t+1}\} - \rho^t\lambda_t = 0, \quad X_t > 0$$

In steady state, where the forest economy chooses to preserve some old-growth forest, it will be the case that both $h = 0$ and $\rho\lambda = N$. This implies that $\lambda = (1 + \delta)N$. Evaluating the last expression in steady state implies

$$A'(X) - \delta\pi + N - (1+\delta)N = 0$$

or

$$A'(X) = \delta(\pi + N) \tag{4.9}$$

This is one equation in one unknown, the optimal stock of old-growth forest, X^*. The economic interpretation is straightforward. It says cut old-growth forest until the *marginal amenity flow*, $A'(X)$ is equal to the interest payment on the sum of the present value of an additional hectare of new-growth forest plus the net revenue from old-growth timber, $\delta(\pi + N)$. It can also be shown that the approach from $X_0 > X^*$ to X^* is "most rapid." If h_{MAX} is the maximum rate at which old-growth can be cut, then there will be an interval $\tau \geq t \geq 0$ where $h_t = h_{MAX}$ and $\tau = (X_0 - X^*)/h_{MAX}$.

Marginal amenity flow is difficult to measure. It would include the incremental benefits of habitat, watershed protection, and recreation that an additional hectare of old-growth forest would provide, per period. The term $\delta(\pi + N)$ can be regarded as the opportunity cost of preservation. It is the interest payment forgone by not cutting another hectare of old-growth forest. It is more amenable to measurement. In fact, if one can estimate $\delta(\pi + N)$, one will have a lower-bound value which $A'(X)$ must *exceed* in order to justify the preservation of all remaining old-growth forest.

Table 4.3 contains estimates of $\delta(\pi + N)$ for four important commercial species, on high-quality sites, in coastal British Columbia, circa 1990. The per hectare market value for old-growth timber provides considerable incentive for logging. A mixed stand of old-growth cedar/hemlock would have yielded a net revenue of $50,199 (Canadian dollars). The Faustmann rotations, for $\delta = 0.04$ and $\delta = 0.06$, are given in the third and fourth columns and range from 52 to 79 years. The present value of all future rotations for a recently replanted hectare is given for both discount rates in the fifth and sixth columns. Finally, the opportunity cost of old-growth preservation, $\delta(\pi + N)$, is given for $\delta = 0.04$ and $\delta = 0.06$ in the last two columns. If marginal amenity flow per hectare per year exceeded these values, then the remaining old-growth forest in British Columbia should be preserved.

It is interesting to note that as the discount rate increases from $\delta = 0.04$ to $\delta = 0.06$, π decreases as expected, but the overall opportunity cost, $\delta(\pi + N)$, *increases*. This happens because the net revenue from cutting old-growth timber is so large relative to π that the increased interest payment on N more than offsets the decline in $\delta\pi$. For higher discount rates, land expectation or site value, $(\pi - c)$, becomes negative, indicat-

Table 4.3. *The Opportunity Cost of Old-Growth Forest Preservation on High-Quality Sites in Coastal British Columbia, circa 1990*

Species	N Net Revenue from Standing Old-Growth	Faustmann Rotation When		π When		Opportunity Cost, δ(π + N), When	
		δ=0.04	or δ=0.06	δ=0.04	or δ=0.06	δ=0.04	or δ=0.06
Douglas fir	$24,517	76 yrs.	69 yrs.	$718	$162	$1,009	$1,480
Cedar/Hemlock	$50,199	57 yrs.	52 yrs.	$2,222	$707	$2,096	$3,054
Balsam	$17,383	62 yrs.	57 yrs.	$735	$211	$724	$1,055
Spruce	$48,313	79 yrs.	70 yrs.	$527	$116	$1,953	$2,905

Notes: (1) N, π, and δ(π + N) are in 1990 canadian dollars per hectare. N is a "one-time" net revenue, π is a present value, and δ(π + N) is an annual interest payment.

(2) The Faustmann rotations were calculated after fitting a cubic polynomial to net value at harvest and then maximizing the present value of an infinite series of even-aged rotations.

ing that forest firms would have no interest in replanting. Their *only* interest would be in the value of standing old-growth timber.

4.7   Questions and Exercises

Q4.1 Non-native settlers of the Pacific Northwest found a vast inventory of old-growth forest. What are the conservation and rotational problems confronting a forest-based economy fortunate enough to inherit such an old-growth inventory?

Q4.2 In words, explain the mean annual increment, the optimal single rotation, and the Faustmann rotation.

Q4.3 If the discount rate increases, what happens to the optimal inventory of old-growth forest which a forest economy would choose to preserve?

E4.1 You are the manager of a forest products company with land recently planted ($t = 0$) with a fast-growing species of pine. The merchantable volume of timber at instant $t \geq 0$ is given by $Q(t) = \alpha t + \beta t^2 - \gamma t^3$, where $\alpha = 10$, $\beta = 1$, and $\gamma = 0.01$.
(a) What is the maximum volume and when does it occur?
(b) What rotation length maximizes mean annual increment, $[Q(T)/T]$, and what is the associated volume?
(c) If the net price per unit volume is $p = 1$ and the discount rate is $\delta = 0.05$, what are the optimal *single rotation, T_s*; volume at harvest; and present value at $t = 0$?
(d) If the cost of replanting is $c = 150$, what are the optimal Faustmann rotation, T^*; volume at harvest; and present value at $t = 0$?
(e) If the price increases to $p = 2$, what are the new values for T_s and T^*? Do the new values make sense relative to their values when $p = 1$?

E4.2 Suppose that the inventory of old-growth forest yields an amenity flow given by $A_t = a \ln(X_t)$, where $a > 0$, and $\ln(\bullet)$ is the natural log operator. As in Section 4.6, let δ denote the discount rate, N the net revenue from old-growth timber, and π the present value of recently replanted land under the Faustmann rotation.
(a) What is the expression defining X^*, the optimal amount of old-growth forest to preserve?
(b) Suppose the initial stock of old-growth forest has been normalized to $X_0 = 1$, and you estimate $a = 615$, $\delta = 0.05$, $\pi = 1,000$, and $N = 40,000$. What is the value for X^*?
(c) If the maximum rate at which old growth can be cut is $h_{MAX} = 0.01$, how many years of "old-growth mining" will be allowed before the forest economy must obtain all its timber from "new-growth" forest?

E4.3 A private woodlot owner receives an amenity flow, $A(t)$, while growing trees, where $A'(t) > 0$, $A''(t) < 0$, $A(0) = 0$, and the woodlot was replanted at $t = 0$. Suppose she is interested in both the amenity flow and the present value of net revenue from a *single rotation*. She wishes to maximize

$$\pi = pQ(T)e^{-\delta T} + \int_0^T A(t)e^{-\delta t} dt$$

(a) What is the first-order condition defining the optimal single rotation with nontimber amenity benefits? Hint: The derivative of the integral with respect to T is simply $A(T)e^{-\delta T}$.

(b) What is the marginal value of waiting? What is the marginal cost of waiting?

(c) If $Q(T) = e^{a - b/T}$ ($b > a > 0$) and $A(t) = vt - wt^2$ ($v > w > 0$), what is the implicit expression, $G(T) = 0$, that must be satisfied by the single rotation maximizing π?

(d) If $a = 15$, $b = 180$, $\delta = 0.05$, $p = 1$, $v = 173.167$, and $w = 0.0025$, what is the value for the rotation maximizing π? Denote this rotation T_A.

(e) How does T_A compare with T_s, the optimal single rotation when no amenity value is present?

CHAPTER 5

The Economics of Nonrenewable Resources

5.0   Introduction and Overview

Nonrenewable resources do not exhibit significant growth or renewal over an economic time scale. Examples would include coal, oil, and natural gas and minerals such as copper, tin, iron, silver, and gold. We noted in Chapter 1 that a plant or animal species might be more appropriately viewed as a nonrenewable resource than as a renewable resource. In Chapter 2 we developed a model of a nonrenewable resource to show how Solver might be used to determine the optimal time path of depletion. In Chapter 4 the cutting of old-growth forest was modeled as a nonrenewable resource.

If the initial reserves of a nonrenewable resource are known, the question becomes "How should they be extracted over time?" Is complete depletion (exhaustion) ever optimal? Is it ever optimal to abandon a mine or well with extractable reserves? Does the time path of extraction by a competitive firm differ from that of a price-making monopolist? If exploration allows a firm to find (acquire) more reserves, what are the optimal time paths for extraction and exploration?

In working through the various models of this chapter an economic measure of *resource scarcity* which is different from standard measures based on physical abundance will emerge. From an economic perspective, scarcity should reflect marginal value net of the marginal costs associated with extraction. The Lagrange multiplier, encountered in our models of renewable resources, will once again provide an appropriate economic measure of scarcity.

When a commodity is scarce from an economic perspective, it commands a positive rent: that is, a market price which exceeds the marginal cost of production. "Rent seeking behavior" by firms supplying the commodity, or potential substitutes, and consumers wishing to avoid high prices set in motion market forces which may offset a decline in physical abundance. Economists view scarcity as a constantly changing dynamic condition, in which ingenuity and adaptive behavior allow society to escape the pinch of scarcity in one resource, only to face it in another.

Not all scientists share the economist's optimism about the ingenuity and adaptability of *Homo economicus,* or at least the ability to extend that ingenuity to the protection of environmental quality and the preservation of natural environments. Ecologists often view resource depletion and pollution as irreversible and inevitable results of growth in economic output, as measured by gross domestic product (GDP). There is, however, some evidence to indicate that economic growth might be necessary before a modern society can consider environmental protection and conservation. When a society is free from the threat of starvation and war, resources can be devoted to protecting and improving environmental quality and preserving remaining wilderness. Can nutritional security and political stability be established in less developed countries in time to allow for investment in, and preservation of, their natural environments?

5.1   A Simple Model

Suppose a nonrenewable resource has known initial reserves given by R_0. Denote the level of extraction in period t by q_t. With no exploration and discovery, the dynamics of remaining reserves are given by the simple difference equation $R_{t+1} = R_t - q_t$, where R_t and q_t have the same unit of measure, say, metric tons.

To keep things simple, suppose that society only values extraction, q_t, according to the utility function $U(q_t)$, where $U'(\bullet) > 0$ and $U''(\bullet) < 0$ guarantee strict concavity. Utility is discounted by the factor $\rho = 1/(1 + \delta)$, and society's objective is to select the extraction schedule which maximizes discounted utility subject to the dynamics of remaining reserves.

What is the relevant horizon? For this simple problem, let's suppose that the relevant economic horizon is $t = 0, 1, \ldots, T$, where T is finite and given. (In subsequent problems we will treat T as an unknown that must be optimally determined.) It is also assumed that there is no value assigned to remaining reserves in period $T+1$. In the notation of Chapter 2 we set $\lambda_{T+1} = B = 0$.

With $U_t = U(q_t)$, T given, and $\lambda_{T+1} = 0$, we have no incentive to save or conserve the resource beyond $t = T$, and exhaustion ($R_{T+1} = 0$) is optimal. This permits us to dispense with the difference equation for remaining reserves and to substitute the single constraint

$$R_0 - \sum_{t=0}^{T} q_t = 0 \tag{5.1}$$

Equation (5.1) requires that cumulative extraction exhausts initial reserves. Maximization of discounted utility subject to the exhaustion constraint leads to the Lagrangian

$$L = \sum_{t=0}^{T} \rho^t U(q_t) + \mu \left[R_0 - \sum_{t=0}^{T} q_t \right] \tag{5.2}$$

Let's assume that $q_t > 0$ for $T \geq t \geq 0$, so that exhaustion before $T + 1$ is not optimal. ($U'(0) \to \infty$ will guarantee that this is the case.) The first-order conditions for maximization of discounted utility require

$$\frac{\partial L}{\partial q_t} = \rho^t U'(q_t) - \mu = 0 \tag{5.3}$$

and

$$\frac{\partial L}{\partial \mu} = R_0 - \sum_{t=0}^{T} q_t = 0 \tag{5.4}$$

Equation (5.3) must hold for $t = 0, 1, \ldots, T$, and implies

$$U'(q_0) = \rho U'(q_1) = \rho^2 U'(q_2) = \ldots = \rho^T U'(q_T) = \mu \tag{5.5}$$

Equation (5.5) implies that discounted utility is maximized by scheduling extraction so that discounted marginal utility is equal in every period. Also note that $\mu = \partial L / \partial R_0$ may be interpreted as the shadow price of initial reserves, R_0. It is the value of having one more unit of initial reserves to deplete optimally.

Consider two adjacent periods, t and $t + 1$. Equation (5.5) implies that $\rho^t U'(q_t) = \rho^{t+1} U'(q_{t+1})$, or $U'(q_{t+1}) = (1 + \delta) U'(q_t)$. The implication of this last expression is that the marginal utility of extraction must be growing at the rate of discount, or more generally

$$U'(q_t) = (1 + \delta)^t U'(q_0) \tag{5.6}$$

Finally, note that equations (5.3) and (5.4) constitute a system of $(T + 2)$ equations in $(T + 2)$ unknowns, permitting us to solve, in theory, for q_t, $t = 0, 1, \ldots, T$, and μ.

5.2   Hotelling's Rule

Suppose a market exists for q_t, and in each period $U'(q_t) = p_t$, where p_t is the unit price for q_t. Then we can substitute $p_t = U'(q_t)$ and $p_0 = U'(q_0)$ into equation (5.6) to obtain

$$p_t = (1 + \delta)^t p_0 \tag{5.7}$$

Equation (5.7) says that the price is rising at the rate of interest. Harold Hotelling, an economist writing in 1931, presumed that a competitive industry, which comprised present value maximizing mine owners with perfect foresight, would schedule extractions so that price would rise at the rate of discount. If they did not, they couldn't be maximizing present value, since a reallocation of extraction from a period with a lower discounted price to a period with a higher discounted price would increase present value. From Hotelling's perspective competitive mine owners, maximizing the present value of their initial reserves, would be forced to extract so that price rose at the rate of interest. Another way of expressing Hotelling's rule is to note that (5.7) implies $p_{t+1} = (1 + \delta)p_t$, which can be algebraically manipulated to yield

$$\frac{p_{t+1} - p_t}{p_t} = \delta \tag{5.8}$$

This version says that the capital gain on an extractable unit of q_t in the ground (the LHS) must equal the rate of discount in order to remain indifferent between extracting that unit in period t versus extracting it in period $t + 1$.

This is the simplest form of Hotelling's Rule and it implicitly assumes that there are no costs of extraction, or that the marginal cost of extraction is constant, and that p_t represents the net price per unit. If these assumptions are relaxed we will get modifications of equation (5.8). Before we examine more complex models, let's flesh out the implications of Hotelling's Rule for different inverse demand curves.

5.3   The Inverse Demand Curve

By an inverse demand curve we mean a function mapping aggregate quantity to market price. In general, we will write $p_t = D(q_t)$, where p_t is the unit price in period t given that an aggregate quantity of q_t is supplied to the market. We will assume that $D(q_t)$ does not increase with increases in q_t ($D'(q_t) \leq 0$), and we will often assume that price decreases with increases in $q_t (D'(q_t) < 0)$. Two functional forms we will use in our analysis of nonrenewable resources are the linear inverse demand curve given by

$$p_t = a - bq_t \tag{5.9}$$

and the constant elasticity inverse demand curve given by

$$p_t = aq_t^{-b} \tag{5.10}$$

The linear inverse demand curve has an intercept of $a > 0$ on the price axis and an intercept of $a/b > 0$ on the quantity axis (see Figure 5.1).

The elasticity of demand in period t is given by the general expression

$$\eta_t = \left| \frac{\frac{dq_t}{q_t}}{\frac{dp_t}{p_t}} \right| = \left| \frac{p_t}{q_t} \frac{1}{(dp_t/dq_t)} \right| \tag{5.11}$$

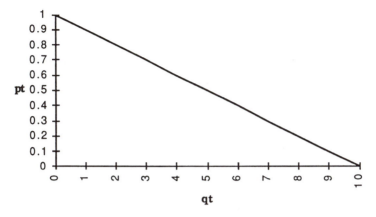

Figure 5.1. The Linear Inverse Demand Curve: $a = 1$ and $b = 0.1$

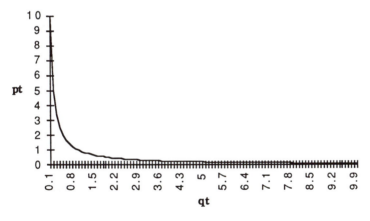

Figure 5.2. The Constant Elasticity Demand Curve: $a = 1$ and $b = 1$

For the linear inverse demand curve you can show that $\eta_t = |1 - a/(bq_t)|$. As $q_t \to 0$, $\eta_t \to \infty$; when $q_t = a/(2b)$, $\eta_t = 1$; and when $q_t = a/b$, $\eta_t = 0$.

The constant elasticity inverse demand curve, with $a > 0$ and $b > 0$, is convex to the origin, with the q_t and p_t axes serving as asymptotes. (See Figure 5.2.) The elasticity of demand does not depend on q_t and is given by $\eta_t = |-1/b|$.

What will be the level of extraction and price (over time) under Hotelling's Rule when the competitive market is characterized by the linear or constant elasticity inverse demand curve? Would the extraction and price paths differ if all reserves of the nonrenewable resource were controlled by a price-making monopolist? We will analyze the competitive industry first.

5.4   Extraction and Price Paths in the Competitive Industry

Let's first consider a competitive mining industry facing a linear inverse demand curve for aggregate output, q_t. An important characteristic of the linear demand curve is the implied maximum (or "choke-off") price at the intercept $p_t = a$ when $q_t = 0$. Such an upper bound may result from the existence of a superabundant substitute, available at a constant marginal cost $MC_s = a$. In scheduling their production, each competitive firm is assumed to know about this "backstop" substitute and to know that price will reach the intercept when all reserves have been collectively exhausted. Suppose exhaustion occurs in $t = T$. At that time remaining reserves and extraction fall to zero ($R_T = q_T = 0$). The date of exhaustion, T, is unknown and must be determined along with the competitive extraction and price paths.

With knowledge of the choke-off price, and optimizing so as to equate the discounted price in each period, price will rise at the rate of discount until $p_T = a$. Knowing where price will end up and knowing its rate of increase imply $p_T = a = (1 + \delta)^T p_0$. We can solve for the initial price, $p_0 = a(1 + \delta)^{-T}$, which upon substitution into equation (5.7) implies

$$p_t = a(1+\delta)^{t-T} \tag{5.12}$$

This is the price path, p_t. With the linear inverse demand curve we also have $p_t = a - bq_t$. Equating these last two expressions and solving for q_t yield the extraction path

$$q_t = (a/b)\left[1-(1+\delta)^{t-T}\right] \tag{5.13}$$

The only problem with the price and extraction paths is that we don't know the date of exhaustion, T. With no reserve-dependent extraction costs exhaustion will be optimal, and cumulative extractions, from $t = 0$ to $t = T - 1$, must equal initial reserves, R_0, implying

$$\sum_{t=0}^{T-1} q_t = \sum_{t=0}^{T-1}(a/b)\left[1-(1+\delta)^{t-T}\right] = R_0 \tag{5.14}$$

Given values for a, b, δ, and R_0, equation (5.14) will imply a value for T, and one could numerically plot the time paths for extraction and price. These time paths are shown in Figures 5.3 and 5.4 when $a = 1$, $b = 0.1$, $\delta = 0.05$, and $R_0 = 75$. The value of T satisfying equation (5.14) is $T = 19.94$. In a discrete-time problem such as this, where T must be an integer, we round T up to 20. The extraction path is concave to the origin start-

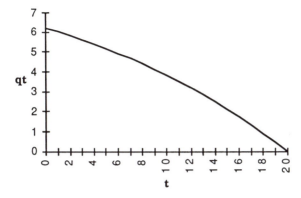

Figure 5.3. The Competitive Extraction Path for the Linear Inverse Demand Curve When $a = 1$, $b = 0.1$, $\delta = 0.05$, and $R_0 = 75$

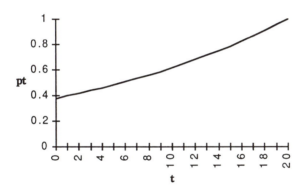

Figure 5.4. The Competitive Price Path for the Linear Inverse Demand Curve When $a = 1$, $b = 0.1$, $\delta = 0.05$, and $R_0 = 75$

ing at $q_0 = 6.22$ and declining to $q_{20} = 0$. The price path is convex from below, starting at $p_0 = 0.38$ and rising at the rate of discount to $p_{20} = 1$.

The derivation of competitive extraction and price paths for the constant elasticity inverse demand curve (equation [5.10]) is made difficult by the lack of a choke-off price. Recall that the q_t and p_t axes were asymptotes for the constant elasticity curve. With no choke-off price, price can continue to rise forever as the rate of extraction becomes infinitesimal. Price will rise at the rate of discount so we know $p_t = (1 + \delta)^t p_0$. Equating this last expression to $p_t = aq_t^{-b}$ and solving for q_t yields

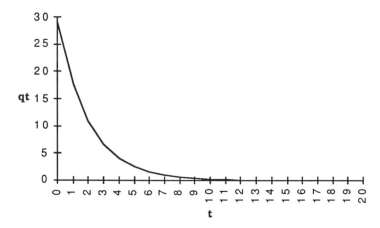

Figure 5.5. The Competitive Extraction Path for the Constant Elasticity Inverse Demand Curve When $a = 1$, $b = 0.1$, $\delta = 0.05$, and $R_0 = 75$

$$q_t = \left[\frac{a}{(1+\delta)^t p_0}\right]^{1/b} \tag{5.15}$$

As $t \to \infty$, $q_t \to 0$, and $p_t \to \infty$ as we surmised from Figure 5.2. Assuming exhaustion as $t \to \infty$, we can equate cumulative extraction (in the limit) to initial reserves and use the resulting expression to solve for p_0. Specifically, it can be shown that

$$\sum_{t=0}^{\infty}\left[\frac{a}{(1+\delta)^t p_0}\right]^{1/b} = \frac{\left[\frac{a(1+\delta)}{p_0}\right]^{1/b}}{\left[(1+\delta)^{1/b}-1\right]} = R_0 \tag{5.16}$$

Solving for p_0 yields

$$p_0 = \frac{a(1+\delta)}{\left\{R_0\left[(1+\delta)^{1/b}-1\right]\right\}^b} \tag{5.17}$$

When this last expression is evaluated for the same parameter values used to illustrate the linear inverse demand curve (i.e., $a = 1$, $b = 0.1$, $\delta = 0.05$, and $R_0 = 75$), one obtains $p_0 = 0.7142$. The competitive extraction and price paths in this case are shown in Figures 5.5 and 5.6.

With the implications of Hotelling's Rule fleshed out for a competitive mining industry facing either a linear or a constant elasticity inverse demand curve we can now ask, "How would the extraction and price paths differ if all reserves were controlled by a monopolist?" The ques-

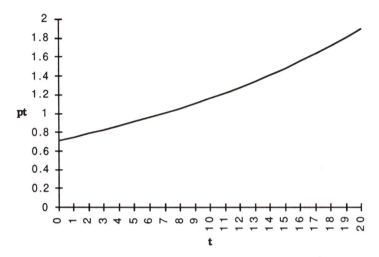

Figure 5.6. The Competitive Price Path for the Constant Elasticity Inverse Demand Curve When $a = 1$, $b = 0.1$, $\delta = 0.05$, and $R_0 = 75$

tion is of historical interest because of the existence of the Organization of Petroleum Exporting Countries (OPEC), which from 1973 to 1981 maintained a monopoly-like cartel, setting production quotas for its members and for a brief period banning the export of oil to the United States. This set off a series of price increases which by 1981 saw the real price of crude oil standing at five times the price level of the early 1970s. It also resulted in the greatest "peaceful" transfer of wealth from the industrialized economies of North America, Europe, and Asia to OPEC members that included Saudi Arabia, Kuwait, Iran, Iraq, Libya, the United Arab Emirates, Algeria, Nigeria, Indonesia, Venezuela, Ecuador, Gabon, and Qatar. By the early 1980s, however, a combination of energy conservation, new (non-OPEC) sources of crude oil, and an economic recession resulted in reduced demand. The cartel itself had experienced internal bickering and, in 1979, the outbreak of hostilities between Iran and Iraq. Saudi Arabia, which had frequently reduced its quota to maintain price while other members were producing in excess of their agreed quota, finally grew tired of what it regarded as greedy, undisciplined overproduction and decided it would produce at its full quota and let the price find a new, lower, market equilibrium. Although OPEC has never regained its previous cohesion, the analysis of monopoly pricing of a nonrenewable resource is still of considerable interest.

5.5   Extraction and Price Paths under Monopoly

As with our analysis of the competitive mining industry, we will assume there is no variable cost to extraction. (Reserve-dependent costs will be examined in the next section.) We assume that the monopolist seeks to maximize the present value of revenues and knows the form of the inverse demand curve. If the monopolist faced a linear inverse demand curve, revenue in period t would be given by $\pi_t = p_t q_t = aq_t - bq_t^2$. Hotelling simply argued that the monopolist, as a price maker, would schedule extraction so as to *equate discounted marginal revenue*. If this were not the case, extraction could be shifted from a period with lower discounted marginal revenue to a period when discounted marginal revenue was higher, and overall present value would be increased.

If the monopolist schedules extraction to equate discounted marginal revenue, then marginal revenue, given by $MR_t = a - 2bq_t$, must be rising at the rate of discount. This implies that $MR_t = (1 + \delta)^t MR_0$. For the linear inverse demand curve, marginal revenue will equal price when extraction drops to zero: that is, $MR_T = p_T = a$ when $q_T = 0$, where $t = T$ is the monopolist's date of exhaustion, which may differ from the date of exhaustion in the competitive industry. Knowing the rate of increase in marginal revenue and its value at $t = T$ one can solve for $MR_0 = a(1 + \delta)^{-T}$, and the second expression for marginal revenue becomes $MR_t = a(1 + \delta)^{t-T}$. Equating this expression to the expression $MR_t = a - 2bq_t$ and solving for q_t yields

$$q_t = [a/(2b)]\left[1 - (1+\delta)^{t-T}\right] \tag{5.18}$$

Compare equation (5.18) with equation (5.13). Although we don't know the monopolist's date of exhaustion, if a, b, δ, and R_0 are the same as in the competitive industry, and if the dates of exhaustion for both are reasonably far into the future, then the monopolist's initial rate of extraction will be approximately one-half that of the competitive industry, because $[a/(2b)]$ is one-half of (a/b). If the monopolist's initial rate of extraction is less than that of the competitive industry, if exhaustion is optimal (as is the case with no reserve-dependent costs), and if R_0 is the same for competitors in aggregate as for the monopolist, then the date of exhaustion for the monopolist, T_m, will be greater than the date of exhaustion for the competitive industry, T_c. When plotted in the same graph, the extraction path for the monopolist will intersect the competitive extraction path from below and there will be an interval where the rate of extraction of the monopolist exceeds the rate of extraction from the competitive industry. The monopolist's date of exhaustion is the value of T which equates

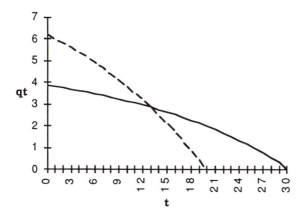

Figure 5.7. The Extraction Paths for the Monopolistic (Solid Curve) and Competitive (Dashed Curve) Mining Industry Facing a Linear Inverse Demand Curve When $a = 1$, $b = 0.1$, $\delta = 0.05$, and $R_0 = 75$

$$\sum_{t=0}^{T-1} q_t = \sum_{t=0}^{T-1} [a/(2b)]\left[1 - (1+\delta)^{t-T}\right] = R_0 \tag{5.19}$$

For $a = 1$, $b = 0.1$, $\delta = 0.05$, and $R_0 = 75$, $T_m \approx 30 > T_c = 20$. The monopolist's extraction path, and that for the competitive industry (from Figure 5.3), are shown in Figure 5.7.

In Figure 5.7, if R_0 is the same for both the competitive and the monopolistic industry, then the area below the competitive extraction path and above the monopolist's extraction path, to the left of their intersection, will equal the area below the monopolist's extraction path and above the competitive extraction path to the right of their intersection. Why?

For the linear inverse demand curve the monopolist is able to increase the present value of its revenues by restricting extraction initially, thus raising price. Since it is optimal to exhaust initial reserves, R_0, the monopolist will extend the period of positive extraction to $T_m - 1$. Although the monopolist spreads extraction over a longer horizon, there is nothing socially desirable about this behavior. In fact, if $U'(q_t) = p_i$; – that is, marginal social welfare is equal to price – then the competitive extraction path is optimal and the monopolist's extraction path reduces the present value of social welfare. Will the monopolist's extraction always be initially restrictive? Let's now consider the monopolist facing a constant elasticity inverse demand curve.

With the constant elasticity inverse demand curve, revenue in period t is given by $\pi_t = aq_t^{-b}q_t = aq_t^{1-b}$, and marginal revenue is given by $MR_t = (1 - b)aq_t^{-b} = (1 - b)p_t$. With marginal revenue (MR) rising at the rate of discount we know that $MR_t = (1 + \delta)^t MR_0 = (1 + \delta)^t(1 - b)p_0$. These last two expressions imply that $p_t = (1 + \delta)^t p_0$: that is, price is rising at the rate of interest, which was our result for the competitive industry. We could solve for q_t, in which case we would get the same expression as given in equation (5.15). The conclusion: If the inverse demand curve exhibits constant elasticity, the time paths for extraction and price are the same for the competitive industry and the monopolist. The key to this unexpected result lies in the fact that the monopolist, facing a constant elasticity inverse demand curve, cannot increase the present value of revenues by restricting the rate of extraction. In fact, points on a constant elasticity inverse demand curve all yield the same revenue. Although the monopolist is still a price-maker, he or she is unable to shift revenue to earlier periods as was the case with the linear inverse demand curve.

We might summarize these last two sections as follows: (i) If the mining industry is competitive, with complete futures markets for q_t, price will rise at the rate of discount. (ii) If marginal social welfare is equal to price ($U'(q_t) = p_t$), then the competitive extraction and price paths are optimal. (iii) If a monopolist can take advantage of changing elasticity of demand to increase the present value of revenues, then he or she will restrict the rate of extraction initially and spread initial reserves over a longer horizon than the competitive industry. The monopolist is not behaving out of any conservation ethic, but is simply trying to maximize the present value of revenues.

5.6   Reserve-Dependent Costs

The nonrenewable resource models considered thus far have assumed that there are no variable costs to extraction and that any fixed costs have been incurred (sunk). Although not realistic, this assumption kept things analytically simple and allowed us to get a feel for the dynamics of extraction and price in the competitive and monopolistic mining industry. We now consider the implications of reserve-dependent costs. Specifically, suppose that the cost of extracting q_t depends on the level of remaining reserves so that $C_t = C(q_t, R_t)$ is the cost of extracting q_t units of ore when remaining reserves are R_t. Using subscripts to denote the partial derivatives of $C(\bullet)$, it is assumed that $C_q(\bullet) > 0$, $C_{qq}(\bullet) > 0$, $C_{qR}(\bullet) = C_{Rq}(\bullet) < 0$, $C_R(\bullet) < 0$, and $C_{RR}(\bullet) > 0$. As in the fishery model of Chapter 3, higher reserves serve to lower total cost $[C_R(\bullet) < 0]$ and the marginal cost of extraction $[C_{qR}(\bullet) < 0]$.

Consider the competitive industry facing per unit prices p_t for $t = 0, 1, \ldots, T$. Each competitive firm is assumed to have information on the "forward prices" for delivery of a unit of q_t in period t. These prices are assumed to be known through the smooth operation of a futures market for q_t. These prices are not affected by the extraction decisions of an individual firm. Net revenue in period t is given by $\pi_t = p_t q_t - C(q_t, R_t)$. The representative firm will try to extract so as to

Maximize $\quad \sum_{t=0}^{T} \rho^t [p_t q_t - C(q_t, R_t)]$

Subject to $\quad R_{t+1} - R_t = -q_t$

$\qquad\qquad R_0$ given, T chosen

The Lagrangian for this problem may be written as

$$L = \sum_{t=0}^{T} \rho^t \{p_t q_t - C(q_t, R_t) + \rho\lambda_{t+1}[-q_t + R_t - R_{t+1}]\} \qquad (5.20)$$

and for q_t, R_t, and λ_t positive, the first-order conditions require

$$\frac{\partial L}{\partial q_t} = \rho^t [p_t - C_q(\bullet) - \rho\lambda_{t+1}] = 0 \qquad (5.21)$$

$$\frac{\partial L}{\partial R_t} = \rho^t [-C_R(\bullet) + \rho\lambda_{t+1}] - \rho^t \lambda_t = 0 \qquad (5.22)$$

$$\frac{\partial L}{\partial [\rho\lambda_{t+1}]} = \rho^t [-q_t + R_t - R_{t+1}] = 0 \qquad (5.23)$$

Dividing through by ρ^t, this system implies $\rho\lambda_{t+1} = p_t - C_q(\bullet)$, $\lambda_t = (1 + \delta)[p_{t-1} - C_q(\bullet)]$, and $\rho\lambda_{t+1} - \lambda_t = C_R(\bullet)$. Substituting the first two expressions into the third implies $[p_t - C_q(\bullet)] - (1 + \delta)[p_{t-1} - C_q(\bullet)] = C_R(\bullet)$. This last expression can be further manipulated to imply

$$\frac{[p_t - C_q(\bullet)] - [p_{t-1} - C_q(\bullet)]}{[p_{t-1} - C_q(\bullet)]} = \delta + \frac{C_R(\bullet)}{[p_{t-1} - C_q(\bullet)]} \qquad (5.24)$$

In this expression the term $[p_t - C_q(q_t, R_t)]$ can be defined as the "rent" on the marginal unit extracted in period t, and $[p_{t-1} - C_q(q_{t-1}, R_{t-1})]$ is the rent on the marginal unit extracted in period $t - 1$. Knowing that $C_R(\bullet) < 0$, equation (5.24) has the following, Hotelling-type, interpretation: In the competitive industry, with reserve-dependent costs, rent rises at *less* than the rate of discount.

How long will the competitive industry operate? The answer will depend on initial reserves, the inverse demand curve, and the cost function. If $t = T$ is the last period for optimal operation ($q_T > 0$, $q_{T+1} = 0$), then we know that any remaining reserves in period $T + 1$ must be worth-

	A	B	C	D
1	p=	1		
2	c=	10		
3	δ =	0.05		
4	ρ =	0.95238095		
5				
6	t	qt	Rt	Discounted πt
7	0	10	100	9
8	1	10	90	8.46560847
9	2	10	80	7.93650794
10	3	10	70	7.40432227
11	4	10	60	6.85585396
12	5	10	50	6.26820933
13	6	10	40	5.59661547
14	7	10	30	4.73787553
15	8	10	20	3.38419681
16	9	0	10	0
17	10	0	10	0
18				
19			π =	59.6491898

Spreadsheet 5.1

less, thus $\lambda_{T+1} = 0$. From equation (5.21) we see that $p_T = C_q(q_T, R_T)$: that is, price equals marginal cost. It will also be the case that R_T, while positive, will have optimally declined so that $p_T = C(q_T, R_T)/q_T$. In the terminal period, the marginal cost of extraction equals price, which also equals the average cost of extraction. With p_T known, this would give us two equations which *may* imply unique values for q_T and R_T. For example, when $p_t = p$ and $C_t = cq_t/R_t$, where p and c are positive constants, $C_q(\bullet) = C(\bullet)/q_t$, and the two terminal conditions collapse to a single condition implying $R_T = c/p$. The Lagrangian in this case is linear in q_t, and the optimal extraction schedule is to drive R_t from R_0 to R_T as rapidly as possible. If $q_{MAX} \geq q_t \geq 0$ then the number of periods with maximum extraction would be given by $(R_0 - R_T)/q_{MAX}$.

Spreadsheet 5.1 shows this linear case when $p = 1$, $c = 10$, $\delta = 0.05$, $R_0 = 100$, and $q_{MAX} = 10$. Although the discount rate is used to calculate present value, it plays no role in determining the optimal extraction schedule, since the most rapid approach path (MRAP) is optimal. Note: The number of periods to reach $R_T = 10$ from $R_0 = 100$, using $q_{MAX} = 10$, is 9. Thus, the last period with positive extraction at q_{MAX} is $t = 8$. It is optimal to abandon the mine with 10 units of remaining reserves. Their extraction would only lower present value.

Equation (5.24) contains our earlier result for the competitive industry with no variable costs, since in that case $C_q(\bullet) = C_R(\bullet) = 0$ (in fact, there is no variable cost function), and price rises at the rate of discount. It also contains the case where costs only depend on the rate of extraction $[C = C(q_t)]$, in which case rent rises at the rate of discount.

By now you might be able to anticipate the analogue of equation (5.24) for the monopolist. You should be able to show that the monopolist will schedule extraction so that

$$\frac{[MR_t - C_q(\bullet)] - [MR_{t-1} - C_q(\bullet)]}{[MR_{t-1} - C_q(\bullet)]} = \delta + \frac{C_R(\bullet)}{[MR_{t-1} - C_q(\bullet)]} \qquad (5.25)$$

In words, the monopolist will schedule extraction so marginal revenue less marginal cost rises at *less* than the rate of discount, where the term $C_R(\bullet)/[MR_{t-1} - C_q(\bullet)] < 0$.

The introduction of reserve-dependent costs resulted in a more realistic model of the competitive or monopolistic mining industry. The model, however, still lacks several important features, most notably the process of exploration for and acquisition of new reserves.

5.7 Exploration

Geological processes typically result in a nonuniform distribution of resources in the earth's crust. The location and size of economically recoverable reserves are uncertain. Firms and individuals must typically explore (search) for recoverable reserves, and their economic value may depend on their grade (concentration), location, technology available for extraction, future price, and cost. Exploration is a costly and risky investment. It is undertaken when a firm believes that the expected present value of discoveries will exceed the cost of prospecting, field development, and extraction. If extraction costs are reserve-dependent, a firm may have an incentive to increase exploration as its known and developed reserves decline. The prospect of future discoveries may also depend on cumulative discoveries to date. If the most obvious locations have been explored, the probability of large future discoveries may decline.

Determining the optimal rates of extraction and exploration, in the face of uncertain discovery, is a formidable problem. To keep things manageable, we will develop a two-period model, $t = 0,1$, where $t = 0$ is the current period and $t = 1$ is the future (period). Current extraction ($q_0 \geq 0$) and exploration ($e_0 \geq 0$) decisions are contemporaneously determined, based on current net revenues, exploration costs, expected discoveries, and the present value of expected future net revenues from optimal extraction in each of two possible future states ($s = 0, s = 1$). A zero–one random variable, conditional on $e_0 > 0$, is used to determine the size of the discovery which augments reserves at the beginning of $t = 1$. It is not optimal to explore in the future ($t = 1$), since there is no third period ($t = 2$) when discoveries could be extracted. Thus, given the structure of this simple two-period model, the firm must optimally determine the level of four variables, $q_{1,0}$ = the level of extraction in future state $s = 0$, $q_{1,1}$ = the level of extraction in future state $s = 1$, q_0 = the level of extraction in $t = 0$, and e_0 = the level of exploration in $t = 0$.

Let's start by specifying the exploration/discovery process. To keep things simple we assume that the random process of discovery can be characterized by the binary variable s, where $s = 0$ with probability ε and $s = 1$ with probability $(1 - \varepsilon)$, $1 > \varepsilon > 0$. If $s = 0$, positive exploratory effort ($e_0 > 0$) results in *no discovery*. If $s = 1$, then positive exploratory effort yields a discovery of size αe_0, where $\alpha > 0$. This permits us to write the size of discovery as $D_s = s\alpha e_0$, where D_s is the size of discovery in state s, $s = 0,1$.

The solution of this two-period, two-state problem will employ the method of *stochastic dynamic programming* (SDP), which can be employed in multiperiod, multistate problems as well. The procedure starts in the terminal period, when it is possible to determine optimal behavior assuming remaining reserves, after extraction and discovery in the previous period, are known with certainty. In state $s = 0$ (no discovery), we know that remaining reserves are simply $R_1 = R_0 - q_0$. Denote the price in $t = 1$ as p_1, and assume that the cost of extracting q_1 units in $t = 1$ (in either state) is given by the term cq_1^2/R_1, where $c > 0$. In $s = 0$ the cost of extracting $q_{1,0}$ becomes $cq_{1,0}^2/(R_0 - q_0)$ and we can write the net revenue in $t = 1$, $s = 0$, as

$$\pi_{1,0} = p_1 q_{1,0} - cq_{1,0}^2 / (R_0 - q_0) \tag{5.26}$$

In state $s = 1$, after a discovery of size αe_0, remaining reserves are $R_1 = R_0 - q_0 + \alpha e_0$, and the net revenue from $q_{1,1}$ is given by

$$\pi_{1,1} = p_1 q_{1,1} - cq_{1,1}^2 / (R_0 - q_0 + \alpha e_0) \tag{5.27}$$

$\pi_{1,0}$ can be maximized with respect to $q_{1,0}$, as can $\pi_{1,1}$ with respect to $q_{1,1}$. Setting the appropriate derivatives equal to zero you should obtain

$$q_{1,0}^* = \frac{p_1(R_0 - q_0)}{2c} \tag{5.28}$$

$$q_{1,1}^* = \frac{p_1(R_0 - q_0 + \alpha e_0)}{2c} \tag{5.29}$$

Equations (5.28) and (5.29) constitute the optimal extraction policy for the future in all possible states. Note that the optimal value of $q_{1,0}$

depends on q_0 and the optimal value of $q_{1,1}$ depends on q_0 and e_0, neither of which is known at this point in the solution algorithm, but when they are known, we will know what to do in either state.

Now take the expressions for $q_{1,0}^*$ and $q_{1,1}^*$ and substitute them into equations (5.26) and (5.27), respectively. After some algebra you should get the following expressions for optimized net revenue:

$$\pi_{1,0}^* = \frac{p_1^2(R_0 - q_0)}{4c} \tag{5.30}$$

$$\pi_{1,1}^* = \frac{p_1^2(R_0 - q_0 + \alpha e_0)}{4c} \tag{5.31}$$

Suppose that the first period decisions $q_0 > 0$ and $e_0 > 0$ have been made, but that the size of the discovery has not been revealed. The expected value, in $t = 1$, of a (q_0, e_0) decision may be calculated as

$$\begin{aligned}\pi_1 &= [p_1^2/(4c)][\varepsilon(R_0 - q_0) + (1 - \varepsilon)(R_0 - q_0 + \alpha e_0]\\&= [p_1^2/(4c)][R_0 - q_0 + (1 - \varepsilon)\alpha e_0]\end{aligned} \tag{5.32}$$

The expression for π_1 depends on q_0 and e_0 and presumes optimal extraction in the future in all possible states. Such expressions are called *value functions*. We can discount π_1 by ρ, add it to the expression for net revenue in $t = 0$, and obtain an expression for the present value of expected net revenues which depends on q_0 and e_0. This expression takes the form

$$\pi = p_0 q_0 - cq_0^2/R_0 - we_0^2 + \rho[p_1^2/(4c)][R_0 - q_0 + (1 - \varepsilon)\alpha e_0] \tag{5.33}$$

Setting the partial derivatives of π with respect to q_0 and e_0 equal to zero yields the following expressions for optimal first-period extraction and exploration:

$$q_0^* = \frac{R_0(4cp_0 - \rho p_1^2)}{8c^2} \tag{5.34}$$

$$e_0^* = \frac{\rho p_1^2 \alpha(1 - \varepsilon)}{8cw} \tag{5.35}$$

Assuming that the optimal levels for q_0 and e_0 are positive, one would wait until the state of the world is revealed, and then use equation (5.28) or (5.29) to determine the optimal levels of extraction in $s = 0$ or $s = 1$.

There are eight parameters in this model: R_0, p_0, p_1, c, w, α, ε, and δ. Spreadsheet 5.2 shows the optimal values for q_0, e_0, $q_{1,0}$, and $q_{1,1}$ when $R_0 = 100$, $p_0 = 1$, $p_1 = 1.1$, $c = 2$, $w = 5$, $\alpha = 250$, $\varepsilon = 0.7$, and $\delta = 0.05$. In cell \$B\$21 we have programmed the expression for π from equation (5.33) and placed guesses for the optimal q_0 and e_0 in cells \$B\$19 and \$B\$20,

	A	B	C	D
1	Optimal Extraction and Exploration in the Two-Period Model			
2				
3	R0=	100		
4	p0=	1		
5	p1=	1.1		
6	c=	2		
7	w=	5		
8	α=	250		
9	ε=	0.7		
10	δ=	0.05		
11	ρ=	0.95238095		
12				
13	q0*=	21.3988095		
14	e0*=	1.08035714		
15	q1,0*=	21.6153274		
16	q1,1*=	95.889881		
17				
18	Using Solver			
19	q0=	21.3988095		
20	e0=	1.08035714		
21	π=	29.3988007		

Spreadsheet 5.2

respectively. As a check on our algebra we asked Solver to maximize π by changing q_0 and e_0, and after a few iterations it converges to the values given by our analytical expressions in cells \$B\$13 and \$B\$14.

By inspection of the optimal expressions for q_0, e_0, $q_{1,0}$, and $q_{1,1}$, or through numerical analysis via Spreadsheet 5.2, one can conduct comparative statics to see how extraction and exploration change as a result of a change in one of the eight parameters. The results are summarized in Table 5.1, where a plus sign (+) indicates that an increase in a parameter increases the optimal value of a variable, a minus sign (−) indicates that an increase in a parameter will decrease the optimal value of the variable, and zero (0) indicates no change.

The comparative statics are, for the most part, consistent with economic intuition. For example, the optimal level of extraction in the first period will (i) increase with increases in initial reserves, R_0, the initial price, p_0, or the discount rate, δ; (ii) decrease with increases in the future price, p_1, or the cost of extraction, c; and (iii) remain unchanged for changes in the cost of exploration, w; the productivity of exploration, α; and the probability of no discovery, ε. The fact that the optimal level of q_0 does not depend on w, α, or ε is a result of the separability of q_0 and e_0 in the expression for the present value of expected net rev-

Table 5.1. *The Comparative Statics of Extraction and Exploration*

	R_0	p_0	p_1	c	w	α	ε	δ
$\dot{q}_0$	+	+	-	-	0	0	0	+
$\dot{e}_0$	0	0	+	-	-	+	-	-
$\dot{q}_{1,0}$	+	-	+	-	0	0	0	-
$\dot{q}_{1,1}$	+	-	+	-	-	+	-	-

enues, π (π is separable in q_0 and e_0 if the second, cross-partial derivative, $\pi_{q,e}$, is zero).

Exploratory effort is not affected by a change in R_0 or p_0, will increase with an increase in p_1 or α, and will decrease with an increase in c, w, ε, or δ. The only surprise here is that exploratory effort is not influenced by the size of initial reserves. In more complex models, it might be the case that low initial reserves would encourage greater initial exploration. The nonresponse of optimal e_0 to a change in p_0 makes sense since one cannot sell discoveries in the initial period.

The comparative statics of $q_{1,0}^*$ and $q_{1,1}^*$ are made complex by their dependency on q_0 and e_0, which are determined first. The logic of the comparative statics for $q_{1,0}^*$ and $q_{1,1}^*$ is more readily deduced by moving vertically down a parameter column in Table 5.1. For example, an increase in initial reserves, R_0, will increase extraction in the current period and in all future states. Basically, an increase in initial reserves is optimally spread across all periods and all states. An increase in current price, because it increases the optimal q_0, will reduce the rate of extraction in either future state. An increase in p_1 will reduce extraction initially and increase it in either state. An increase in the cost of extraction, via an increase in c, reduces all variables. An increase in the cost of exploratory effort, w, reduces the level of exploration and the level of extraction in future state $s = 1$, while leaving extraction in the no-discovery state ($s = 0$) unchanged. If the productivity of exploratory effort increases, the optimal level of e_0 will increase, along with the optimal rate of extraction in $s = 1$, but again, there is no change in the optimal extraction rate in $s = 0$. If the probability of no discovery, ε, increases, the optimal e_0 is reduced, as is the optimal extraction rate in $s = 1$. Finally, an increase in the discount rate increases current extraction and reduces exploration and future extraction in all states.

5.8   The Economic Measure of Scarcity

In our model with reserve-dependent costs, the first-order condition for $q_t > 0$ required $p_t - C_q(\bullet) = \rho\lambda_{t+1}$ (see equation [5.21]). When the optimal extraction schedule has been determined, λ_{t+1} will reflect the value of the marginal unit of remaining reserves in period $t + 1$. Because λ_{t+1} is linked, via a difference equation, to all future $\lambda_{t+1+\tau}$, $\tau = 1, 2, \ldots$, it will reflect the value that the marginal unit conveys in period $t + 1$ *and* in all future periods. Recall that λ_{t+1} was also called a shadow price on the marginal unit of ore in the ground in period $t + 1$, presuming that remaining reserves would be optimally extracted. The equation $p_t - C_q(\bullet) = \rho\lambda_{t+1}$ simply says that the marginal value of a unit of ore at the surface in period t should equal the discounted marginal value if it were left in the ground, and thus available in period $t + 1$.

The economic notion of scarcity is based on net value rather than physical abundance. If we could be confident that a resource were being optimally extracted (say, by a competitive industry with adequate futures markets) then the preferred measure of resource scarcity from an economist's point of view would be $\lambda_{t+1} = (1 + \delta)[p_t - C_q(\bullet)]$. If we could observe the current spot price for q_t and estimate marginal cost $C_q(\bullet)$ and the social rate of discount, δ, we could estimate the time series λ_{t+1} and observe what was happening to resource scarcity over time. This is not as easy as it sounds. Time-series data on marginal cost in extractive industries are either nonexistent or proprietary. In attempting to reconstruct the scarcity index λ_{t+1} it may be easier to estimate the cost function $C(R_t, q_t)$ and take the partial with respect to q_t to obtain a marginal cost function which would provide an estimate of marginal cost.

The economic measure of resource scarcity can indicate growing or declining scarcity, which would be counter to a geologic (abundance-based) notion of scarcity. Note: If marginal costs increase as remaining reserves decline, but market price does not increase as rapidly, then λ_{t+1} is declining, and the resource is becoming *less scarce* from an economic perspective. The fact that remaining reserves are declining would indicate geologic scarcity, but unless the market price increases faster than marginal cost, the resource is not becoming economically scarce. This is precisely what has happened to copper. Copper was once used extensively in plumbing and in the transmission of electricity. It has been replaced by plastic in plumbing and by aluminum for distributing electricity. While the known remaining reserves of copper have declined the real price of copper has fallen, and from an economic perspective, copper is less scarce.

On the cost side of scarcity, if technology lowers the cost of exploration or extraction, but price remains high, the resource is becoming more scarce. This is what happened to crude oil in the last half of the nineteenth century. Although geological and engineering applications led to the discovery of more oil and reduced the cost of extraction and refinement, the demand for kerosene and other distillates increased at a greater rate, and from an economic point of view the resource, though known reserves were more abundant, was becoming more scarce. The opposite forces were at work in the 1980s, when the demand for crude oil declined as a result of improved efficiency in automobiles, appliances, heating, and air conditioning. Since 1981 crude oil has become less scarce, in terms of our economic measure of scarcity.

The development of substitute commodities, in the case of copper, or the substitution of capital and labor, in the case of energy, can reduce economic scarcity. As the OPEC experience has shown, it may be possible to create a short-term economic scarcity, but innovators, entrepreneurs, and consumers will react to high prices by trying to provide lower-cost substitutes or by adapting their economic behavior to reduce the demand for an economically scarce commodity. These forces have been effective at ameliorating resource scarcity throughout human history. Although scarcity is an ever-present economic fact of life, it is a dynamic condition, at least for the resources and commodities that flow through organized markets.

What about species extinction? Was the passenger pigeon economically scarce when the last member of that species died in a zoo in 1914? We could argue that our economic notion of scarcity is equally valid for endangered species, and that what we need to do is replace p_t with the collectively held marginal preservation value for the species in question, and replace $C_q(\bullet)$ with the marginal cost of preservation. Is the freshwater snail darter more or less scarce than the right whale? Species that are highly valued and easy to protect (conserve) would be the most scarce, and perhaps the ones on which conservation efforts should be focused. In reality, the problem is more complex, genetically, economically, and politically.

What about environmental quality? Is potable fresh water more scarce than clean air? Could we modify our commodity-based notion of economic scarcity and apply it to environmental goods? Would it help us prioritize an agenda for environmental action? Perhaps, but the more "public" or nonmarket the environmental service or attribute, the more difficult it will be to adapt our economic notion of scarcity, which is best suited to private commodities that pass through markets. We could argue that if a species or environmental attribute tends toward the private/market side of the commodity spectrum, the market or nongovernmental organizations (NGOs) might be active and effective in reducing economic scarcity. Such a perspective might imply that safe drinking water or animals that are prized by hunters or photographers are more amenable to provision or protection through markets or private conservation efforts than the species or environmental attributes which tend to be purely public and nonmarket. These may require national or multinational conservation efforts to reduce economic scarcity.

5.9   Questions and Exercises

Q5.1 Indicate whether each of the following statements is true or false and briefly explain why.

(a) In the simple model of a nonrenewable resource, discounted marginal utility should be equated for all periods when extraction is positive. _____

(b) If price equals marginal utility, then, in the simple model, price should rise at the rate of discount. _____

(c) A monopolist would deplete a nonrenewable resource faster than a competitive industry. _____

(d) The choke-off price is a price that is so low that it causes the competitive mining industry to shut down before exhaustion. _____

(e) With reserve-dependent costs, price less marginal cost is rising at less than the rate of discount in the competitive mining industry. _____

(f) An increase in the current (spot) price for oil will cause an increase in exploration. _____

(g) An increase in extraction cost will reduce extraction and exploration. _____

(h) An increase in the discount rate will increase the current rate of extraction and reduce exploration. _____

(i) If, as a resource is being physically depleted, its price does not increase, it is becoming less scarce economically. _____

(j) If the price of a resource increases, substitution, conservation, and exploration might cause the price to fall in the future. _____

E5.1 You are a present value maximizing monopolist facing a downward-sloping demand curve for diamonds extracted from your mine. The price for diamonds in period t is given by $p_t = a - bq_t$, where q_t is the rate of diamond extraction in period t, and $a > b > 0$. Your remaining diamond reserves change according to $R_{t+1} = R_t - q_t$. You face reserve-dependent extraction costs given by the function $C_t = cq_t/R_t, c > 0$. Your net revenue in period t is given by the expression $\pi_t = aq_t - bq_t^2 - cq_t/R_t$. You wish to maximize the present value of net revenue over the horizon $t = 0$, $1, \ldots, T$, for a discount rate of δ, assigning no value to remaining reserves in period $T + 1$ ($\lambda_{T+1} = 0$). You may treat R_0 and T as given constants.

(a) Write the Lagrangian expression for this problem and derive the first-order necessary conditions.

(b) Suppose $a = 1$, $b = 0.5$, $c = 0.001$, $\delta = 0.05$, $R_0 = 1$, and $T = 9$. Use Solver to maximize the present value of net revenues subject to $q_t \geq 0$ for $t = 0, 1, 2, \ldots, 9$, $q_{10} = 0$, $R_{10} \geq 0$. As an initial guess for the optimal rates of extraction set $q_t = 0.1$ for $t = 0, 1, 2, \ldots, 9$. Is the diamond mine abandoned before $T = 9$?

(c) Suppose the rate of discount increases to $\delta = 0.1$. Resolve for the optimal rates of extraction. What does the increase in the discount rate do to the optimal extraction rate?

E5.2 A nonrenewable resource yields net benefits according to the function $\pi(q_t) = \alpha q_t^\beta$. Positive levels of extraction are desired for $t = 0,1,2,3,4$, from initial reserves R_0 (given). $R_{t+1} = R_t - q_t$ and at $t = 5$, $q_5 = R_5 = 0$.

(a) With $\rho = 1/(1 + \delta)$, solve for the expression defining the optimal extraction rate q_t^* as a function of β, δ, q_0, and t.

(b) Making use of the exhaustion condition

$$\sum_{t=0}^{4} q_t = R_0$$

solve for the expression defining q_0^*.

(c) For $\alpha = 1$, $\beta = 0.5$, $\delta = 0.1$, and $R_0 = 1$, solve for the numerical values of q_t^* and R_t^* for $t = 0, 1, 2, 3, 4, 5$.

(d) What is the value of an increment to initial reserves, R_0?

E5.3 You are managing a mine which has entered into a contract to sell all ore to another company at a fixed unit price for the life of the mine. The cost of extracting q_t units is given by the cost function $C_t = cq_t^2$. Denoting the constant unit price by p, the net revenue in period t is $\pi_t = pq_t - cq_t^2$. Although the contract specifies the unit price, the number of units extracted and sold in a particular period and the date when the mine is closed are decisions to be made by you. Let $t = T$ denote the period when the mine is closed and $q_T = 0$. You wish to

$$\text{Maximize} \quad \sum_{t=0}^{T-1} \rho^t \left[pq_t - cq_t^2 \right]$$

$$\text{Subject to} \quad R_0 - \sum_{t=0}^{T-1} q_t = 0$$

$$R_0 \text{ given and } q_T = 0$$

where R_0 is the given level of initial reserves. The Lagrangian for this problem may be written as

$$L = \sum_{t=0}^{T-1} \rho^t \left[pq_t - cq_t^2 \right] + \mu \left[R_0 - \sum_{t=0}^{T-1} q_t \right]$$

(a) What are the first-order necessary conditions?

(b) With $q_T = 0$, what is the expression for μ and q_t?

(c) Making use of the constraint requiring exhaustion of R_0, and noting that $\sum_{t=0}^{T-1}(1+\delta)^{(t-T)} = \left[1-(1+\delta)^{-T}\right]/\delta$, what is the implicit equation which could be used numerically to solve for the optimal exhaustion date, T?

(d) If $R_0 = 1$, $p = 1$, $c = 1.14$, and $\delta = 0.05$, what is the optimal date of exhaustion and extraction levels, q_t^*, $t = 0, 1, \ldots, T-1$?

(e) Set up an Excel Spreadsheet with a horizon longer than the value of T obtained in part **(d)**. Give Solver the option of optimizing the present value of net revenue over this longer horizon subject to the constraint that $R_t \geq 0$ for all t. Does Solver opt for your solution in part **(d)**?

CHAPTER 6

Stock Pollutants

6.0   Introduction and Overview

This chapter is concerned with the wastes from production or consumption that might accumulate over time. We will refer to any accumulated waste as a stock pollutant. Returning to Figure 1.1, extracted ore, q_t, was seen to generate a waste flow, αq_t, which might accumulate as the stock pollutant, Z_t, where $\alpha > 0$ was a coefficient (parameter) with a dimension which converted the units used to measure q_t into the units used to measure Z_t. For example, if q_t were measured in metric tons (mt) and Z_t were measured in parts per million (ppm), then α would have the dimension parts per million/metric ton (ppm/mt).

For *degradable wastes*, there is often a biological or chemical process whereby a portion of the pollution stock is decomposed (degraded) into constituent compounds that might pose little or no threat to the environment. In Figure 1.1, the rate at which the stock pollutant degrades is γZ_t, where $1 > \gamma > 0$ is a degradation coefficient indicating the fraction of the pollution stock degraded during period t. The net effect of the rates of waste flow and degradation will determine the change in the stock pollutant as given by the difference equation

$$Z_{t+1} - Z_t = -\gamma Z_t + \alpha q_t \tag{6.1}$$

As noted in Chapter 1, if the rate of waste flow exceeds the rate of degradation, the stock pollutant will increase; if the degradation rate exceeds the flow of new waste, the stock pollutant will decrease. If the rate of waste flow precisely equals the rate of degradation, the stock pollutant will be unchanged. If such an equality can be maintained, the pollution stock will be in a steady state.

Not all stock pollutants are degradable. If $\gamma = 0$, positive waste flows can only increase the level of the stock pollutant. *Nondegradable wastes* might be subject to *diffusion*, as they are spread by physical, or perhaps biological, processes and become more evenly distributed within the overall environment. Diffusion may reduce the "local" concentration of a nondegradable stock pollutant, but the overall mass of such pollutants, in a closed environment, cannot decrease. To model the diffusion of a

101

nondegradable stock pollutant, one must typically construct a model that has both a temporal and a spatial dimension. In this chapter we will examine some simple models for both degradable and nondegradable stock pollutants.

The rate of waste generation might be more complex than a simple coefficient of proportionality, such as α. In the next section we will introduce the *commodity-residual transformation frontier*, where an economy must implicitly allocate its resources to choose the rate of output for a positively valued commodity and the rate of flow for a negatively valued residual (waste).

This is followed by a section which formulates a measure of welfare in which the damage from a stock pollutant is subtracted from the value of the commodity which generates the residual waste flow. Such a measure is consistent with the recommendation by environmental economists that the national income accounts be adjusted to reflect the depletion of nonrenewable resources and the cost of environmental damage.

Sections 6.3 through 6.6 present some simple models of degradable and nondegradable stock pollutants. The emphasis is on the optimal control of stock pollutants by (i) the implicit allocation of resources between commodity production and waste reduction, (ii) the rate and location of residual deposition, (iii) the rate of extraction of a nonrenewable resource, and (iv) the rate of waste generation and recycling. These models collectively cover many of the dynamic and spatial aspects of real-world pollutants.

Section 6.7 analyzes two environmental policies advocated by economists: emission taxes and marketable pollution permits. Section 6.8 ends the chapter with some questions and exercises.

6.1   The Commodity-Residual Transformation Frontier

Suppose, within the context of Figure 1.1, we defined $S_t = \alpha q_t$ to be the flow of residual waste from the extraction of q_t units of ore in period t. The presumption would be that the rate of residual waste (or simply residual) is proportional to the rate of extraction. This is but one possible relationship. In general, let Q_t denote the rate of production of some positively valued commodity in period t and S_t the rate of flow of a jointly produced, negatively valued residual. The residual is negatively valued because it might accumulate as a damage-inducing stock pollutant.

Within the economy, suppose there is a fixed bundle of resources which can be used to produce Q_t or reduce S_t. (Since the underlying bundle of resources is fixed, we don't need to represent them as a time-

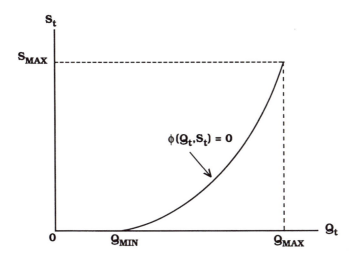

Figure 6.1. The Commodity-Residual Transformation Frontier

varying variable.) Given the fixed bundle of resources, let $\phi(Q_t, S_t) = 0$ denote the commodity-residual transformation frontier. This implicit function indicates the minimum level of S_t for a given level of Q_t, or equivalently, the maximum level of Q_t for a given level of S_t. What would the commodity-residual transformation frontier look like in Q_t–S_t space? One possible curve is shown in Figure 6.1.

In Figure 6.1 the commodity rate $Q_{MIN} > 0$ represents the largest rate of output that can be achieved when $S_t = 0$. If S_t were a residual that accumulated as a highly toxic stock pollutant, then the economy might find it optimal to allocate the available resources to locate at $(Q_{MIN}, 0)$. If, on the other hand, S_t and its associated stock pollutant produced only mild discomfort, the economy might opt for a larger level for Q_t. To produce $Q_t > Q_{MIN}$ the economy would have to divert some of the fixed resources from residual prevention and to commodity production. This would result in a positive flow of residuals $(S_t > 0)$. At the other extreme from $(Q_{MIN}, 0)$, if all resources were devoted to production of Q_t, the economy could achieve $Q_t = Q_{MAX}$, but it would have to accept a flow of residuals at $S_t = S_{MAX}$. Points along the curve connecting $(Q_{MIN}, 0)$ with (Q_{MAX}, S_{MAX}) represent the *trade-off menu* for Q_t and S_t, given the fixed bundle of resources. This is the commodity-residual transformation frontier implied by $\phi(Q_t, S_t) = 0$. It is a relative of the production possibility (PP) curve from introductory economics. The PP curve depicted the trade-off between two positively valued commodities, whereas the commodity-residual transformation frontier shows the trade-off between a commodity and its jointly produced residual.

6.2   Damage Functions and Welfare

In this book a damage function will relate the size of the stock pollutant, Z_t, to the monetary damage suffered by an economy in period t. In static models of pollution, damage might depend on the level of emissions or waste flow, S_t. With the pollution stock changing according to $Z_{t+1} - Z_t = -\gamma Z_t + S_t$, residual wastes emitted in period t will not become part of the pollution stock until period $t + 1$, when they will make their first "contribution" to a future flow of environmental damage.

Denoting the level of monetary damage in period t by D_t, the damage function will be written as $D_t = D(Z_t)$. The shape of the damage function will depend on the toxicity of Z_t. In a spatial model, damage might depend on location. One would generally think that larger pollution stocks would result in higher damage, $D'(\bullet) > 0$, and that damage might be "smoothly" increasing at an increasing rate, $D''(\bullet) > 0$. Positive first and second derivatives would imply that the damage function is strictly convex. As it turns out, empirical studies seem to indicate that damage functions, from exposing a single individual to higher doses of some pollutant, might resemble a discontinuous step-function, as shown in Figure 6.2. The step-function would imply that damage is constant for a certain level (dose) of Z_t, and then jumps discontinuously at a critical threshold. When individual step-functions are aggregated across a large, diverse population, a smooth, strictly convex function might be a reasonable way to approximate total damage.

Empirical estimation of damage functions is made difficult by the need to assign dollar values to the damage to an ecosystem. This might involve estimating the value of a particular plant or animal species within that system, or attempting to value human morbidity or a shortened life. What is the monetary damage from an oil-soaked sea otter? What is the loss from a life shortened by emphysema exacerbated by air pollution? These questions pose difficult valuation problems. Damages might be imperfectly estimated by lost earnings, hospitalization costs, and the "willingness-to-pay" of humans to remain healthy or prevent despoliation of marine or other ecosystems. Various methods exist to estimate environmental damage (or the value of improving environmental quality). Two methods frequently employed are the *travel cost method* and *contingent valuation*.

The travel cost method attempts to value a favored or preferred environmental attribute by observing the additional costs that users (hikers,

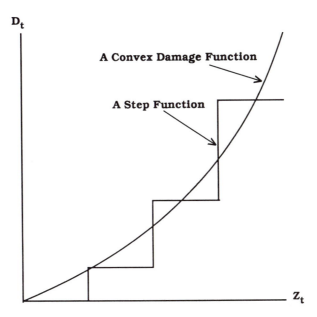

Figure 6.2. Damage as a Step Function and as a Smooth, Convex Function

bikers, campers, etc.) are willing to incur for recreation in a site with the preferred attribute. It is also possible to estimate the loss to users if the attribute or environmental quality is impaired. For example, clean and less congested beaches may require visitors to expend more time and money in travel and accommodations than if they visited less clean or more congested beaches closer to home. If wastes or an oil spill were to sully the more distant, pristine beach, the travel cost premium, summed over all potential visitors, might provide an estimate of one component of the environmental damage.

Contingent valuation methods might be used to estimate other components of damage. Contingent valuation employs surveys to directly ask individuals their willingness-to-pay for certain attributes, or the level of compensation which the individual would require to forgo certain attributes. Returning to our less-than-clean, congested urban beach, a contingent valuation survey might show a visitor pictures of the beach after refuse pickup and under less congested conditions and ask the individual how much he or she would be willing to pay for a day of refuse-free, reduced-congestion beach time. Alternatively, visitors to the more distant, pristine beach might be shown pictures of washed-up medical wastes or oil-stained sand and asked what compensation payment they would require if a garbage scow or oil barge were to disgorge its contents onto the beach during the last day of their vacation.

The preceding examples involved observing travel cost or administering surveys to visitors at a site. Such research might provide estimates of the value of cleanup or the damage from pollution to "users." Contingent valuation, because it employs survey techniques, can be used to estimate *nonuse values* as well. Most economists would agree that individuals with a low or zero probability of visiting (using) a pristine environment might still be willing to pay something for its preservation or protection. Accurately measuring these values is much more difficult because of the tendency that a respondent might have to embed broader environmental values into a question about a particular inlet in Alaska or beach on Cape Cod. Although the value that current nonusers place on the option of future use (including the options of generations yet unborn) is seen as valid, its measurement by contingent valuation methods is imprecise and controversial. In this text we need not resolve these measurement issues. In the optimization problems of this chapter, we will typically assume a convex damage function and then solve for the optimal flow of waste, disposal site, or rate of recycling. In empirical work dynamic models might be useful in determining the environmental value implied by a certain ambient standard. For example, if the costs of waste treatment are known and if an ambient standard is binding, it may be possible to estimate the smallest marginal environmental damage which would optimally justify the ambient standard.

Mathematically we might hypothesize that the welfare of society in period t depends on the flow of output, Q_t, and the level of the stock pollutant, Z_t, and write $W_t = W(Q_t, Z_t)$. The welfare function might be additively separable, where $W_t = \pi(Q_t) - D(Z_t)$, with $\pi(\bullet)$ strictly concave $[\pi'(\bullet) > 0$ and $\pi''(\bullet) < 0]$ and $D(\bullet)$ strictly convex $[D'(\bullet) > 0, D''(\bullet) > 0]$.

The additively separable form could reflect a national accounting philosophy in which environmental damage is deducted from the value of newly produced goods and services. Such a revision to the national income accounts has been advocated by environmental economists for at least three decades. Although such deductions from gross domestic product are conceptually well founded, the aforementioned difficulty of measuring environmental damage on an annual basis causes other economists to view such proposals as impractical. The dynamic models we will now consider will clarify the economic notion of damage, and suggest how such damages might be measured, by making use of shadow prices, in a fashion similar to that proposed for measuring the scarcity of a nonrenewable resource.

6.3   A Degradable Stock Pollutant

For a degradable stock pollutant, with dynamics $Z_{t+1} - Z_t = -\gamma Z_t + S_t$, the degradation coefficient, γ, is positive. We will assume that the economy faces a commodity-residual transformation frontier implied by $\phi(Q_t, S_t)$ $= 0$. The partial derivative of $\phi(\bullet)$ with respect to the rate of output, Q_t, will be denoted by $\phi_Q(\bullet)$ and, by convention, will be positive, $(\phi_Q(\bullet) > 0)$. The partial with respect to the residual rate, S_t, will be negative $(\phi_S(\bullet) < 0)$. Assume a separable welfare function, whereby economic well-being in period t is given by $W_t = \pi(Q_t) - D(Z_t)$, with $\pi(\bullet)$ strictly concave and $D(\bullet)$ strictly convex. The optimization problem of interest seeks to

$$\text{Maximize}\quad W = \sum_{t=0}^{\infty} \rho^t [\pi(Q_t) - D(Z_t)]$$

$$\text{Subject to}\quad Z_{t+1} - Z_t = -\gamma Z_t + S_t$$

$$\phi(Q_t, S_t) = 0$$

$$Q_{\text{MAX}} \geq Q_t \geq Q_{\text{MIN}}$$

$$Z_0 \text{ given}$$

The Lagrangian for this problem may be written as

$$L = \sum_{t=0}^{\infty} \rho^t \{\pi(Q_t) - D(Z_t) + \rho\lambda_{t+1}[(1-\gamma)Z_t + S_t - Z_{t+1}] - \mu_t \phi(Q_t, S_t)\}$$

Note that the commodity-residual transformation frontier is premultiplied by $-\mu_t$ and included within the summation operator. This implies that the shadow price on the resources implicit in the transformation frontier may be changing over time. The negative sign, $-\mu_t \phi(\bullet)$, is also convention, but chosen because it will lead to logical signs for λ_{t+1} and μ_t (specifically, $\lambda_{t+1} < 0$ and $\mu_t > 0$).

The first-order necessary conditions imply

$$\mu_t = \pi'(\bullet)/\phi_Q(\bullet) > 0 \tag{6.2}$$

$$\rho\lambda_{t+1} = \mu_t \phi_s(\bullet) = \pi'(\bullet)\phi_s(\bullet)/\phi_Q(\bullet) < 0 \tag{6.3}$$

$$(1-\gamma)\rho\lambda_{t+1} - \lambda_t = D'(\bullet) \tag{6.4}$$

$$Z_{t+1} - Z_t = -\gamma Z_t + S_t \tag{6.5}$$

$$\phi(Q_t, S_t) = 0 \tag{6.6}$$

Equations (6.2)–(6.6) are obtained by setting the partial derivatives of L with respect to Q_t, S_t, Z_t, $\rho\lambda_{t+1}$, and μ_t equal to zero. It is assumed that $Q_{\text{MAX}} > Q_t > Q_{\text{MIN}} > 0$; S_t, Z_t, and μ_t are positive; and λ_{t+1} is negative.

We next consider the conditions at a steady-state optimum and then the likely approach path if $Z_0 \neq Z^*$. In steady state $\mu = \pi'(\bullet)/\phi_Q(\bullet)$ and $\rho\lambda = \pi'(\bullet)\phi_S(\bullet)/\phi_Q(\bullet)$. Evaluating (6.4) in steady state and factoring out $\rho\lambda$ imply $\rho\lambda[(1 - \gamma) - (1 + \delta)] = D'(\bullet)$. Substituting in the expression for $\rho\lambda$, and simplifying, imply $-\pi'(\bullet)[\phi_S(\bullet)/\phi_Q(\bullet)] = D'(\bullet)/(\delta + \gamma)$. Although this last expression may appear to be nothing more than notational gibberish, it does have a logical economic interpretation. The term $-[\phi_S(\bullet)/\phi_Q(\bullet)]$ is equal to dQ/dS and is called a *marginal rate of transformation* (MRT); in this case it is the marginal rate at which S can be transformed into Q. In other words, if you are willing to put up with slightly higher residual emissions, how much more Q can you get? $\pi'(\bullet)$ is the marginal value of that additional unit of steady-state Q. Thus, the LHS is the marginal value of a slight increase in S which will allow a slight increase in Q. What is the cost? The cost is that a slight increase in S will lead to a slight increase in steady-state Z, which leads to an increase in marginal damage, $D'(\bullet)$. That marginal damage is sustained over an infinite horizon and has a present value (adjusted by the degradation coefficient) of $D'(\bullet)/(\delta + \gamma)$. Thus, this last equation says that in steady state you want to choose the mix of Q and S so that the marginal value in transformation is precisely equal to the present value of marginal damage. Makes perfect sense, right?

Equations (6.6) and (6.5) can be evaluated in steady state and imply $\phi(Q,S) = 0$ and $Z = S/\gamma$. We will bundle these last three equations together, because they can be used to solve for the steady-state levels of Q, S, and Z, and simply state that

$$-\pi'(\bullet)[\phi_S(\bullet)/\phi_Q(\bullet)] = D'(\bullet)/(\delta + \gamma)$$
$$\phi(Q,S) = 0$$
$$Z = S/\gamma \tag{6.7}$$

define (Q^*, S^*, Z^*).

If $\pi(\bullet)$ and $\phi(\bullet)$ are strictly concave in Q_t, the approach from $Z_0 \neq Z^*$ will be asymptotic, with $Z_t \to Z^*$ as $t \to \infty$. If $Z_0 > Z^*$, the economy will select rates of output and residual emission where $\gamma Z_t > S_t$, and the pollution stock will decline toward Z^*. If $Z_0 < Z^*$, the economy can indulge in rates of output and residual emission in excess of those at the steady-state optimum, S_t will be greater than γZ_t, and the pollution stock will grow toward Z^*.

If the Lagrangian is linear in Q_t and S_t, the approach to Z^* may be most rapid. Consider the case when (i) $\pi(\bullet) = pQ_t$, where $p > 0$ is the unit price for Q_t; (ii) $D(\bullet) = cZ_t^2$, where $c > 0$ is a damage coefficient; and (iii) the transformation frontier is given by $\phi(Q_t, S_t) = Q_t - nS_t - Q_{MIN} = 0$,

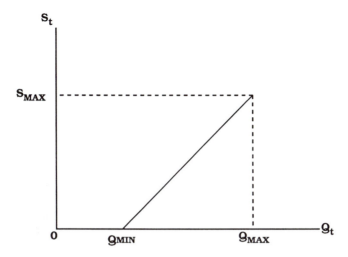

Figure 6.3. $\phi(Q_t, S_t) = Q_t - nS_t - Q_{MAX} = 0$, with $Q_{MAX} \geq Q_t \geq Q_{MIN}$

where $n > 0$ is a coefficient indicating the incremental increase in commodity Q_t if one is willing to put up with an incremental increase in the residual S_t. It is assumed that $Q_{MAX} \geq Q_t \geq Q_{MIN}$. The commodity-residual transformation frontier is drawn in Figure 6.3. In this case $\phi(Q_t, S_t) = 0$ implies $S_t = (Q_t - Q_{MIN})/n$.

The optimal steady-state pollution stock, Z^*, is immediately implied by the first equation in the group (6.7). This can be shown by noting that $\phi_Q(\bullet) = 1$, $\phi_S(\bullet) = -n$, $D'(\bullet) = 2cZ$, and $\pi'(\bullet) = p$. Substituting these derivatives into $-\pi'(\bullet)[\phi_S(\bullet)/\phi_Q(\bullet)] = D'(\bullet)/(\delta + \gamma)$ one obtains $pn = 2cZ/(\delta + \gamma)$ or

$$Z^* = \frac{pn(\delta + \gamma)}{2c} \tag{6.8}$$

Given the expression for Z^*, one can obtain expressions for S^* and Q^* by noting $S^* = \gamma Z^*$ and $Q^* = Q_{MIN} + nS^*$. Spreadsheet 6.1 shows the numerical values when $p = 2$, $n = 10$, $\delta = 0.05$, $\gamma = 0.2$, $c = 0.1$, $Q_{MIN} = 10$, $Q_{MAX} = 100$, and $Z_0 = 0$. These parameter values imply a unique steady-state optimum where $Z^* = 25$, $S^* = 5$, $Q^* = 60$. In the body of the spreadsheet we set up a 21-period horizon ($t = 0, 1, \ldots, 20$) in which we will ask Solver to determine how it wants to go from $Z_0 = 0$ to $Z^* = 25$. The choice variables will be Q_t, $t = 0, 1, \ldots, 19$, and in cell $C$14 we define S_t in terms of the choice for Q_t by typing =(B14 – $B$6)/$B$2 and fill down accordingly. In cell $D$15 we program the dynamics of the stock

	A	B	C	D	E	F
1	ρ=	2				
2	n=	10				
3	δ =	0.05				
4	γ =	0.2				
5	c=	0.1				
6	Qmin=	10				
7	Qmax=	100				
8						
9	Z*=	25				
10	R*=	5				
11	Q*=	60				
12						
13	t	Qt	St	Zt	Discounted πt	
14	0	100	9	0	200	
15	1	100	9	9	182.761905	
16	2	100	9	16.2	157.601814	
17	3	100	9	21.96	131.109677	
18	4	100	9	26.568	106.469331	
19	5	100	9	30.2544	84.986833	
20	6	100	9	33.20352	66.9747914	
21	7	100	9	35.562816	52.2554116	
22	8	100	9	37.4502528	40.4397011	
23	9	100	9	38.9602022	31.0767661	
24	10	100	9	40.1681618	23.7289001	
25	11	100	9	41.1345294	18.0052273	
26	12	100	9	41.9076235	13.5729727	
27	13	100	9	42.5260988	10.1572935	
28	14	100	9	43.0208791	7.53581407	
29	15	100	9	43.4167033	5.53120976	
30	16	100	9	43.7333626	4.00357381	
31	17	100	9	43.9866901	2.84339331	
32	18	100	9	44.1893521	1.96546106	
33	19	100	9	44.3514817	1.30378807	
34	20	0	0	44.4811853	0.5315223	
35						
36				π =	1142.85539	
37						

Spreadsheet 6.1

pollutant by typing =(1 − $B$4)*D14 + C14. In column E we program the discounted net revenues. In cell $E$14 we type =((1/(1 + $B$3))^A14)*($B$1*B14 − $B$5*(D14^2)) and fill down through cell $E$33. The terminal function in cell $E$34 requires some explanation.

In this example we are going to tell Solver that whatever it selects for Z_{20}, it has to adopt that value as a steady-state pollution stock and live with it forever. This terminal condition is similar in spirit to the terminal condition discussed in Chapter 2 for the optimal harvest problem. (Review Section 2.2.) This approach implies that $S = \gamma Z_{20}$ and $Q = Q_{MIN} + n\gamma Z_{20}$ for the rest of time, as well. The discounted terminal value in cell $E$34 is the expression

$$\rho^T \left(\sum_{t=T}^{\infty} \rho^{t-T} [pQ - cZ^2] \right) = \rho^T [pQ - cZ^2][1 + \rho + \rho^2 + \rho^3 + \ldots]$$

$$= \rho^T [pQ - cZ^2] \left[\frac{1}{(1-\rho)} \right]$$

$$= \rho^T [pQ - cZ^2] \left[\frac{(1+\delta)}{\delta} \right]$$

$$= \rho^{T-1} [pQ - cZ^2]/\delta$$

where $Z = Z_{20}$ and $Q = Q_{MIN} + n\gamma Z_{20}$. Thus in cell $E$34 we type

=((1/(1+$B$3))^A33)*($B$1*($B$6+$B$2*$B$4*D34)
−$B$5*(D34^2))/$B$3

This terminal function tells Solver that although it is free to choose values for Q_0 through Q_{19}, it must live with Z_{20} and its steady-state companions $S = \gamma Z_{20}$ and $Q = Q_{MIN} + n\gamma Z_{20}$ for the rest of time. As an initial guess we set $Q_t = 100 = Q_{MAX}$ for $t = 0, 1, \ldots, 19$, which results in a terminal pollution stock of $Z_{20} = 44.48$ and a total present value of $\pi = 1{,}142.855$. The time paths for Q_t, Z_t, and S_t are shown in the chart at the bottom of the spreadsheet. In setting up Solver you will specify $E$36 as the Set Cell to be maximized and $B$14:$B$33 as the changing cells. In the constraint box enter two constraints (the minimum and maximum levels for Q_t) by typing $B$14:$B$33 <= 100 and $B$14:$B$33 >= 10.

How does Solver change Q_t to maximize π? The results are shown in Spreadsheet 6.2. We see that Solver opts to go on a short binge, setting $Q_t = 100$ for $t = 0, 1, 2$ and $Q_3 = 84.33$. This results in the pollution stock's growing from $Z_0 = 0$ to $Z_4 = Z^* = 25$ (which was calculated via equation [6.8] prior to optimization). Solver then stays at the steady-state optimum from $t = 4$ through $t = 19$ and, given our terminal function, for the rest of time. The chart at the bottom of Spreadsheet 6.2 depicts this most rapid approach to Z^*.

	A	B	C	D	E	F
1	p=	2				
2	n=	10				
3	δ =	0.05				
4	γ =	0.2				
5	c=	0.1				
6	Qmin=	10				
7	Qmax=	100				
8						
9	Z*=	25				
10	R*=	5				
11	Q*=	60				
12						
13	t	Qt	St	Zt	Discounted πt	
14	0	100	9	0	200	
15	1	100	9	9	182.761905	
16	2	100	9	16.2	157.601814	
17	3	84.3302394	7.43302394	21.96	104.03742	
18	4	59.9704683	4.99704683	25.0010239	47.2525887	
19	5	59.9759991	4.99759991	24.997866	45.0235038	
20	6	60.0684483	5.00684483	24.9958927	43.0248631	
21	7	59.9530238	4.99530238	25.003559	40.7847589	
22	8	59.9839796	4.99839796	24.9981496	38.9028389	
23	9	60.0307598	5.00307598	24.9969176	37.1146028	
24	10	60.0221871	5.00221871	25.0006101	35.3253813	
25	11	59.9864265	4.99864265	25.0027068	33.5952735	
26	12	59.9602281	4.99602281	25.0008081	31.9716087	
27	13	59.9659759	4.99659759	24.9966693	30.4662214	
28	14	60.0064833	5.00064833	24.993933	29.0632757	
29	15	60.0455069	5.00455069	24.9957947	27.7123755	
30	16	60.0157751	5.00157751	25.0011865	26.3531483	
31	17	59.9519743	4.99519743	25.0025267	25.0396404	
32	18	60.0884672	5.00884672	24.9972188	23.9717355	
33	19	59.941098	4.9941098	25.0066217	22.6949795	
34	20	0	0	24.9994072	455.098742	
35						
36				π =	1637.79668	
37						
38						

Spreadsheet 6.2

6.4   Diffusion and a Nondegradable Stock Pollutant

Among the major environmental problems in the United States are the identification, assessment, and possible remediation of sites where toxic substances had been legally or illegally dumped prior to the enactment of legislation requiring environmentally secure disposal. These sites might contain a variety of pollutants which can contaminate soils and groundwater. In the vicinity of some sites there have been suspiciously high rates of leukemia and other cancers. Often the firms or individuals responsible for the dump site are no longer in existence or are financially incapable of paying for damages and remediation. The U.S. government has established a fund (called the "Superfund") under the control of the Environmental Protection Agency (EPA) to clean up such sites, but the sheer number of sites and the cost of remediation have resulted in what many regard as unacceptably slow progress. How should the EPA prioritize the known Superfund sites? Given the limited funds for cleanup what is the optimal schedule for remediation?

Let Z_i denote the stock (mass) of one or more pollutants at site i, $i = 1, 2, \ldots, I$. Although some of the pollutants may be subject to biodegradation, we will assume, in this model, that the initial mass of accumulated pollutants can only be diffused into surrounding soils or groundwater by precipitation (rain or snowmelt). The initial volume (sphere) of contamination is assumed given and is denoted by $V_{i,0}$. Over time, the volume of contamination is assumed to grow according to the equation $V_{i,t+1} = (1 + \alpha_i)V_{i,t}$, where $1 > \alpha_i > 0$ is the rate at which the volume of contamination grows.

Within a volume of contaminated soil or water the concentration of the pollutant will typically vary. The actual dynamics of a pollutant moving through nonuniform soil or a "plume" of contaminated groundwater can be quite complex. We will simplify things by defining average concentration in period t as $C_{i,t} = Z_i/V_{i,t}$ and assume that the damage at site i in period t is a function of both the volume contaminated and the average concentration, and let $D_{i,t} = D_i(V_{i,t}, C_{i,t})$ denote the damage at site i if nothing is done and the volume of contamination grows unchecked. Intuitively, one would think that an increase in the volume of contaminated soil or water would increase damage. If no additional pollutants are deposited at the ith site, the growth in the volume of contamination will reduce average concentration, and the dynamics of damage at a particular site will depend on the weight given to $V_{i,t}$ and $C_{i,t}$ in $D_i(\bullet)$.

Let $X_{i,t} = 0$ indicate that the ith site has *not* been cleaned up during or before period t, and let $X_{i,t} = 1$ indicate that the ith site has been cleaned up during or before period t. If $X_{i,t} = 1$, $X_{i,\tau} = 1$ for all $\tau > t$: that is, once a site is cleaned, it stays cleaned.

If and when a site is cleaned, the damage in the period of remediation and all future periods is assumed to go to zero. Damage with or without remediation becomes $D_{i,t} = (1 - X_{i,t})D_i(V_{i,t}, C_{i,t})$. Let K_i denote the cost of cleanup at the ith site, and K the total funds available for remediation.

In our allocation problem we will assume that funds not spent in period t may be placed in an interest bearing account where they will increase by the factor $(1 + \delta)$ per period, where $\delta > 0$ is the rate of discount. This introduces a scheduling dimension to our problem, where initial remediation at some sites might be optimal, while waiting for unspent funds to compound to the point where other sites can be cleaned up at a later date. Alternatively, the environmental agency can contract with a remediation firm for cleanup of a particular site at a future date and make a reduced, present-value payment today.

The optimal schedule of remediation becomes a *binary dynamic optimization problem* which seeks to

$$\text{Minimize} \quad \sum_{t=0}^{T} \rho^t \left\{ \sum_{i=1}^{I} [(X_{i,t+1} - X_{i,t})K_i + (1 - X_{i,t})D_i(V_{i,t}, C_{i,t})] \right\}$$

In words, the optimal cleanup schedule seeks to minimize the discounted sum of remediation costs and environmental damage. In determining the optimal schedule, the first time that $X_{i,t} = 1$ the environmental agency commits to make a payment of K_i dollars in period t or a present value payment of $\rho^t K_i$ today (in $t = 0$). If and when $X_{i,t} = 1$, $X_{i,\tau} = 1$ for $\tau > t$, and the future coefficients on K_i are zero, thus ensuring only a one-time payment for remediation at any site. Initially, it is assumed that no remediation has taken place, $X_{i,0} = 0$, and that $Z_i > 0$ and $V_{i,0} > 0$ for all i. The budget constraint may be written

$$\sum_{t=0}^{T} \rho^t \left\{ \sum_{i=1}^{I} (X_{i,t+1} - X_{i,t})K_i \right\} \leq K$$

Insight into the optimal scheduling of remediation will be enhanced through a numerical example. Consider the problem with five toxic sites $(I = 5)$ over a 21-year horizon $(T = 20)$. For a damage function with no remediation, let $D_{i,t} = \beta_i C_{i,t} V_{i,t}^2$, where $\beta_i > 0$ is a coefficient indicating the relative financial damage from pollutants at the ith site. With $C_{i,t} = Z_i/V_{i,t}$, the damage function becomes $D_{i,t} = \beta_i Z_i V_{i,t}$. The initial conditions and parameters are Z_i, $V_{i,0}$, α_i, K_i, β_i, K, and δ, and their numerical values are summarized at the top of Spreadsheet 6.3. Note that Site #1 is relatively small in terms of the mass of toxics $(Z_1 = 5)$ and the initial volume of contamination ($V_{1,0} = 10$). Site #1 has a relatively slow rate of growth in the volume of contaminated soil or water ($\alpha_1 = 0.01$), but it is relatively damaging ($\beta_1 = 1$). Site #1 is the least costly to clean up ($K_1 = 50$).

Site #2 is the largest site in terms of the mass of pollutants ($Z_2 = 50$) and volume already contaminated ($V_{2,0} = 500$) and the most rapid in dispersion ($\alpha_2 = 0.1$). Site #2 is the most costly to clean up ($K_2 = 500$) but relatively low in damage ($\beta_2 = 0.01$). Sites #3, #4, and #5 fall between Sites #1 and #2 in these attributes. The overall (present-value) budget for remediation is $K = \$400$ million and the discount rate is $\delta = 0.05$.

In cells B15 through F35 we introduce the initial conditions indicating that no sites have been cleaned ($X_{i,0} = 0$) and set $X_{i,t} = 0$ for $t = 1, 2, \ldots,$ 20, to see what will happen to the present value of damages at each site in each future period. In row 38 we program the initial damage level $D_{i,0} = \beta_i Z_i V_{i,0}$ for the five sites. For example, in B38 we have typed =$B$8*$B$4*$B$5. In cells B39 through F58 we program the expression for the discounted sum of remediation cost and environmental damage. For example, in cell B39 we have typed =($B$12^A39)*((B16-B15)*$B$7 + (1-B16)*$B$8*$B$4*$B$5*(1 + $B$6)^A39). Note that the initial damage grows according to $(1 + \alpha_1)$ and we can fill down through cell B58 to get discounted cost and damage through $t = 20$. Also note that discounted remediation cost will enter at most once, in the period when cleanup is initiated. Reading down a column in the block B38 through F58 you can see what is happening to discounted damages at each site if no remediation takes place. In row 60 we sum the discounted remediation cost and environmental damage for each site. For Site #1 the sum of discounted damage is $731.90 million, whereas for Site #2 it is $8695.38 million. The sum of discounted remediation cost and environmental damages over all sites is given in cell B62. This will be the sum we will ask Solver to minimize.

In cells G15 through K15 we enter zeros, indicating that remediation cost is zero in $t = 0$ for all sites. Then in cells G16 through K35 we program the formula for discounted remediation cost. For example in cell G16 we have typed =($B$12^A16)*(B16-B15)*$B$7 and fill down through G35. When we optimize by changing cells $B$16 through $F$35, the block of cells G16 through K35 will indicate if and when remediation is undertaken, and the present value of the costs K_i. In G38 through K38 the discounted remediation costs are summarized by site. They are summed to get total discounted clean up costs in cell E62. These costs needed to be broken out separately from environmental damages in order to specify the overall budget (Superfund) constraint.

We are now ready to call Solver. We indicate that we wish to minimize

	A	B	C	D	E	F
1	Optimal Sequential Clean-up of Toxic Sites					
2						
3	Parameter	Site i=1	Site i=2	Site i=3	Site i=4	Site i=5
4	Zi	5	50	20	10	30
5	Vi,o	10	500	100	10	50
6	α	0.01	0.1	0.02	0.02	0.04
7	Ki	50	500	200	100	300
8	β	1	0.01	0.4	0.5	0.2
9						
10	K=	400				
11	δ =	0.05				
12	ρ =	0.95238095				
13						
14	t	X1,t	X2,t	X3,t	X4,t	X5,t
15	0	0	0	0	0	0
16	1	0	0	0	0	0
17	2	0	0	0	0	0
18	3	0	0	0	0	0
19	4	0	0	0	0	0
20	5	0	0	0	0	0
21	6	0	0	0	0	0
22	7	0	0	0	0	0
23	8	0	0	0	0	0
24	9	0	0	0	0	0
25	10	0	0	0	0	0
26	11	0	0	0	0	0
27	12	0	0	0	0	0
28	13	0	0	0	0	0
29	14	0	0	0	0	0
30	15	0	0	0	0	0
31	16	0	0	0	0	0
32	17	0	0	0	0	0
33	18	0	0	0	0	0
34	19	0	0	0	0	0
35	20	0	0	0	0	0
36						
37	t	#1:PV(K+D)	#2: PV(K+D)	#3: PV(K+D)	#4: PV(K+D)	#5:PV(K+D)
38	0	50	250	800	50	300
39	1	48.0952381	261.904762	777.142857	48.5714286	297.142857
40	2	46.2630385	274.376417	754.938776	47.1836735	294.312925
41	3	44.5006371	287.441961	733.369096	45.8355685	291.509945
42	4	42.8053747	301.129673	712.415693	44.5259808	288.73366
43	5	41.1746938	315.469182	692.060959	43.25381	285.983815
44	6	39.606134	330.491524	672.287789	42.0179868	283.26016
45	7	38.0973289	346.229215	653.079567	40.8174729	280.562444
46	8	36.6460021	362.716321	634.42015	39.6512594	277.890421
47	9	35.2499639	379.988526	616.29386	38.5183663	275.243845
48	10	33.9071081	398.083218	598.685464	37.4178415	272.622475
49	11	32.6154088	417.039562	581.580165	36.3487603	270.026071
50	12	31.372917	436.898589	564.963589	35.3102243	267.454394
51	13	30.1777583	457.703283	548.821772	34.3013608	264.907209
52	14	29.0281294	479.498678	533.14115	33.3213219	262.384284
53	15	27.9222959	502.331948	517.908546	32.3692841	259.885386
54	16	26.8585894	526.252517	503.111159	31.4444474	257.410287
55	17	25.835405	551.312161	488.736554	30.5460347	254.95876
56	18	24.8511991	577.565121	474.772653	29.6732908	252.530582
57	19	23.9044868	605.068222	461.20772	28.8254825	250.125528
58	20	22.9938397	633.880994	448.030357	28.0018973	247.74338
59						
60	PV K+D at Site	731.905549	8695.38187	12766.9679	797.935492	5734.68843
61						
62	SUM of All PV	28726.8792		SUM OF PVKi	0	

Spreadsheet 6.3

G	H	I	J	K
PV(K1)	PV(K2)	PV(K3)	PV(K4)	PV(K5)
0	0	0	0	0
0	0	0	0	0
0	0	0	0	0
0	0	0	0	0
0	0	0	0	0
0	0	0	0	0
0	0	0	0	0
0	0	0	0	0
0	0	0	0	0
0	0	0	0	0
0	0	0	0	0
0	0	0	0	0
0	0	0	0	0
0	0	0	0	0
0	0	0	0	0
0	0	0	0	0
0	0	0	0	0
0	0	0	0	0
0	0	0	0	0
0	0	0	0	0
0	0	0	0	0
0	0	0	0	0
PVK1	PVK2	PVK3	PVK4	PVK5
0	0	0	0	0

the Set Cell $B$62 by changing cells $B$16 through $F$35. The binary constraints on $X_{i,t}$ are achieved by using three statements.

$B$16:$F$35 <= 1
$B$16:$F$35 = integer
$B$16:$F$35 >= 0

The constraint that if $X_{i,t} = 1$, $X_{i,\tau} = 1$, for $\tau > t$, can be imposed by the following statements:

$B$17:$B$35 >= $B$16:$B$34
$C$17:$C$35 >= $C$16:$C$34
$D$17:$D$35 >= $D$16:$D$34
$E$17:$E$35 >= $E$16:$E$34
$F$17:$F$35 >= $F$16:$F$34

Finally, the constraint requiring that the present value of remediation costs not exceed the total funds available is achieved by entering $E$62 <= $B$10

You can now click on the Solve button and Solver will embark on an agonizingly long search for the optimal remediation schedule, which will be revealed in the 1's and 0's in the block B16 through F35 and by the present values for cleanup costs in block G16 through K35. It turns out that using your economic intuition you can beat Solver to the solution.

Take a close look at Spreadsheet 6.3, in particular row 58, which contains the discounted damages for our five sites. If you could reduce the damages at one site to zero in $t = 20$, which site would you choose? It would be Site #2, weighing in with discounted damages of $633.88 million. For Site #2, with $\alpha_2 > \delta$, the discounted environmental damages actually grow over time. If this were the case for the other sites we could move backward in time, from $t = 20$ to $t = 0$, looking for the largest marginal reduction in damage. For the other sites, however, $\alpha_i < \delta$, and discounted environmental damage declines from $t = 0$ to $t = 20$.

We can see that of the other sites, Site #3 has the next highest damages, starting at $D_{3,0} = \$800$ million and declining to $D_{3,20} = \$448.03$ million. In checking out the remediation costs for Sites #2 and #3, we see that $K_2 = \$500$ million, and thus we could not afford immediate remediation at Site #2, since our entire budget is only $K = \$400$ million. Site #3 has a cleanup cost of $200 million, which is reduced to a present value of $190.47 million in $t = 1$, the first period that remediation can be implemented. Change the 0 in cell D16 to a 1 and fill down to D35. By making a commitment to the cleanup of Site #3 in $t = 1$ we will eliminate all future environmental damages at that site. We then have ($400 − $190.47) = $209.53 million in uncommitted cleanup funds to use in the future cleanup of Site #2, which we could not afford to do in $t = 1$ anyway.

When should we schedule Site #2, or, more accurately, when can we afford to schedule Site #2? Proceed to column C, row 35, and change the 0 to a 1. Examination of cell H35 shows that cleaning up Site #2 in $t = 20$ only has a present value cost of $188.44 million. This is less than the uncommitted balance of $209.53 million after cleaning up Site #3 in $t = 1$, so we can consider an earlier date for remediation of Site #2. In fact, committing to the cleanup of Site #2 in $t = 18$ has a present-value cost of $207.76 million, which results in a combined present value for Sites #2 and #3 of $398.23 million, which is less than our present value budget of $400 million. There is no other combination of timing and sites which will yield a lower present value for cleanup costs and environmental damage. This result is shown in Spreadsheet 6.4. If you use this spreadsheet as an initial guess for Solver, it will stop after the first iteration and indicate that it could not improve upon your solution. Perhaps you should earn the remaining $1.77 million as your consulting fee. Not bad for a day's work!

6.5 Optimal Extraction with a Nondegradable Waste

Suppose that the extraction of a nonrenewable resource generates a nondegradable waste. In particular, suppose remaining reserves change according to $R_{t+1} = R_t − q_t$, while the stock pollutant accumulates according to $Z_{t+1} = Z_t + \alpha q_t$. It is assumed that the stock pollutant is relatively immobile, so we need not concern ourselves with diffusion. The welfare of the economy in period t is given by $W_t = pq_t − cZ_t^2$, where $p > 0$ is the per unit price for q_t and $c > 0$ is a cost parameter. (This might be the case for a region or small country extracting q_t for export at a world price of p, while having to contend with the local environmental damages caused by Z_t.) Finally, assume that the rate of extraction is subject to a capacity constraint so that $q_{MAX} \geq q_t \geq 0$.

Given the structure of this problem, there will be only two possible outcomes. Either initial reserves, R_0, will be completely exhausted by some period $t = T$, in which case the nondegradable pollution stock, $Z_T = \alpha R_0$, will continue to impose damages over the remaining (infinite) horizon, or the economy will stop extraction before exhaustion in order to prevent the pollution stock from exceeding its "optimal" level. In the first case $\alpha R_0 \leq Z^*$; in the second case $\alpha R_0 > Z^*$, where Z^* is the optimal pollution stock. In either case, if $Z_0 < Z^*$, the approach to Z^* is most rapid and will involve some initial periods where $q_t = q_{MAX}$.

	A	B	C	D	E	F
1	Optimal Sequential Clean-up of Toxic Sites					
2						
3	Parameter	Site i=1	Site i=2	Site i=3	Site i=4	Site i=5
4	Zi	5	50	20	10	30
5	Vi,o	10	500	100	10	50
6	α	0.01	0.1	0.02	0.02	0.04
7	Ki	50	500	200	100	300
8	β	1	0.01	0.4	0.5	0.2
9						
10	K=	400				
11	$\delta =$	0.05				
12	$\rho =$	0.95238095				
13						
14	t	X1,t	X2,t	X3,t	X4,t	X5,t
15	0	0	0	0	0	0
16	1	0	0	1	0	0
17	2	0	0	1	0	0
18	3	0	0	1	0	0
19	4	0	0	1	0	0
20	5	0	0	1	0	0
21	6	0	0	1	0	0
22	7	0	0	1	0	0
23	8	0	0	1	0	0
24	9	0	0	1	0	0
25	10	0	0	1	0	0
26	11	0	0	1	0	0
27	12	0	0	1	0	0
28	13	0	0	1	0	0
29	14	0	0	1	0	0
30	15	0	0	1	0	0
31	16	0	0	1	0	0
32	17	0	0	1	0	0
33	18	0	1	1	0	0
34	19	0	1	1	0	0
35	20	0	1	1	0	0
36						
37	t	#1:PV(K+D)	#2: PV(K+D)	#3: PV(K+D)	#4: PV(K+D)	#5:PV(K+D)
38	0	50	250	800	50	300
39	1	48.0952381	261.904762	190.47619	48.5714286	297.142857
40	2	46.2630385	274.376417	0	47.1836735	294.312925
41	3	44.5006371	287.441961	0	45.8355685	291.509945
42	4	42.8053747	301.129673	0	44.5259808	288.73366
43	5	41.1746938	315.469182	0	43.25381	285.983815
44	6	39.606134	330.491524	0	42.0179868	283.26016
45	7	38.0973289	346.229215	0	40.8174729	280.562444
46	8	36.6460021	362.716321	0	39.6512594	277.890421
47	9	35.2499639	379.988526	0	38.5183663	275.243845
48	10	33.9071081	398.083218	0	37.4178415	272.622475
49	11	32.6154088	417.039562	0	36.3487603	270.026071
50	12	31.372917	436.898589	0	35.3102243	267.454394
51	13	30.1777583	457.703283	0	34.3013608	264.907209
52	14	29.0281294	479.498678	0	33.3213219	262.384284
53	15	27.9222959	502.331948	0	32.3692841	259.885386
54	16	26.8585894	526.252517	0	31.4444474	257.410287
55	17	25.835405	551.312161	0	30.5460347	254.95876
56	18	24.8511991	207.760327	0	29.6732908	252.530582
57	19	23.9044868	0	0	28.8254825	250.125528
58	20	22.9938397	0	0	28.0018973	247.74338
59						
60	PV K+D at Site	731.905549	7086.62786	990.47619	797.935492	5734.68843
61						
62	SUM of All PV	15341.6335		SUM OF PVKi	398.236518	

Spreadsheet 6.4

G	H	I	J	K
PV(K1)	PV(K2)	PV(K3)	PV(K4)	PV(K5)
0	0	0	0	0
0	0	190.47619	0	0
0	0	0	0	0
0	0	0	0	0
0	0	0	0	0
0	0	0	0	0
0	0	0	0	0
0	0	0	0	0
0	0	0	0	0
0	0	0	0	0
0	0	0	0	0
0	0	0	0	0
0	0	0	0	0
0	0	0	0	0
0	0	0	0	0
0	0	0	0	0
0	0	0	0	0
0	0	0	0	0
0	207.760327	0	0	0
0	0	0	0	0
0	0	0	0	0
PVK1	PVK2	PVK3	PVK4	PVK5
0	207.760327	190.47619	0	0

The Lagrangian expression for this problem may be written as

$$L = \sum_{t=0}^{T-1} \rho^t \{ pq_t - cZ_t^2 + \rho\lambda_{t+1}[R_t - q_t - R_{t+1}] + \rho\mu_{t+1}[Z_t + \alpha q_t - Z_{t+1}] \}$$
$$- \rho^{T-1} cZ_T^2 / \delta$$

where the last term represents the present value of damages from a pollution stock of Z_T which will never degrade. We are again making use of a terminal condition similar in philosophy to that employed in Section 2.2. It is derived in the same manner as the terminal value function in cell \$E\$34 of Spreadsheet 6.1, only in this case q_t drops to 0 when reserves are exhausted or the optimal pollution stock is reached.

Suppose the relevant solution is one in which we stop extracting to prevent the pollution stock from exceeding its optimal value $Z^* > 0$. In this case we know that a steady state has been reached where $q^* = 0$, $R^* > 0$, and $\lambda^* = 0$, since remaining reserves are worthless. Take the partial of L with respect to q_t. Suppose $t = T - 1$ is the last period when extraction is positive. Then $\partial L/\partial q_{T-1} = 0$ would imply that $p - \rho\lambda_T + \rho\mu_T\alpha = 0$. But $\lambda_T = \lambda^* = 0$, implying that $\mu_T = \mu^* = -(1 + \delta)p/\alpha < 0$. Now take the partial of L with respect to Z_t and set it equal to 0. It will imply $-2cZ_t + \rho\mu_{t+1} - \mu_t = 0$. In steady state this implies $Z^* = -\delta\mu/[2c(1 + \delta)] = \delta p/[2\alpha c]$ as the expression for the optimal pollution stock. The optimal extraction path in this case will have $q_t = q_{MAX}$ for $t = 0, 1, \ldots, T - 2$, and $0 < q_{T-1} \le q_{MAX}$, with $Z_T = Z^* = \delta p/[2\alpha c]$.

In Spreadsheet 6.5 we show a numerical example of the case in which depletion is not optimal because of damage from the stock pollutant. The parameter values are $\alpha = 0.1$, $p = 100$, $c = 0.5$, and $\delta = 0.05$, with initial conditions $R_0 = 1,000$ and $Z_0 = 0$. These parameter values imply $Z^* = 50$. In this initial spreadsheet we specify $q_t = q_{MAX} = 100$ for $t = 0, 1, 2, \ldots,$ 9, which causes depletion in period $t = 10$ ($R_{10} = 0$) and causes the pollution stock to reach $Z_{10} = 100$. In cell E8 we type =(\$B\$5^A8)*(\$B\$2*B8 – \$B\$3*(D8^2)) and fill down to E17. In cell E18 we type =(\$B\$5^A17)*(-\$B\$3*(\$D\$18^2)/\$B\$4), which is the present value of damage from Z_{10}. In cell E20 we type =SUM(\$E\$8:\$E\$18) to calculate the present value of welfare for this initial depletion schedule. This yields the value $W = 6{,}501.09454$.

Can Solver increase the present value of welfare by changing q_t? We tell Solver to maximize \$E\$20 by changing cells \$B\$8:\$B\$17, subject to \$B\$8:\$B\$17 <= 100 and \$B\$8:\$B\$17 >= 0. As we would predict, Solver recognizes that Z_t should not exceed $Z^* = 50$, and in Spreadsheet 6.6 sets $q_5 = \ldots = q_9 = 0$, yielding a present value of welfare of $W = 23{,}616.0293$.

	A	B	C	D	E
1	$\alpha =$	0.1			
2	p=	100			
3	c=	0.5			
4	$\delta =$	0.05			
5	$\rho =$	0.95238095			
6					
7	t	qt	Rt	Zt	PVWt
8	0	100	1000	0	10000
9	1	100	900	10	9476.19048
10	2	100	800	20	8888.88889
11	3	100	700	30	8249.64907
12	4	100	600	40	7568.86277
13	5	100	500	50	6855.85396
14	6	100	400	60	6118.96625
15	7	100	300	70	5365.64404
16	8	100	200	80	4602.50766
17	9	100	100	90	3835.42305
18	10	0	0	100	-64460.8916
19					
20				W =	6501.09454

Spreadsheet 6.5

	A	B	C	D	E
1	$\alpha =$	0.1			
2	p=	100			
3	c=	0.5			
4	$\delta =$	0.05			
5	$\rho =$	0.95238095			
6					
7	t	qt	Rt	Zt	PVWt
8	0	100	1000	0	10000
9	1	100	900	10	9476.19048
10	2	100	800	20	8888.88889
11	3	100	700	30	8249.64907
12	4	100	600	40	7568.86277
13	5	0	500	50	-979.407708
14	6	0	500	50	-932.769246
15	7	0	500	50	-888.351663
16	8	0	500	50	-846.049203
17	9	0	500	50	-805.761145
18	10	0	500	50	-16115.2229
19					
20				W =	23616.0293

Spreadsheet 6.6

6.6   Recycling

Many products have scrap value because they contain materials that can be recycled into the same or different products. Various metals, plastic, and newsprint are common examples. We will consider a nonrenewable resource that can be recycled once. In particular, let R_t denote remaining reserves and q_t extraction in period t so that $R_{t+1} = R_t - q_t$. Suppose q_t is a commodity which is used and immediately recycled, or processed into another commodity, u_t, which can be consumed in period t or inventoried. Let I_t denote the inventory of u_t where $I_{t+1} = I_t + \beta q_t - u_t$, and $1 > \beta > 0$.

Suppose q_t is sold in a competitive market at unit price $p_1 > 0$, and likewise for u_t, but at unit price p_2. To keep things simple, we assume that the extraction costs of q_t are not reserve dependent and that the net revenue in period t may be written as $\pi_{1,t} = p_1 q_t - C_1(q_t)$. The cost of recycling or processing q_t into u_t depends on the levels of both q_t and u_t according to $C_2(q_t, u_t)$, leading to a second stream of net revenues given by $\pi_{2,t} = p_2 u_t - C_2(q_t, u_t)$. (This model can also be thought of as a *transfer pricing model*, in which one division of a company extracts q_t and sells it at price p_1 to a second division, which then processes q_t for storage as I_{t+1} or sale as u_t.) Let $t = T$ be the first period that both q_t and u_t go to 0. We will assume that this happens because the nonrenewable resource, R_t, and the inventory, I_t, have been exhausted.

The Lagrangian for this problem may be written as

$$L = \sum_{t=0}^{T-1} \rho^t \{ p_1 q_t - C_1(q_t) + p_2 u_t - C_2(q_t, u_t) + \rho \lambda_{t+1}[R_t - q_t - R_{t+1}]$$
$$+ \rho \mu_{t+1}[I_t + \beta q_t - u_t - I_{t+1}] \}$$

and for the periods when q_t, u_t, R_t, and I_t are positive, we have first-order necessary conditions that require

$$\frac{\partial L}{\partial q_t} = \rho^t \{ p_1 - \partial C_1(\bullet)/\partial q_t - \partial C_2(\bullet)/\partial q_t - \rho \lambda_{t+1} + \rho \mu_{t+1} \beta \} = 0$$

$$\frac{\partial L}{\partial u_t} = \rho^t \{ p_2 - \partial C_2(\bullet)/\partial u_t - \rho \mu_{t+1} \} = 0$$

$$\frac{\partial L}{\partial R_t} = \rho^t \{ \rho \lambda_{t+1} \} - \rho^t \lambda_t = 0$$

$$\frac{\partial L}{\partial I_t} = \rho^t \{ \rho \mu_{t+1} \} - \rho^t \mu_t = 0$$

The last two equations imply that $\lambda_{t+1} = (1 + \delta)\lambda_t$ and $\mu_{t+1} = (1 + \delta)\mu_t$. This says that both the shadow prices on remaining reserves and remaining inventories are growing at the rate of discount. Substituting the expressions for λ_{t+1} and μ_{t+1} into the first and second equations we obtain

$$p_1 - \partial C_1(\bullet)/\partial q_t - \partial C_2(\bullet)/\partial q_t - \lambda_t + \beta\mu_t = 0$$
$$p_2 - \partial C_2(\bullet)/\partial u_t - \mu_t = 0$$

We can use these last two equations to determine the terminal values for λ_T and μ_T. If in $t = T$, when $q_T = u_T = 0$, the marginal costs are also zero – i.e., $\partial C_1(\bullet)/\partial q_T = \partial C_2(\bullet)/\partial q_T = \partial C_2(\bullet)/\partial u_T = 0$ – then $\mu_T = p_2$ and $\lambda_T = p_1 + \beta p_2$. Having these expressions for the terminal values for λ_T and μ_T, and knowing that the shadow prices are rising at the rate of discount, we can in turn show that $\mu_t = \rho^{T-t} p_2$ and $\lambda_t = \rho^{T-t}[p_1 + \beta p_2]$. Thus, although we do not know the terminal period, T, we do know how the shadow prices will behave over time and where they will end up when $q_T = u_T = 0$. To solve the problem in its entirety we could substitute $\mu_t = \rho^{T-t}p_2$ and $\lambda_t = \rho^{T-t}[p_1 + \beta p_2]$ into the last two equations and select a candidate value (a guess) for T. Then we could solve for q_t and u_t, simultaneously, for the horizon $t = 0, 1, \ldots, T-1$. Since depletion will be optimal, we would then check to see if

$$\sum_{t=0}^{T-1} q_t = R_0$$

If the sum of extraction is greater than (less than) R_0, we shorten (lengthen) T and resolve the previous two equations for the new values of q_t and u_t. Alternatively, for a numerical problem, we can summon Solver and check its solution to see if λ_t and μ_t are behaving as they should on the basis of our analytic understanding of the problem.

In Spreadsheet 6.7 we show the setup for an optimal extraction/recycling problem. In this problem $C_1(q_t) = c_1 q_t^2$ and $C_2(q_t, u_t) = c_2(q_t + u_t)^2$, where $c_1 = 0.01$ and $c_2 = 0.001$. The market price for q_t is $p_1 = 2$, while the market price for u_t is $p_2 = 1$. The recovery rate is $\beta = 0.7$, the discount rate is $\delta = 0.05$, initial reserves are $R_0 = 100$, and initial inventories are $I_0 = 0$. In this worksheet, extraction is spread out over 20 periods ($t = 0, 1, 2, \ldots, 19$) with $q_t = 5$. Recycling is initially set at $\beta q_t = 3.5$, for the same horizon. The values for q_{20} and u_{20} are set at 0 and Solver will be allowed to change only the earlier values of these variables. Of interest is whether Solver will find it optimal to deplete reserves and inventories before $T = 20$.

In cell F10 we type

=($B$7^A10)*($B$1*B10+$B$2*D10-$B$3*(B10^2)
   -$B$4*(B10+D10)^2)

	A	B	C	D	E	F	G	H
1	p1=	2						
2	p2=	1						
3	c1=	0.01						
4	c2=	0.001						
5	β=	0.7						
6	δ=	0.05						
7	ρ=	0.95238095						
8								
9	t	qt	Rt	ut	It	Discounted πt	μ	λ
10	0	5	100	3.5	0	13.17775	0.983	2.5711
11	1	5	95	3.5	0	12.5502381	0.983	2.5711
12	2	5	90	3.5	0	11.9526077	0.983	2.5711
13	3	5	85	3.5	0	11.3834359	0.983	2.5711
14	4	5	80	3.5	0	10.8413675	0.983	2.5711
15	5	5	75	3.5	0	10.3251119	0.983	2.5711
16	6	5	70	3.5	0	9.83343994	0.983	2.5711
17	7	5	65	3.5	0	9.3651809	0.983	2.5711
18	8	5	60	3.5	0	8.9192199	0.983	2.5711
19	9	5	55	3.5	0	8.49449515	0.983	2.5711
20	10	5	50	3.5	0	8.08999538	0.983	2.5711
21	11	5	45	3.5	0	7.7047575	0.983	2.5711
22	12	5	40	3.5	0	7.33786429	0.983	2.5711
23	13	5	35	3.5	0	6.98844218	0.983	2.5711
24	14	5	30	3.5	0	6.65565922	0.983	2.5711
25	15	5	25	3.5	0	6.33872306	0.983	2.5711
26	16	5	20	3.5	0	6.03687911	0.983	2.5711
27	17	5	15	3.5	0	5.74940868	0.983	2.5711
28	18	5	10	3.5	0	5.47562731	0.983	2.5711
29	19	5	5	3.5	0	5.21488315	0.983	2.5711
30	20	0	0	0	0	0	1	2.7
31						172.435087		
32					π =			

Spreadsheet 6.7

which is the expression for discounted net revenue. This expression is filled down to cell F30. Cell F32 contains the sum of cells $F$10 through $F$30, which for the initial guess $q_t = 5$ and $u_t = 3.5$ for $t = 0, \ldots, 19$, yields 172.435087. Solver is then asked to maximize the value in cell $F$32 by changing the values in $B$10:$B$29 and $D$10:$D$29, subject to the nonnegativity constraint that $B$10:$E$30 >= 0.

Spreadsheet 6.8 shows Solver's optimal solution. Initial extraction is increased and reserves are depleted by the beginning of $t = 7$. (The values for q_t, u_t, R_t, and I_t for $t \geq 7$ are so small that they are regarded as 0 by Solver.) It is optimal to sell all units of u_t as they become available; thus $u_t = \beta q_t$, and no inventories accumulate. Examination of the values for λ_t will show that they grow from $\lambda_0 = 2.00465$ at a rate of approximately $\delta = 0.05$, reaching $\lambda_T = \lambda_7 = p_1 + \beta p_2 = 2.7$. Because inventories, I_t, are never positive, μ_t is not required to grow at the rate of discount. Only when $I_t > 0$ will $\mu_{t+1} = (1 + \delta)\mu_t$. The maximized present value is $\pi = 224.430795$.

6.7 Emission Taxes and Marketable Pollution Permits

Environmental policy constitutes an attempt by government to correct for economic behavior which generates unacceptable environmental damage. Deterioration of air and water quality in the United States in the 1950s and 1960s led to the passage of laws by state and federal governments which established a system of standards and permits which sought to control the amount and type of wastes disposed of via smokestack and outfall. The federal government also subsidized the construction of primary and secondary municipal wastewater treatment plants. Although progress has been made in improving the quality of many lakes and rivers, improving the quality of air in the major metropolitan areas of the United States has proved to be a more difficult problem. A combination of pollutants from point sources (factories and utilities) and mobile sources (cars, trucks, and buses) makes the formulation of effective air quality policies more difficult than in the case of wastewater treatment. Economists have long advocated the use of *emission taxes* or *marketable pollution permits*. This section will focus on these two policies.

We begin with the emission tax. Consider an industry that comprises many identical firms, each employing a technology characterized by a commodity-residual transformation function $\phi(Q_t, S_t) = 0$, as described in Section 6.1. We assume that $Q_{MAX} \geq Q_t \geq Q_{MIN}$, $\partial\phi(\bullet)/\partial Q_t = \phi_Q > 0$, $\partial\phi(\bullet)/\partial S_t = \phi_S < 0$, $\phi(Q_{MIN}, 0) = 0$, and $\phi(Q_{MAX}, S_{MAX}) = 0$ as in Figure 6.1. Suppose no firm is concerned with the dynamics of the stock pollutant and each is exclusively interested in maximizing after-tax revenue in each

	A	B
1	p1 =	2
2	p2 =	1
3	c1 =	0.01
4	c2 =	0.001
5	β =	0.7
6	δ =	0.05
7	ρ =	0.95238095

	A	B	C	D	E	F	G	H
9	t	qt	Rt	ut	It	Discounted πt	μ	λ
10	0	26.9720976	100	18.8804683	0	63.4472652	0.90829487	2.00465932
11	1	23.0846301	73.0279024	16.1592411	0	52.8184937	0.92151226	2.10487824
12	2	19.0027122	49.9432723	13.3018985	3.5527E-15	42.3153781	0.93539078	2.21011008
13	3	14.7155298	30.9405601	10.3008709	7.1054E-15	31.9107155	0.9499672	2.32063364
14	4	10.2162819	16.2250303	7.15139733	1.0658E-14	21.5865617	0.96526464	2.43662425
15	5	5.48686541	6.00874838	3.84080579	6.2172E-15	11.3035201	0.98134466	2.55854861
16	6	0.52188288	0.52188296	0.36531802	7.1054E-15	1.04886025	0.9982256	2.68654586
17	7	5.4286E-09	7.8019E-08	-1.1206E-08	7.3275E-15	-2.4755E-10	1	2.7
18	8	6.6852E-09	7.259E-09	4.6796E-09	1.5006E-08	1.2217E-08	1	2.7
19	9	1.6821E-08	6.5905E-08	1.1775E-08	1.5006E-08	2.9276E-08	1	2.7
20	10	4.6399E-08	4.9084E-08	3.2479E-08	1.5006E-08	7.6909E-08	1	2.7
21	11	-2.3611E-10	2.6854E-10	-1.6527E-10	1.5006E-08	-3.7273E-10	1	2.7
22	12	-8.0988E-08	2.9216E-08	-5.6692E-08	1.5006E-08	-1.2176E-07	1	2.7
23	13	1.1319E-08	8.391E-08	7.9234E-09	1.5006E-08	1.6208E-08	1	2.7
24	14	2.3506E-08	7.259E-08	1.6454E-08	1.5006E-08	3.2055E-08	1	2.7
25	15	4.6162E-08	4.9084E-08	3.2314E-08	1.5006E-08	5.9953E-08	1	2.7
26	16	-6.9669E-08	2.9216E-09	-4.8768E-08	1.5006E-08	-8.6173E-08	1	2.7
27	17	6.9669E-08	7.259E-08	4.8768E-08	1.5006E-08	8.207E-08	1	2.7
28	18	-1.4172E-09	2.9216E-09	-2.5489E-07	1.5006E-08	-1.0709E-07	1	2.7
29	19	-1.0674E-09	4.3388E-09	-7.4719E-10	2.6891E-07	-1.1405E-09	1	2.7
30	20	0	5.4061E-09	0	2.6891E-07	0	1	2.7
31								
32		π =				224.430795		

Spreadsheet 6.8

period. Each firm is a price-taker, receiving $p > 0$ for each unit of Q_t. Each firm faces a tax rate of $\tau_t > 0$ for each unit of S_t emitted. This tax rate might change over time, hence the subscript. In each period, each firm faces a static optimization problem associated with the Lagrangian

$$L_t = pQ_t - \tau_t S_t - \mu_t \phi(Q_t, S_t) \tag{6.9}$$

with first-order conditions for $Q_{\text{MAX}} > Q_t > Q_{\text{MIN}}$ that require

$$\partial L_t / \partial Q_t = p - \mu_t \phi_Q = 0 \tag{6.10}$$

$$\partial L_t / \partial S_t = -\tau_t - \mu_t \phi_S = 0 \tag{6.11}$$

$$\partial L_t / \partial \mu_t = -\phi(Q_t, S_t) = 0 \tag{6.12}$$

Equations (6.10) and (6.11) imply that $p/\tau_t = -\phi_Q/\phi_S$, which along with $\phi(Q_t, S_t) = 0$ provides the representative firm with two equations to solve for the levels of Q_t and S_t which maximize after-tax revenue. For example, suppose that

$$\phi(Q_t, S_t) = (Q_t - m)^2 - nS_t = 0 \tag{6.13}$$

where $Q_{\text{MIN}} = m$ and n are positive parameters. The partials of this function are $\phi_Q = 2(Q_t - m) \geq 0$ and $\phi_S = -n < 0$, and $p/\tau_t = 2(Q_t - m)/n$ implies that

$$Q_t = \frac{np}{2\tau_t} + m \tag{6.14}$$

which upon substitution into (6.13) implies

$$S_t = \frac{n}{4}\left(\frac{p}{\tau_t}\right)^2 \tag{6.15}$$

Note that as $\tau_t \to \infty$, $Q_t \to m = Q_{\text{MIN}}$, and $S_t \to 0$. As $\tau_t \to 0$, $Q_t \to Q_{\text{MAX}}$ and $S_t \to S_{\text{MAX}}$. In fact, τ_t must be greater than $np/[2(Q_{\text{MAX}} - m)]$ before each competitive firm would choose $Q_t < Q_{\text{MAX}}$ and $S_t < S_{\text{MAX}}$.

To summarize, given the form of the commodity-residual transformation function in equation (6.13), after-tax revenue maximization by each firm will imply that each will operate so as to produce Q_t and S_t as given by equations (6.14) and (6.15), subject to $Q_{\text{MAX}} \geq Q_t \geq m$ and $S_{\text{MAX}} \geq S_t \geq 0$.

What is the optimal tax τ_t? Let's suppose that the environmental regulator has studied the industry and knows the form of $\phi(Q_t, S_t) = 0$. Suppose that aggregate emissions contribute to the accumulation of the stock pollutant Z_t and that there are $N > 0$ firms in the industry. The regulator wants to set τ_t so as to cause each firm to adopt the levels for Q_t and S_t which will

$$\text{Maximize} \quad \sum_{t=0}^{\infty} \rho^t \left[pNQ_t - cZ_t^2 \right]$$

$$\text{Subject to} \quad Z_{t+1} - Z_t = -\gamma Z_t + NS_t$$

$$\phi(Q_t, S_t) = 0$$

$$Q_{\text{MAX}} \geq Q_t \geq Q_{\text{MIN}}$$

$$Z_0 \text{ given}$$

Note that pNQ_t is the value of aggregate output in period t and that NS_t is the aggregate waste loading from our N identical firms. We are also assuming that damage is quadratic in the pollution stock with $c > 0$. The Lagrangian for the regulator may be written

$$L = \sum_{t=0}^{\infty} \rho^t \{ pNQ_t - cZ_t^2 + \rho\lambda_{t+1}[(1-\gamma)Z_t + NS_t - Z_{t+1}$$

$$-\mu_t \phi(Q_t, S_t) \}$$

The first-order necessary conditions for $Q_{\text{MAX}} > Q_t > m$, $S_t > 0$, and $Z_t > 0$ require

$$\partial L / \partial Q_t = \rho^t \{ pN - \mu_t \phi_Q \} = 0 \tag{6.16}$$

$$\partial L / \partial S_t = \rho^t \{ N\rho\lambda_{t+1} - \mu_t \phi_S \} = 0 \tag{6.17}$$

$$\partial L / \partial Z_t = \rho^t \{ -2cZ_t + \rho\lambda_{t+1}(1-\gamma) \} - \rho^t \lambda_t = 0 \tag{6.18}$$

Equation (6.16) implies $\mu_t = Np/\phi_Q$, and upon substitution into equation (6.17) gives $\rho\lambda_{t+1} = p\phi_S/\phi_Q$. Equation (6.18) implies $\rho\lambda_{t+1}(1-\gamma) - \lambda_t = 2cZ_t$. We will evaluate these last three expressions in steady state to determine expressions for the optimal pollution stock, rate of output, and rate of residual emissions. Knowing the optimal steady-state rate of output, Q^*, for the representative firm, the regulator can calculate the steady-state optimal emissions tax according to $\tau^* = np/[2(Q^* - m)]$. The expression for the optimal tax comes from solving equation (6.14) for τ_t and presumes that all firms maximize after-tax revenue.

In steady state we have $\mu = Np/\phi_Q$, $\rho\lambda = p\phi_S/\phi_Q$, and $-\rho\lambda(\delta + \gamma) = 2cZ$. Substituting $\rho\lambda$ into the last expression yields $-p[\phi_S/\phi_Q](\delta + \gamma) = 2cZ$. To make things concrete, assume that the commodity-residual transformation frontier is again given by equation (6.13) with $\phi_Q = 2(Q_t - m)$ and $\phi_S = -n$. Substituting these partials into the last steady-state equation implies

Table 6.1 *Steady-State Optimum with an Emission Tax*

Variable	Base Case	n = 20	p = 400	δ = 0.1	γ = 0.4	c = 0.04
Q*	15	17.94	16.30	15.31	17.66	13.97
τ*	200	251.98	317.48	188.21	130.50	251.98
S*	2.5	3.15	3.97	2.82	5.87	1.57
Z*	1,250	1,574.90	1,984.25	1,411.55	1,468.08	787.45

$$Z^* = \frac{np(\delta+\gamma)}{4c(Q^*-m)} \tag{6.19}$$

which is the analogue to equation (6.8), but for the quadratic commodity-residual transformation frontier given by (6.13). In steady state we also know that $S^* = (Q^* - m)^2/n$ and that $NS^* = \gamma Z^*$. These last two expressions combine with equation (6.19) to imply

$$\frac{N(Q^*-m)^2}{\gamma n} = Z^* = \frac{np(\delta+\gamma)}{4c(Q^*-m)}$$

which can be solved for Q^* yielding

$$Q^* = \sqrt[3]{\frac{n^2 p(\delta+\gamma)\gamma}{4cN}} + m \tag{6.20}$$

Knowing Q^* the environmental regulator can set $\tau^* = np/[2(Q^* - m)]$, which will induce firms to operate at (Q^*,S^*), where $NS^* = \gamma Z^*$ at the steady-state optimum. Because the commodity-residual transformation frontier is nonlinear the optimal approach from $Z_0 < Z^*$ would require the environmental regulator to solve in advance for Q_t^* and then calculate and announce τ_t^*. From $Z_0 < Z^*$ the optimal emission tax will asymptotically rise to τ^* as the steady-state equilibrium is approached.

Table 6.1 reports on the comparative statics of the steady-state optimum to changes in various parameters. The base-case parameters are $n = 10, p = 200, \delta = 0.05, \gamma = 0.2, c = 0.02, N = 100$, and $m = 10$. Columns 3 through 7 give the new values for Q^*, τ^*, S^*, and Z^* for a change in a single parameter to the value reported at the top of that column.

For example, when n is increased from 10 to 20 the optimal level of output for the representative firm increases from 15 to 17.94. The optimal tax increases from 200 to 251.98. Each firm now emits 3.15 units of waste each period and the optimal pollution stock increases from 1,250 to

Table 6.2 *Elasticities of the Steady-State Variables for a 100% Increase in Various Parameters in the Emission Tax Model*

Variable	n	p	δ	γ	c	N
Q^*	0.20	0.09	0.02	0.18	- 0.07	- 0.07
τ^*	0.26	0.59	- 0.06	- 0.35	0.26	0.26
S^*	0.26	0.59	0.13	1.35	- 0.37	- 0.37
Z^*	0.26	0.59	0.13	0.17	- 0.37	0.25

1,574.90. Note: Increases in p, δ, and γ increase the optimal pollution stock; increases in n, p, and c raise the optimal emission tax, τ^*; and increases in δ and γ lower it. The level of emissions from the representative firm increases with increases in n, p, δ, and γ and declines with an increase in c.

Another way of showing numerical comparative statics is to construct a table showing the percentage change in a variable divided by the percentage change in the parameter. Such ratios may be interpreted as elasticities. The absolute changes in Table 6.1 are converted to elasticities in Table 6.2. Such a table has the advantage of conveying both the direction and the relative size of the change. The calculations in Table 6.2 are made easier by the fact that in Table 6.1 all parameters were increased by 100%. Table 6.2 also contains the elasticities of the steady-state variables for changes in N, the number of firms in the industry.

All of the elasticities in Table 6.2 are less than 1, with the exception of the response of S^* to a change in γ. An increase in γ from 0.2 to 0.4 causes an 18% increase in Q^*, a 35% decrease in τ^*, a 135% increase in S^*, and a 17% increase in Z^*.

The second environmental policy advocated by economists is marketable pollution permits. Such permits are now being used to reduce SO_2 emissions, which are a precursor to acid rain. The Chicago Board of Trade currently administers the auction for both "spot" (current year) and futures markets. The market was initially set up for fossil fuel burning utilities but is being expanded to other industries and air pollutants. Since its inception in 1993, the price of a permit to emit one ton of SO_2 has fallen from about $150 to about $68. This would seem to indicate that the cost of reducing SO_2 emissions has fallen as firms have looked for a least-cost way to avoid having to purchase permits.

With a slight modification, we can make use of the emission tax model to examine firm behavior when there is access to a market for pollution permits. Let $\phi_i(Q_{i,t}, S_{i,t}) = 0$ denote the commodity-residual transformation frontier for the ith firm in a competitive industry. We will assume that the ith firm is endowed with $M_{i,t}$ permits in period t. Each permit entitles the firm to emit one ton of some pollutant, or to sell that right to another firm, with the permit price being determined through a competitive auction. Each firm, though technologically different from every other, wishes to maximize net revenue in each period. If the firm chooses to emit residuals beyond $M_{i,t}$, it must purchase permits at a per unit price of $p_{m,t} > 0$. If the firm chooses to emit at a rate less than $M_{i,t}$, it can sell the unused permits and augment its revenue. This market structure leads to the Lagrangian

$$L_{i,t} = pQ_{i,t} - p_{m,t}(S_{i,t} - M_{i,t}) - \mu_{i,t}\phi_i(Q_{i,t}, S_{i,t}) \tag{6.21}$$

where for $Q_{i,\mathrm{MAX}} > Q_{i,t} > Q_{i,\mathrm{MIN}}$ the first-order conditions require

$$\partial L_{i,t}/\partial Q_{i,t} = p - \mu_{i,t}\phi_{i,Q} = 0 \tag{6.22}$$

$$\partial L_{i,t}/\partial S_{i,t} = -p_{m,t} - \mu_{i,t}\phi_{i,S} = 0 \tag{6.23}$$

$$\partial L_{i,t}/\partial \mu_{i,t} = -\phi_i(Q_{i,t}, S_{i,t}) = 0 \tag{6.24}$$

Equations (6.22) and (6.23) imply $p/p_{m,t} = -\phi_{i,Q}/\phi_{i,S}$. Recall in the emission tax model that our representative firm sought to equate the ratio of price to emission tax to the same marginal rate of transformation (i.e., $p/\tau_t = -\phi_Q/\phi_S$). Thus, we can see that the price for a marketable pollution permit, $p_{m,t}$, is playing a role similar to that of the emission tax τ_t. Given $M_{i,t}$, the equations $p/p_{m,t} = -\phi_{i,Q}/\phi_{i,S}$ and $\phi_i(Q_{i,t}, S_{i,t}) = 0$ will permit each firm to determine its optimal levels for $Q_{i,t}$ and $S_{i,t}$, and to determine whether it will be a buyer or seller in the market for pollution permits. With a given price, p, for $Q_{i,t}$ (faced by all our heterogeneous but competitive firms), there will exist a demand function $S_i(p_{m,t})$, and the price which clears the pollution permit market must satisfy the following equation:

$$\sum_{i=1}^{I}(S_i(p_{m,t}) - M_{i,t}) = 0 \tag{6.25}$$

where the excess demand, $(S_i(p_{m,t}) - M_{i,t})$, for a particular firm may be positive, zero, or negative, and I is the number of firms in the industry.

If we adopt the commodity-residual transformation frontier specified in equation (6.13), the ith firm's rate of output and residual emissions will be determined by

$$Q_{i,t} = \frac{n_i p}{2p_{m,t}} + m_i \tag{6.26}$$

$$S_{i,t} = \frac{n_i}{4}\left(\frac{p}{p_{m,t}}\right)^2 \tag{6.27}$$

Note the similarity between equations (6.14)–(6.15) and (6.26)–(6.27). With a heterogeneous industry we have firm-specific transformation parameters, n_i and m_i, and again note the similar roles played by the emission tax and the price in the permit market.

There is a difference between these two sets of equations. In equations (6.14)–(6.15) the firm would wait for the environmental regulator to announce this period's emission tax, τ_t. In our model of marketable pollution permits each firm must have received its allotment, $M_{i,t}$; know p, n_i, and m_i; and then participate in an auction where they offer to buy or sell, on the basis of the candidate market clearing price, which the auctioneer announces and then modifies until there is no further desire to trade among the I firms in the industry.

Mathematically, we are able to solve for the market clearing price, $p_{m,t}$, and don't need an auctioneer. Return to equation (6.25) and assume we are dealing with an emission demand function given by (6.27). Substituting (6.27) into (6.25) implies

$$\sum_{i=1}^{I} \frac{n_i}{4} \left(\frac{p}{p_{m,t}} \right)^2 = M_t = \sum_{i=1}^{I} M_{i,t} \tag{6.28}$$

where M_t is the known total of permits which have been issued by the environmental regulator. Although still unknown, the market clearing price in the permit market will be a constant. Some algebra will reveal

$$p_{m,t} = \frac{0.5 p}{\sqrt{\dfrac{M_t}{\displaystyle\sum_{i=1}^{I} n_i}}} \tag{6.29}$$

Although the environmental regulator would be able to tell the auctioneer M_t, and possibly p, it is probably a stretch for her to know all the n_i. Thus the auctioneer, even in this model, might have to stick around to help find $p_{m,t}$. Once found, however, it will be consistent with the emission decisions by the I firms and the total number of permits available.

6.8   Questions and Exercises

Q6.1 What is the difference between a degradable and a nondegradable stock pollutant? If the initial pollution stock is positive ($Z_0 > 0$), what happens to Z_t over time if $\gamma > 0$ and $\gamma = 0$ when no further wastes are generated?

Q6.2 What is the definition of the commodity-residual transformation frontier?

Q6.3 What are the travel cost method and the method of contingent valuation? Why are they used by environmental economists?

E6.1 Consider a commodity, Q_t, which generates a residual waste flow according to αQ_t, which may accumulate as a stock pollutant, Z_t, according to $Z_{t+1} - Z_t = -\gamma Z_t + \alpha Q_t$, where α and γ are both positive but less than 1. The stock pollutant adversely affects the growth of a renewable resource according to $X_{t+1} - X_t = rX_t(1 - X_t/K)/(1 + \beta Z_t) - Y_t$, where r, K, and β are positive parameters and Y_t is the rate of harvest of the renewable resource in period t. The rates of commodity production and harvest of the renewable resource are both constrained according to $Q_{MAX} \geq Q_t \geq 0$ and $Y_{MAX} \geq Y_t \geq 0$. The welfare of the economy in period t is given by $W_t = \varepsilon \ln(Q_t) + (1 - \varepsilon)\ln(Y_t)$, where $\ln(\bullet)$ is the natural log operator and $1 > \varepsilon > 0$. Consider the Lagrangian

$$L = \sum_{t=0}^{\infty} \rho^t \{\varepsilon \ln(Q_t) + (1 - \varepsilon)\ln(Y_t) + \rho\lambda_{t+1}[(1 - \gamma)Z_t + \alpha Q_t - Z_{t+1}]$$
$$+ \rho\mu_{t+1}[X_t + rX_t(1 - X_t/K)/(1 + \beta Z_t) - Y_t - X_{t+1}]\}$$

where $\rho = 1/(1 + \delta)$, $\delta > 0$.
(a) What are the first-order conditions assuming that Z_t and X_t are positive, $Q_{MAX} > Q_t > 0$, and $Y_{MAX} > Y_t > 0$? What are the signs of λ_{t+1} and μ_{t+1}?
(b) Evaluate the first-order conditions in steady state and derive the analytic expression for Z^*, the steady-state optimal pollution stock. What is the expression for X^* as a function of Z^*, K, r, δ, and β?
(c) If your algebra is correct, you should get the values for Z^*, X^*, Y^*, and Q^* as given in cells \$B\$9:\$B\$12 on the initial spreadsheet for E6.1, when $\alpha = 0.2$, $\beta = 1$, $\delta = 0.1$, $\gamma = 0.2$, $\varepsilon = 0.25$, $r = 1$, and $K = 1$. In columns C through H we set up an initial spreadsheet to determine the optimal values for Q_t and Y_t for $t = 0, 1, \ldots, 24$. The initial conditions are $Z_0 = 0$ and $X_0 = 1$. The equations for Z_{t+1} and X_{t+1} are programmed in cells \$F\$3 and \$G\$3, respectively, and filled down through \$F\$27 and \$G\$27. In cell \$H\$2 we have typed =((1/(1+\$B\$3))^C2)*(\$B\$5*LN(D2)+ (1-\$B\$5)*LN(E2)) and we fill down to \$H\$26. In cell \$H\$27 we have typed the final function

=((1/(1+\$B\$3))^\$C\$26)*(\$B\$5*LN((\$B\$4/\$B\$1)*\$F\$27)+
(1-\$B\$5)*LN(\$B\$6*\$G\$27*
(1-\$G\$27/\$B\$7)/(1+\$B\$2*\$F\$27)))/\$B\$3

This is the expression for the present value of maintaining $Q = (\gamma/\alpha)Z_{25}$ and $Y = rX_{25}(1 - X_{25}/K)/(1 + \beta Z_{25})$ over the infinite horizon $t = 25, 26, \ldots, \infty$. (See Section 2.2, Section 6.3, and Spreadsheet 6.1.) This is yet

	A	B	C	D	E	F	G	H
1	α =	0.2	t	Qt	Yt	Zt	Xt	πt
2	β =	1	0	2	0.05	0	1	-2.07351241
3	δ =	0.1	1	2	0.05	0.4	0.95	-1.88501128
4	γ =	0.2	2	2	0.05	0.72	0.93392857	-1.71364662
5	ε =	0.25	3	2	0.05	0.976	0.91980415	-1.55786056
6	r =	1	4	2	0.05	1.1808	0.90713435	-1.41623688
7	K =	1	5	2	0.05	1.34464	0.89576312	-1.28748807
8			6	2	0.05	1.475712	0.88558653	-1.1704437
9	Z* =	1	7	2	0.05	1.5805696	0.87651335	-1.06403973
10	X* =	0.4	8	2	0.05	1.66445568	0.86845669	-0.96730884
11	Y* =	0.12	9	2	0.05	1.73156454	0.86133211	-0.87937167
12	Q* =	1	10	2	0.05	1.78525164	0.85505764	-0.7994288
13			11	2	0.05	1.82820131	0.84955418	-0.72675345
14			12	2	0.05	1.86256105	0.84474611	-0.66068495
15			13	2	0.05	1.89004884	0.84056177	-0.60062269
16			14	2	0.05	1.91203907	0.83693389	-0.54602062
17			15	2	0.05	1.92963126	0.83379986	-0.49638239
18			16	2	0.05	1.943705	0.83110194	-0.45125671
19			17	2	0.05	1.954964	0.82878726	-0.41023338
20			18	2	0.05	1.9639712	0.82680779	-0.37293943
21			19	2	0.05	1.97117696	0.82512023	-0.33903585
22			20	2	0.05	1.97694157	0.82368577	-0.30821441
23			21	2	0.05	1.98155326	0.82246991	-0.28019492
24			22	2	0.05	1.9852426	0.82144209	-0.25472265
25			23	2	0.05	1.98819408	0.82057544	-0.23156605
26			24	2	0.05	1.99055527	0.81984647	-0.21051459
27			25	0	0	1.99244421	0.8192347	-2.11394842
28								
29							π =	-22.8174391
30								
31								
32								
33								

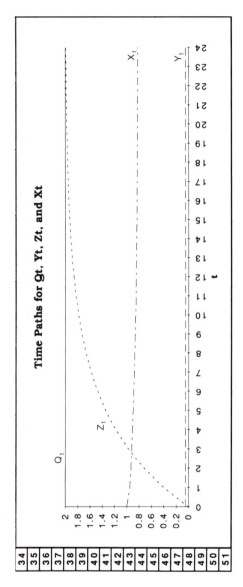

Time Paths for g_t, Y_t, Z_t, and X_t

Initial Spreadsheet for E6.1

another example of approximating the infinite-horizon approach path in a finite-horizon problem. Can you replicate this spreadsheet?

(d) Now call up Solver and maximize the set cell $H\$29$ by changing cells $\$D\$2:\$E\$26$ subject to $\$D\$2:\$D\$26 <= 2$, $\$D\$2:\$G\$27 >= 0$, and $\$E\$2:\$E\$26 <= 0.15$. These constraints imply $Q_{MAX} = 2$ and $Y_{MAX} = 0.15$. When you send Solver off on its mission it will hit the time limit and it will want to stop, after 21 iterations, at a "current solution." Use that current solution as a new initial spreadsheet and tell Solver to keep looking. After 42 more iterations it should converge to an optimal solution and the values for Z_{25} and X_{25} should be very close to the previously calculated values for Z^* and X^* in cells $\$B\$9$ and $\$B\$10$, respectively. (This problem is not robust for all plausible parameter values. For Z^* to be positive, it must be the case that $\gamma > (\delta + 2\gamma)\varepsilon$.)

E6.2 Consider a nonrenewable resource, such as that depicted in Figure 1.1. Welfare in period t is given by $W_t = (a - (b/2)q_t)q_t - cZ_t^2$, where a, b, and c are positive parameters. Pollution dynamics are given by $Z_{t+1} - Z_t = -\gamma Z_t + \alpha q_t$, where γ and α are positive, but less than 1. The nonrenewable resource changes according to $R_{t+1} = R_t - q_t$. When $q_t > 0$ results in a waste flow, we would expect a slower rate of extraction than if there were no waste ($\alpha = 0$) or zero damage ($c = 0$). Consider the initial spreadsheet for E6.2. The parameters are $a = 10$, $b = 1$, $c = 1$, $\alpha = 0.5$, $\delta = 0.05$, and $\gamma = 0.1$. The initial conditions are $R_0 = 1$ and $Z_0 = 0$. In cells $\$C\$11$ and $\$D\$11$ we have programmed in the expressions R_1 and Z_1, respectively, and filled down to $\$C\$30$ and $\$D\$30$. The expression for W_0 is programmed in cell $\$E\$10$ as $=(\$B\$7^\wedge A10)*((\$B\$1-(\$B\$2/2)*B10)*B10-\$B\$3*(D10^\wedge 2))$. This is filled down to cell $\$E\$29$. We specify a final function in cell $\$E\$30$ which tells Solver that the discounted damage from Z_{20}, for $t = 20, 21, \ldots \infty$, is $-\rho^{19}cZ_{20}^2/(\delta + \gamma)$. In cell $\$E\$32$ we sum the flow of discounted welfare and the discounted damage of the degrading pollution stock, Z_{20}. The initial values are $q_t = 0.05$, for $t = 0, 1, \ldots, 19$.

(a) Replicate this initial spreadsheet.

(b) Call Solver and ask it to maximize $\$E\$32$ by changing $\$B\$10:\$B\$29$, subject to $\$B\$10:\$D\$30 >= 0$. Plot the optimal time paths for q_t, R_t, and Z_t.

(c) Reset the optimal spreadsheet to the initial spreadsheet and set $c = 0$. Resolve for the optimal extraction path. Do you deplete sooner?

E6.3 In the marketable pollution permit model of Section 6.7, we derived the optimal residual rate for the ith firm facing a commodity-residual transformation frontier given by $\phi(Q_{i,t}, S_{i,t}) = (Q_{i,t} - m)^2 - n_i S_{i,t} = 0$ and a permit price of $p_{m,t}$. This gave rise to the expression

	A	B	C	D	E	F
1	a=	10				
2	b=	1				
3	c=	1				
4	α =	0.5				
5	δ =	0.05				
6	γ =	0.1				
7	ρ =	0.95238095				
8						
9	t	qt	Rt	Zt	π t	
10	0	0.05	1	0	0.49875	
11	1	0.05	0.95	0.025	0.47440476	
12	2	0.05	0.9	0.0475	0.45033447	
13	3	0.05	0.85	0.06775	0.42687393	
14	4	0.05	0.8	0.085975	0.40424169	
15	5	0.05	0.75	0.1023775	0.38257142	
16	6	0.05	0.7	0.11713975	0.36193557	
17	7	0.05	0.65	0.13042578	0.342363	
18	8	0.05	0.6	0.1423832	0.32385208	
19	9	0.05	0.55	0.15314488	0.30638046	
20	10	0.05	0.5	0.16283039	0.2899121	
21	11	0.05	0.45	0.17154735	0.27440256	
22	12	0.05	0.4	0.17939262	0.25980268	
23	13	0.05	0.35	0.18645335	0.24606123	
24	14	0.05	0.3	0.19280802	0.23312677	
25	15	0.05	0.25	0.19852722	0.22094892	
26	16	0.05	0.2	0.2036745	0.20947914	
27	17	0.05	0.15	0.20830705	0.19867126	
28	18	0.05	0.1	0.21247634	0.18848175	
29	19	0.05	0.05	0.21622871	0.17886983	
30	20	0	-3.1919E-16	0.21960584	-0.12723301	
31						
32				π =	6.14423062	
33						
34						
35			**Extraction with a Degradable Stock Pollutant**			
36						
37	1					
38	0.9		R_t			
39	0.8					
40	0.7					
41	0.6					
42	0.5					
43	0.4					
44	0.3				Z_t	
45	0.2					
46	0.1				q_t	
47	0					
48		0 1 2 3 4 5 6 7 8 9 10 11 12 13 14 15 16 17 18 19				
49						
50			t			

Initial Spreadsheet for E6.2

$$S_{i,t} = \frac{n_i}{4} \left(\frac{p}{p_{m,t}} \right)^2$$

as the optimal emission rate for the ith firm. If a total of M_t permits were available in period t, the market clearing permit price would have to satisfy

$$p_{m,t} = \frac{0.5p}{\sqrt{\dfrac{M_t}{\displaystyle\sum_{i=1}^{I} n_i}}}$$

Suppose $n_1 = 1$, $n_2 = 2$, $n_3 = 3$, $M_t = 600$, $M_{i,t} = 200$, $i = 1,2,3$, and $p = 400$. What are the market clearing permit price, $p_{m,t}$; the level of emissions for each of the three firms; and the permits bought or sold by each?

CHAPTER 7

Option Value and Risky Development

7.0   Introduction and Overview

In this chapter we consider the desirability and timing of projects which might irreversibly alter a natural environment. A large hydroelectric or irrigation project might necessitate the construction of a reservoir, which may inundate a sizable area behind a dam, alter the hydrological processes of a free-flowing river, and be very costly to remove. The cutting of an old-growth forest and the conversion of land to agriculture or other uses might also be viewed as irreversible developments. Risk or uncertainty is present if the future net benefits of development, or the benefits of continued preservation, are not known when a decision about starting the project must be made.

Evaluating the desirability of an investment project has traditionally drawn upon a body of economic theory and methods referred to as *cost-benefit analysis*. This is a sizable literature examining (i) the theoretical foundations of cost–benefits analysis, (ii) the appropriate formulas to evaluate the desirability of a project and, (iii) the complications that arise when there is unemployment, imperfect competition, government regulation, or different opportunity costs for resources that are diverted from the private sector of an economy. It is not possible to cover all these topics, and the next section will review the basic formulas used to calculate a benefit–cost ratio, the present value of net benefits, a project's internal rate of return, and the return on invested capital.

Traditional cost–benefit analysis is oriented toward making a simple decision: should an investment project be undertaken today? The decision is basically a "now-or-never" decision. Missing from the traditional analysis was the possibility (or option) of delay. More recent literature in financial economics is concerned with the optimal timing of a project, or when to exercise an investment option. The option of optimally investing in the future should be of value today. By undertaking a risky project, which is costly to reverse, we incur the construction costs (real resource costs) and we "kill" the option of investing if and when conditions are more favorable in the future. If we do invest today, we would want the

141

present value of expected benefits to equal or exceed the present value of expected costs plus the value of the option to wait.

The models and mathematics of option value are fairly technical. In Section 7.2 we consider a simple two-period model. This model is extended to an infinite horizon in Section 7.3. Critical "trigger values" are examined in Section 7.4; these are values that must be observed (reached) before making a risky and irreversible investment or development decision. Section 7.5 provides some questions and exercises.

7.1   Cost–Benefit Analysis

In our discussion of discounting in Chapter 1, we noted that the present value of net benefits over the horizon $t = 0, 1, 2, \ldots, T$, could be calculated according to the formula

$$N = \sum_{t=0}^{T} \rho^t N_t \qquad (7.1)$$

where $\rho = 1/(1 + \delta)$ was our discount factor, $\delta > 0$ was the discount rate, and $N_t = B_t - C_t$ was the level of net benefits in period t. In previous chapters the benefits (B_t) and costs (C_t) in a particular period depended on the rate of harvest or extraction and the size of the resource stock. In cost–benefit analysis it is usually presumed that the construction of a project will result in a flow of benefits over some future horizon. In addition to the construction costs, which typically dominate the initial periods, there may be operation and maintenance costs, and in the terminal period, a scrap value or "decommissioning cost." The time path for net benefits might look like the one plotted in Figure 7.1.

The data for this plot are given in Spreadsheet 7.1. The first two periods are characterized by construction costs of $100 million and no benefits. In the third period $(t = 2)$ benefits of $40 million are realized, and in periods $t = 3$ through $t = 8$ the benefits are $50 million per period before falling to $40 million in period $t = 9$. In periods $t = 2$ through $t = 9$ the operation and maintenance costs are $10 million per period. In period $t = 10$ the project is shut down while major maintenance of $50 million is performed. The project is now showing its age, and although the operation and maintenance costs are the same as before the shutdown, the output and benefits decline to $20 million in $t = 18$ and the project is decommissioned, at a cost of $50 million, in $t = 19$.

It is important to note that numbers entered under the columns B_t and C_t in Spreadsheet 7.1 are the best estimates of future benefits and costs from our perspective in period $t = 0$. There will always be some uncertainty about any future financial flow, but in this example it is assumed that these benefit and cost values are known and given.

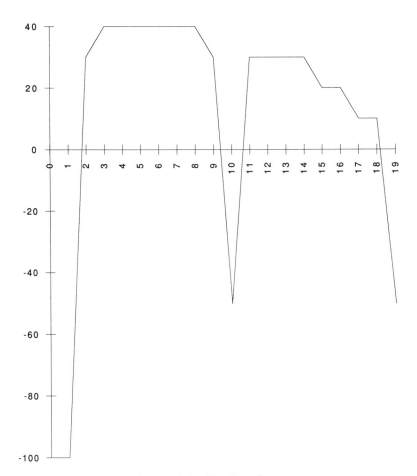

Figure 7.1. A Time Path for Net Benefits

Suppose the agency conducting the cost–benefit analysis is instructed to use a discount rate of $\delta = 0.05$ per period. This rate might reflect the opportunity cost of the resources (funds) used in constructing and maintaining the project. Such resources might have been invested in private investments or they might have provided a flow of utility to consumers. With a mandated discount rate and values for $N_t = B_t - C_t$, it is a relatively simple task to calculate the present value of net benefits according to formula (7.1). The values for $\rho^t N_t$ are calculated in column G in Spreadsheet 7.1, and they sum to $77.5887154 million, as reported in cell $G$27. The fact that the present value of net benefits is positive is taken as an indication that the project in question provides a positive net

	A	B	C	D	E
1	Benefit-Cost Ratio, PVNB, Internal Rate of Return, The RIC				
2					
3	$\delta =$	0.05			
4					
5	t	Bt	Ct	Nt	Discounted Bt
6	0	0	100	-100	0
7	1	0	100	-100	0
8	2	40	10	30	36.2811791
9	3	50	10	40	43.1918799
10	4	50	10	40	41.1351237
11	5	50	10	40	39.1763083
12	6	50	10	40	37.3107698
13	7	50	10	40	35.5340665
14	8	50	10	40	33.8419681
15	9	40	10	30	25.7843566
16	10	0	50	-50	0
17	11	40	10	30	23.3871716
18	12	40	10	30	22.2734967
19	13	40	10	30	21.212854
20	14	40	10	30	20.2027181
21	15	30	10	20	14.4305129
22	16	30	10	20	13.7433457
23	17	20	10	10	8.72593375
24	18	20	10	10	8.3104131
25	19	0	50	-50	0
26					
27				SUMs	424.542098
28					
29				B/C=	1.22362865
30					
31				r =	0.11296595
32					
33				RIC =	0.11186959
34					
35					
36					
37					
38					
39					
40					
41					

Spreadsheet 7.1

F	G	H	I	J	K
Discounted Ct	Discounted Nt	Nt for IRR	PBt-1	(1+?)*PBt-1	PBt
100	-100	-100	0	0	-100
95.2380952	-95.2380952	-89.8500087	-100	-111.186959	-211.186959
9.07029478	27.2108844	24.2190722	-211.186959	-234.812356	-204.812356
8.63837599	34.5535039	29.0144512	-204.812356	-227.72463	-187.72463
8.22702475	32.908099	26.069487	-187.72463	-208.725306	-168.725306
7.83526166	31.3410467	23.4234363	-168.725306	-187.600537	-147.600537
7.46215397	29.8486159	21.0459595	-147.600537	-164.112547	-124.112547
7.1068133	28.4272532	18.9097965	-124.112547	-137.996967	-97.9969668
6.76839362	27.0735745	16.9904538	-97.9969668	-108.959847	-68.9598469
6.44608916	19.3382675	11.4494431	-68.9598469	-76.6743565	-46.6743565
30.6956627	-30.6956627	-17.1455427	-46.6743565	-51.8957974	-101.895797
5.84679289	17.5403787	9.24316298	-101.895797	-113.294838	-83.2948381
5.56837418	16.7051225	8.30498273	-83.2948381	-92.6129971	-62.6129971
5.30321351	15.9096405	7.4620277	-62.6129971	-69.6174872	-39.6174872
5.05067953	15.1520386	6.70463254	-39.6174872	-44.0494791	-14.0494791
4.81017098	9.62034196	4.01607528	-14.0494791	-15.6211885	4.37881151
4.58111522	9.16223044	3.60844398	4.37881151	4.59775208	24.5977521
4.36296688	4.36296688	1.62109362	24.5977521	25.8276397	35.8276397
4.15520655	4.15520655	1.45655275	35.8276397	37.6190217	47.6190217
19.7866979	-19.7866979	-6.54356388	47.6190217	49.9999728	-2.7243E-05
346.953383	77.5887154	-4.4163E-05			

benefit to society, above the opportunity cost of the resources needed to implement the project. *It is important to note that there has been no consideration of who pays the costs and who receives the benefits.* The issue of who pays the costs and who receives the benefits may be hotly debated or deliberately obfuscated within the political process in which public projects are proposed, designed, and funded. In the real world, projects with a positive present value for net benefits have been rejected because they were seen as inequitable (unfair) in their distribution of costs and benefits. Projects of questionable net present value have been approved because they are viewed as an acceptable way of helping a deserving segment of society (for example, farmers).

Many resource development agencies are instructed to calculate a benefit–cost ratio. The formula for this ratio is given as

$$B/C = \frac{\sum\limits_{t=0}^{T} \rho^t B_t}{\sum\limits_{t=0}^{T} \rho^t C_t} \tag{7.2}$$

and is simply the ratio of the present value of benefits to the present value of costs. If a project provides a net benefit to society it should have a benefit–cost ratio greater than 1 ($B/C > 1$). For our hypothetical project, at a discount rate of $\delta = 0.05$, the benefit–cost ratio is 1.22362865 as calculated in cell \$E\$29 in Spreadsheet 7.1. Given the inherent uncertainty in real world estimates of B_t and C_t, and the incentive of some agencies to justify their continued existence with a slate of apparently desirable projects, the benefit–cost ratio is sometimes required to exceed a value greater than 1, say 1.3, to provide a greater measure of confidence that the project in question would actually provide positive net benefits to society.

A third criterion that is sometimes used to evaluate a project is the *internal rate of return* (IRR). Given N_t, a project's internal rate of return is the rate r which when used as a discount rate would reduce the present value of net benefits to 0. The internal rate of return must satisfy the equation

$$\sum_{t=0}^{T} \frac{N_t}{(1+r)^t} = 0 \tag{7.3}$$

In column H of Spreadsheet 7.1 we calculate the present value of net revenues for rate r given in cell \$E\$31. The value $r = 0.11296595$ was actually obtained using Solver. Initially, in cell \$E\$31, we specified the value $r = 0.05$ and we obtained the same values in column H as were obtained in column G for $\delta = 0.05$. We then summoned Solver and asked it to drive the value in cell \$H\$27 to 0 by changing the value in the cell \$E\$31. Solver quickly iterates to the value $r = 0.11296595$. This would seem to make intuitive sense. Since the present value of net benefits was positive at $\delta = 0.05$, and given the time path of net benefits shown in Figure 7.1, it seems quite logical that a higher rate, $r > \delta$, would be required to drive the present value of net benefits to zero.

When using the internal rate of return as an investment criterion, a project must satisfy the rule $r > \delta$ to justify construction today. The internal rate of return might be thought of as an average rate of return for a project, presuming that the horizon and underlying values of B_t and C_t cannot be altered. (For example, it presumes that it is not possible to terminate the project at the end of period $t = 9$.)

There are several potential problems with the internal rate of return criterion. Specifically, equation (7.3) can be transformed into a polynomial of order T in r with the possibility of T distinct roots. If the time path for net benefits changes sign more than once then there may be more than one rate, r, which will reduce the present value of net benefits to 0. In our time profile for net benefits in Figure 7.1, there are four sign changes.

In addition to the possibility that the internal rate of return will not be unique, there is a question about the "availability" of positive balances, prior to $t = T$, and whether these balances have re-investment options. These potential problems have caused some project analysts to use the *return on invested capital* (RIC) as the preferred criterion when comparing two or more investment projects or when calculating an internal return for a project with decommissioning or cleanup costs.

To solve for the RIC we need to define a project's balance in $t = \tau$ as

$$PB_\tau = \sum_{t=0}^{t=\tau} N_t(1+i_t)^{\tau-t} \tag{7.4}$$

where the rate i_t will be either the risk-free discount rate, δ, or the RIC according to the following rule:

$$PB_\tau = (1+RIC)PB_{\tau-1} + N_\tau \quad \text{if} \quad PB_{\tau-1} < 0, \quad \text{or}$$
$$PB_\tau = (1+\delta)PB_{\tau-1} + N_\tau \quad \text{if} \quad PB_{\tau-1} > 0 \tag{7.5}$$

In equation (7.5) we have defined the project's balance in *recursive form* and the presumption is that if the project's balance in τ-1 is negative, no balance is available for re-investment, and the project's RIC is the appropriate marginal return. If the project's balance in τ-1 is positive, that balance is invested for one period at the risk-free discount rate, δ. Thus, depending on the project's balance in τ-1, that balance will be compounded forward to τ by either the RIC (if $PB_{\tau-1} < 0$)) or the risk-free discount rate, δ (if $PB_{\tau-1} > 0$). At this point, however, the RIC is still unknown.

In columns I, J, and K of Spreadsheet 7.1 we set about trying to find the RIC. The column headings are PB_{t-1}, the project's balance in t-1; $(1 + ?)PB_{t-1}$, indicating that at this point we don't know which rate we will use in compounding PB_{t-1}; and PB_t. In $t = 0$ there is no prior project balance and therefore nothing to compound, so we enter 0 in cells I6 and J6. In cell K6 we define the project's balance to equal the compounded prior balance plus current period net benefit and we type =J6 + D6. In $t = 0$ the project's balance is simply $N_0 = -100$. In cell I7 we type =K6, which brings down the previous period balance for inspection and compounding. In J7 we will make use of an Excel IF Statement and we type

$$=IF(I7<0,(1+\$E\$33)*I7,(1+\$B\$3)*I7 \tag{7.6}$$

This tells Excel that if the project balance in I7 is negative, then use the value of the RIC in cell $E$33 for compounding. The initial guess for the RIC was 0.10 and the value now appearing in cell $E$33 is actually Solver's solution for the RIC. In cell K7 we fill down from cell K6 or type =J7 + D7. We can then highlight cells I7:K7 and fill down to cells I25: K25. The value in cell K25 is the project balance in the terminal period, $T = 19$. If you programmed everything correctly you should have a value of 57.5966556 in cell K25. *The RIC is defined as the rate of return which drives the project's balance in the terminal period to 0.* Thus, we can use Solver to drive the value in cell K25 to 0 by changing the value in cell $E$33 from our initial guess of 0.1. When you set Solver to work it quickly finds the real RIC to be 0.11186959. The fact that the traditional internal rate of return, $r = 0.11296595$, was close to the $RIC = 0.11186959$ was a result of the hypothetical data for B_t and C_t in Spreadsheet 7.1, and for other examples the internal rate of return and the RIC may be significantly different.

The RIC has many nice properties. It exits, it is unique, and when there is only one sign change in the time profile of net benefits (going from negative initial values to positive values), it is equal to the traditional IRR. The RIC depends on the risk-free rate of discount and is monotonically increasing in δ. It has an upper bound (called the "crushing rate of return"). The decision: invest if $RIC > \delta$; do not invest if $RIC < \delta$.

7.2   Option Value in a Simple Two-Period Model

In general, the cost–benefit formulas in the preceding section should include estimates of any environmental damage or forgone amenity benefits which the project might cause or induce. These would need to be estimated for each period in the project's horizon ($t = 0.1, \ldots, T$) and added to the costs of construction and operation. If there were environmental damages beyond the project's horizon, it would be appropriate to add the present value of environmental damage from $t = T + 1, \ldots,$ ∞, to the decommissioning cost in period $t = T$. Uncertainty and the fact that a project may be economically costly or ecologically impossible to reverse are two aspects that are not easily introduced into the traditional cost–benefit framework. Dynamic programming, although more difficult analytically, has the advantage of being able to consider uncertainty and irreversibility explicitly. We'll begin with a simple two-period model to get a feel for these two important aspects of resource development.

Consider an old-growth forest not far from the capital city of a developing country. The forest could be clear-cut today ($t = 0$), producing timber with a known net revenue of T_0. If this is done, the remaining vegetation will be burned and the land converted to agriculture with a known net revenue in the future ($t = 1$) of D_1. The present value of clear-cutting today is $D = T_0 + \rho D_1$, where $\rho = 1/(1 + \delta)$ is the discount factor.

If the forest is not cut today, residents of the capital city will visit the forest to view the majestic trees, birds, and wildlife. It has been estimated that the amenity value in the current period is A_0. In the future, both amenity value and net revenue from timber are uncertain. Suppose there are only two possible future "states of world." In state 1 ($s = 1$) the market price of tropical hardwood has drastically increased, resulting in a net revenue from timber of $T_{1,1}$, which exceeds domestic amenity value, $A_{1,1}$. In state 2 ($s = 2$) an international boycott on the import of tropical hardwoods has resulted in a drastically reduced demand, and the net value of the timber is $T_{1,2}$, which is less than amenity value, $A_{1,2}$. Thus, in future state 1 $T_{1,1} > A_{1,1}$, and in future state 2 $A_{1,2} > T_{1,2}$. Suppose that planners advising the country's president believe that future state 1 will occur with probability π, and that state 2 will occur with probability $(1 - \pi)$. We will assume that $T_0 > A_0 > 0$ and that the other net timber, agricultural, and amenity values are positive.

The president, although aware of the amenity value derived by her fellow citizens, is also aware that the sale of logs, particularly in state 1, will provide needed foreign exchange that can be used to improve the water and sanitation system within the capital city. If the forest is not cut today, the president feels that it is optimal to cut if state 1 occurs, but to preserve the forest if state 2 occurs. With this optimal, state-contingent decision rule, the expected present value of preservation today is given by $P = A_0 + \rho[\pi T_{1,1} + (1 - \pi)A_{1,2}]$. If $D > P$ the president will order the timber cut today and the land converted to agriculture. If $D < P$ the president will spare the forest today and wait to see which state obtains in the future. The point of indifference, where $D = P$, implies

$$T_0 + \rho D_1 - A_0 = \rho[\pi T_{1,1} + (1 - \pi)A_{1,2}] \qquad (7.7)$$

On the LHS we have the net value of cutting the forest today, where the forgone amenity value in $t = 0$ has been deducted from $T_0 + \rho D_1$. On the RHS the term $\rho[\pi T_{1,1} + (1 - \pi)A_{1,2}]$ is the option value of preservation in $t = 0$. If the forest is not cut today, the president preserves her option of behaving optimally in the future, cutting the forest in state 1 and preserving it in state 2. *Note: Option value is the discounted expected net value of behaving optimally in the future.* With $1 > \rho > 0$, $1 > \pi > 0$, and $T_{1,1}$ and $A_{1,2}$ both positive, option value is unambiguously positive.

Comparative statics in this simple model are relatively straightforward. An increase in $T_{1,1}$ or $A_{1,2}$ will increase option value and tend to increase the incentive to preserve the forest today. An increase in T_0, D_1, or a decrease in A_0 will increase the LHS and tend to increase the likelihood of cutting today. An increase in the discount rate, δ, will reduce the RHS more than it reduces the LHS, thus tipping the scale toward cutting today.

One interesting, but not obvious, feature of the model is the sign of $d\pi/d\delta$ which would preserve the president's indifference between cutting today and waiting. Multiply both sides of (7.7) by $(1 + \delta)$ and consider the changes in π which must counter an increase in δ in order to preserve indifference. You should obtain the equation $(T_0 - A_0)d\delta = (T_{1,1} - A_{1,2})d\pi$, or

$$\frac{d\pi}{d\delta} = \frac{(T_0 - A_0)}{(T_{1,1} - A_{1,2})} \qquad (7.8)$$

We have assumed that $T_0 > A_0$. If $T_{1,1} > A_{1,2}$, it will be the case that $d\pi/d\delta > 0$. If, however, $A_{1,2} > T_{1,1}$, then $d\pi/d\delta < 0$. Some reflection should reveal that this result is logical. Since an increase in the discount rate reduces option value, we would need to increase the probability of the higher-valued future state in order to maintain indifference. If $T_{1,1} > A_{1,2}$, then π must go up, whereas if $A_{1,2} > T_{1,1}$, π must go down in order for $(1 - \pi)$ to go up.

7.3   Option Value: An Infinite-Horizon Model

What would be the option value of preserving the forest in $t = 0$ with an infinite future horizon? The analysis becomes more complex, but manageable, with the following assumptions: (i) If the forest is cut today, or in any period, t, D_1 is the net agricultural benefit per period over the infinite future, $t+1$, $t+2$, ... ∞. (ii) If the forest has not been cut in period t, there are only two possible states in period $(t + 1)$, and it will be optimal to cut the first time state 1 ($s = 1$) occurs. (iii) The probability of state 1 is "stationary": that is, it remains constant at π. (iv) The expected value of entering the next period with the forest intact is $[\pi T_1 + (1 - \pi)A_2]$, where T_1 and A_2 are the stationary optimal net benefits in state 1 and state 2, respectively.

What is the net present value of a decision to cut the forest today? This is given by $D = T_0 + \rho D_1(1 + \rho + \rho^2 + ...) = T_0 + \rho D_1[(1 + \delta)/\delta]$ or $D = T_0 + D_1/\delta$. (This present value is likely to be an overstatement of the net value of future agricultural production, since it is well known that without fertilizers, production falls off rapidly after soil nutrients from the "slash and burn" are depleted. The level of soil nutrients might be viewed as an inventory and managed as a renewable resource.)

What is the net present value of a decision to preserve the forest today? The expression for P is complex because it must account for the possibility that the forest could be cut in any of the future periods $t = 1$, $2, \ldots, \infty$. We will write out the expression, explain the logic of the various terms, and then note that the expression comprises two convergent series.

The initial expression for P is

$$P = A_0 + \rho[\pi T_1 + (1 - \pi)A_2]$$
$$+ \pi\rho^2 D_1(1 + \rho + \rho^2 + \ldots) + (1 - \pi)\rho^2[\pi T_1 + (1 - \pi)A_2]$$
$$+ (1 - \pi)\pi\rho^3 D_1(1 + \rho + \rho^2 + \ldots) + (1 - \pi)^2\rho^3[\pi T_1 + (1 - \pi)A_2]$$
$$+ (1 - \pi)^2\pi\rho^4 D_1(1 + \rho + \rho^2 + \ldots) + (1 - \pi)^3\rho^4[\pi T_1 + (1 - \pi)A_2]$$
$$+ \ldots$$

In the first line we have A_0, the known amenity value received in $t = 0$, plus the discounted expected value in period $t = 1$. These terms are identical to those in the two-period model, except that we have suppressed the time subscript for net timber value in state 1 (T_1) and amenity value in state 2 (A_2) since they are assumed to be the stationary optimal decisions.

In the second line we have the discounted expected value in $t = 2$. If the forest has been cut in period $t = 1$, we obtain the known present value of an infinite flow of net agricultural benefits, D_1, for $t = 2, 3, \ldots, \infty$. The probability of this stream is π and we multiply it by ρ^2 to bring it back to $t = 0$. The second term represents the expected value in period $t = 2$ if we have not cut in $t = 1$. The probability of not having cut in $t = 1$ is $(1 - \pi)$ and the stationary expected value $[\pi T_1 + (1 - \pi)A_2]$ is also discounted by ρ^2, since we are in period $t = 2$. (Note: In period $t = 2$, the discounted expected value of cutting is $[1 - \pi]\pi\rho^2 T_1$ and the expected discounted value of not cutting is $(1 - \pi)^2\rho^2 A_2$, which is what you get if you expand the second term in the second line.)

If the forest was not cut in period $t = 1$, line 3 of our expression for P calculates the discounted present value in $t = 3$ of a decision to cut or preserve in $t = 2$. Specifically, if the forest is cut in $t = 2$, then in period $t = 3$ we obtain the known present value of D_1 for $t = 3, 4, \ldots, \infty$. The probability of not cutting in $t = 1$ is $(1 - \pi)$, the probability of cutting in period $t = 2$ is π, and the present value in $t = 3$ is discounted back to $t = 0$ by ρ^3. The second term in line 3 is the discounted expected value if the forest has not been cut in $t = 1$ or $t = 2$. The stationary expected value of entering $t = 3$ with the forest still standing is $[\pi T_1 + (1 - \pi)A_2]$. The probability we will enter $t = 3$ with the forest intact is $(1 - \pi)^2$, and given that we're in $t = 3$, we discount this term by ρ^3 as well.

The fourth line in the expression for P calculates the discounted expected value in $t = 4$ from a decision to cut or not to cut in period $t = 3$. As in lines 2 and 3, the first term is the discounted expected value of net agricultural benefits, now from $t = 4, 5, \ldots, \infty$, if the forest was cut in $t = 3$. The second term is the discounted expected net benefits if the forest was not cut in $t = 3$ and we enter $t = 4$ with our option intact. If the logic of these four lines is shaky, a useful exercise is to construct a decision tree, which has the advantage of providing a visualization of the possible decision sequences, their joint probabilities, and their discounted expected values.

Because both ρ and π are positive fractions, the processes of computing joint probabilities and discounting will often result in terms which converge as $t \to \infty$. A close inspection of our expression for P will reveal

$$P = A_0 + \rho[\pi T_1 + (1 - \pi)A_2]\left[1 + (1 - \pi)/(1 - \delta) + [(1 - \pi)/(1 + \delta)]^2 + \ldots\right]$$
$$+ \rho^2\pi D_1\left(1 + \rho + \rho^2 + \ldots\right)\left[1 + (1 - \pi)/(1 + \delta) + [(1 - \pi)/(1 + \delta)]^2 + \ldots\right]$$

The term $(1 + \rho + \rho^2 + \ldots)$ converges to $[(1 + \delta)/\delta]$ while the term $[1 + [(1 - \pi)/(1 + \delta)] + [(1 - \pi)/(1 + \delta)]^2 + \ldots]$ converges to $[(1 + \delta)/(\delta + \pi)]$. These results permit us to write the expression for P one last time as

$$P = A_0 + [\pi T_1 + (1 - \pi)A_2]/(\delta + \pi) + \pi D_1/[\delta(\delta + \pi)] \tag{7.9}$$

We have waded through a lot of algebra to obtain this expression for the expected present value of not cutting in $t = 0$. As a check on the validity of equation (7.9) we can ask, "What happens when $\pi \to 1$?" As π goes to 1, the probability of cutting in $t = 1$ goes to 1, and the present value

	A	B
1	T0=	20
2	D1=	5
3	δ =	0.05
4	A0=	3
5	π =	0.5
6	T1=	25
7	A2=	3.7
8		
9	D=	120
10	P=	120
11	Option Value	117

Spreadsheet 7.2

of not cutting today ($t = 0$) should be $P = A_0 + \rho[T_1 + D_1/\delta]$, which is in fact what happens to equation (7.9).

As with the two-period model, it is instructive to consider the point of indifference where $D = P$, implying

$$T_0 + D_1/\delta - A_0 = [\pi T_1 + (1-\pi)A_2]/(\delta+\pi) + \pi D_1/[\delta(\delta+\pi)] \quad (7.10)$$

On the LHS we again have the present value of cutting and conversion to agriculture, less the forgone amenity benefits in $t = 0$. On the RHS we have the infinite-horizon expression for the option value of not cutting in $t = 0$. Some numerical analysis can illustrate the magnitude and potential importance of option value.

Suppose that the forest, if cut today, would yield $T_0 = \$20$ million in net revenue from logs, and when the land was devoted to intensive agriculture it would yield net benefits of $D_1 = \$5$ million per period ad infinitum. Assume the current amenity flow is $A_0 = \$3$ million, the value of logs in state 1 is $T_1 = \$25$ million, and the amenity flow in state 2 is $A_2 = \$3.7$ million. Let $\delta = 0.05$ and $\pi = 0.5$. In Spreadsheet 7.2 we have programmed the expressions for $D = T_0 + D_1/\delta$, P, as given in equation (7.9), and option value, as given on the RHS of equation (7.10). For these parameter values, $D = P = \$120$ million and option value equals $\$117$ million or 97.5% of the value of P. In this base case, the president would be indifferent between development and preservation in $t = 0$.

If π were to increase to $\pi = 0.75$, the scale would be tipped toward preservation today, with D unchanged and P increasing to \$121.34375 million. In this case it is the higher probability of larger net revenues for the timber which causes the president to wait.

If π falls to $\pi = 0.25$, the probability of state 2 increases to 0.75. In state 2, amenity value of $A_2 = \$3.7$ million was assumed to exceed the net revenue from logs. Decreasing π to 0.25 lowers P to \$116.41667 million, and the president would cut the forest today.

If the discount rate increases from $\delta = 0.05$ to $\delta = 0.1$, D falls to \$70 million, but P falls by more to $P = \$68.583333$ million. At the higher discount rate it is optimal to cut today.

Finally, if D_1 falls to \$2.5 million, D falls to \$70 million, but P falls by a lesser amount to $P = \$74.5454545$ million, implying that it would be optimal to delay cutting at least one period.

7.4   The Trigger Values for Irreversible Decisions

Many resource development projects are costly or impossible to reverse. If the future benefits or costs of such projects are uncertain, one would intuitively think that a more cautious or conservative investment rule would be appropriate. In this section we will explore two models, one in which an irreversible project has uncertain future net benefits and a second in which a stand of old-growth forest provides uncertain amenity value. These are continuous-time models, and a complete derivation of the value functions inherent in each problem requires mathematics beyond the basic calculus used in this book. You will be asked to take certain results on faith. Nevertheless, the trigger values which emerge from these models have intuitive appeal, and the approach taken is important in resource economics, in which irreversibility and uncertainty go hand in hand.

Consider a development project that can be constructed at instant τ for a cost of K million dollars. The net benefits, N, at $t > \tau$ are unknown but are thought to "evolve" according to the stochastic differential equation

$$dN = \mu N dt + \sigma N dz \qquad (7.11)$$

This particular equation implies that net benefits are changing according to a process of *geometric Brownian motion* (GBM). Dividing both sides by N we have $dN/N = \mu dt + \sigma dz$. The term μdt is the mean or expected percentage change in N for the time increment dt, and μ is called the *mean drift rate*. The term σdz introduces a random component to the drift in N because $dz = \varepsilon(t)\sqrt{dt}$, where $\varepsilon(t)$ is a normally distributed random variable with 0 mean and standard deviation of 1. The random variables $\varepsilon(t)$ are independent and identically distributed (*iid*), and the stochastic process $z(t)$ is called a *standard Wiener process* or "white noise." Net benefit is also a random process (because it depends on the change in z), and σ is called the *standard deviation rate*.

A discrete-time approximation of (7.11) is given by the stochastic difference equation

$$N_{t+1} = (1+\mu)N_t + \sigma N_t \varepsilon_{t+1} \tag{7.12}$$

where the ε_{t+1} are standard normal random variates, and the implied time increment is $dt = 1$. From a known value of N_0, and given values for μ and σ, it is possible to use Excel to generate several *sample paths or realizations for N_t*. This is done in Spreadsheet 7.3.

In $A\$7:$A\$37 we specify the period index $t = 0, 1, \ldots, 30$. We then select cells $B\$8:\$D\$37 and choose Analysis Tools from the Options Menu. When the Analysis Tools Menu is loaded, choose Random Number Generation. A dialogue box should appear, indicating that the output range is $B\$8:\$D\$37, and there are to be three random variables (or samples in columns B, C, and D) of 30 random numbers each. In the distribution option, select the normal distribution with mean 0 and variance 1, since it corresponds to the distribution for ε_{t+1}. Click the OK button and Excel will generate the 3 random samples, which we have labeled First Epsilon, Second Epsilon, and Third Epsilon. We can program equation (7.12) to obtain three realizations or sample trajectories for N_t. In cells $E\$7, $F\$7, and $G\$7 we enter $=\$B\$1$ to specify that $N_0 = 5$ for all three realizations. In cell $E\$8 we enter $=(1+\$B\$2)*E7+\$B\$3*E7*B8$ and fill down to $E\$37, giving us the first realization based on the first sample of ε_{t+1}.

In cell $F\$7 we enter $=(1+\$B\$2)*F7+\$B\$3*F7*C8$ and fill down to $F\$37 to obtain our second realization for N_t, and in cell $G\$7 we type $=(1+\$B\$2)*G7+\$B\$3*G7*D8$ and fill down to $G\$37 to obtain the third realization. The three realizations are then plotted in the figure at the bottom of the spreadsheet. Although all three realizations start at $N_0 = 5$ and employ the same values for μ and σ, the future values for N_t are determined by the ε_{t+1} values, which are random and independent within and between sample realizations. The first realization is plotted as the solid line ending with a value of $N_{30} = 15.0168643$. The second realization is plotted as the dashed line ending in $N_{30} = 16.4299634$, and the third realization is drawn as a dotted line ending in $N_{30} = 15.9367308$.

In this model the expected net benefit in period t is $E\{N_t\} = (1 + \mu)^t N_0$. The fact that the ε_{t+1} are *iid* standard normal means that the variance about $E\{N_t\}$ grows with t while the standard deviation grows with the square root of t. This means that as we look further into the future we should expect the realizations to diverge. Also shown in the figure at the

	A	B	C	D	E	F	G	H	I
1	N0 =	5							
2	μ =	0.04							
3	σ =	0.1							
4	α =	1.96							
5									
6	t	First Epsilon	Second Epsilon	Third Epsilon	First Nt	Second Nt	Third Nt	UB	LB
7	0				5	5	5	5	5
8	1	-0.07657263	0.37647396	-0.30167257	5.16171368	5.38823698	5.04916371	6.2192	4.34782609
9	2	-0.79242341	1.37450115	-0.42128931	4.95915596	6.34438026	5.03841439	6.9657065	4.1986357
10	3	-0.57229045	-1.50617325	0.92424671	4.87371444	5.64258188	5.70562476	7.66839322	4.12511129
11	4	0.59428203	-0.06825076	-0.16902163	5.35829911	5.82977411	5.83741235	8.36692201	4.08922495
12	5	0.5533343	0.18082915	0.01690751	5.86912414	6.16838438	6.08077845	9.07713726	4.07684781
13	6	1.65872734	-0.44642093	-2.39271685	7.07741677	6.13975017	4.86905148	9.80780375	4.08101614
14	7	1.34245511	1.1791235	1.53125711	8.31062487	7.10929255	5.80939051	10.5647871	4.09775519
15	8	-0.20014795	0.42204192	-0.13415956	8.47671441	7.6937062	5.9638276	11.3525571	4.1245801
16	9	0.56931867	-0.65457471	-1.16189767	9.29837817	7.4978439	5.50944497	12.1748494	4.15983897
17	10	-0.30119281	-0.24169708	0.91857601	9.39025283	7.61653696	6.23590716	13.034998	4.20238487
18	11	1.12074076	1.01296791	0.71093154	10.8182669	8.69272919	6.92867376	13.9361205	4.25139619
19	12	-0.22636527	0.38482199	-0.27909095	11.0061095	9.37495369	7.01244769	14.8812283	4.30627114
20	13	-0.44017497	-2.42040187	0.60572916	10.9618925	7.4808363	7.71771	15.873298	4.3665623
21	14	0.43575483	-0.52845053	0.79541223	11.878038	7.38474456	8.64029449	16.9153192	4.43193428
22	15	1.07027972	-0.4877154	0.28410568	13.6244418	7.31996898	9.23138195	18.0103295	4.50213517
23	16	-1.10991095	-0.40056307	-0.95820042	12.6572278	7.31955682	8.71608582	19.1614404	4.57697684
24	17	-0.60059165	-0.36193796	1.56121587	12.4033344	7.34741654	10.4254984	20.3718578	4.65632096
25	18	-0.57851821	0.52221594	-1.90488208	12.1819122	8.02500701	8.85658383	21.644997	4.74006881

19	0.45768957	0.12424607	0.37528366	13.2267421	8.44571485	9.5432203	22.9840103	4.82815378
20	1.3533645	-0.41715566	0.6112532	15.545722	8.43122566	10.5082815	24.3927741	4.9205357
21	-0.24618885	-0.17946832	0.61994342	15.784985	8.6171609	11.5800668	25.8749277	5.01719655
22	0.59140802	-0.49237315	-1.56471742	17.3499211	8.53756148	10.2313162	27.4343717	5.11813714
23	-1.07517508	0.32715207	0.53232498	16.1784977	9.15837202	11.1852074	29.0751825	5.22337452
24	-0.96933718	0.09173505	1.09823304	15.2573956	9.60872127	12.8610121	30.8016231	5.33293994
25	-0.46198352	1.81204996	0.76573997	15.1628249	11.7342184	14.3602717	32.6181545	5.44687725
26	-0.41098701	0.22821041	0.1367448	15.1461655	12.4713742	15.1310518	34.5294474	5.56524162
27	0.49756181	1.56628175	-0.67946758	16.5056275	14.9235978	14.708188	36.5403937	5.68809849
28	0.04851927	0.5765753	0.42447049	17.2459367	16.3809995	15.9215701	38.6561187	5.81552281
29	-0.03328296	0.19831418	0.66904931	17.8783746	17.3610979	17.6236644	40.8819928	5.94759833
30	-2.00054274	-0.93633389	-1.35719802	15.0168643	16.4299634	15.9367308	43.2236451	6.0844171

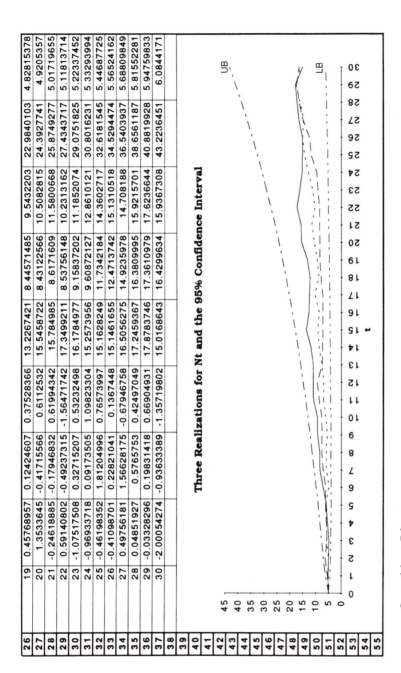

Three Realizations for Nt and the 95% Confidence Interval

Spreadsheet 7.3

bottom of Spreadsheet 7.3 is the 95% confidence interval for $E\{N_t\}$. This interval is given by the upper bound (UB) and lower bound (LB)

$$UB = (1+\mu)^t (1+\alpha\sigma)^{\sqrt{t}} N_0 \quad LB = (1+\mu)^t (1+\alpha\sigma)^{-\sqrt{t}} N_0$$

where the value of α is selected from the standard normal distribution for the level of confidence desired. For example, in Spreadsheet 7.3 we plot the 95% confidence interval with $\alpha = 1.96$. These bounds become quite wide for distant t; the implication is that N_t becomes less certain the further we forecast into the future.

If net benefits evolve according to equation (7.11), what is the level for N which would trigger the construction of a project we could never abandon? Equation (7.11) implies that future net benefits are log normally distributed and if N is the level of net benefit currently observed in $t = 0$, then the expected net benefit at future instant t is $E\{N(t)\} = Ne^{\mu t}$, where e is the base of the natural log, which is also used in the process of continuous discounting (see Section 1.1). This is a happy coincidence because we can get an analytic expression for the present value of expected net benefits by noting

$$\int_0^\infty Ne^{\mu t} e^{-\delta t} dt = N \int_0^\infty e^{-(\delta-\mu)t} dt = \frac{N}{(\delta-\mu)}$$

In general, if the project is constructed when net benefits are currently estimated to be N, its discounted expected value is given by

$$V_I = \frac{N}{(\delta-\mu)} \tag{7.13}$$

where it is assumed that $\delta > \mu$. If this were not the case, if $\mu > \delta$, then the project should be constructed immediately because expected net benefits are growing faster than the rate of discount and the expected value of such a project is infinite.

Suppose we have not constructed the project, but have the option of doing so. What is the value of being able to exercise that option optimally at the trigger value N^*? If the current net benefit is N, the value of the option to invest optimally can be shown to equal

$$V_W = \gamma N^\beta \tag{7.14}$$

where V_W denotes the value of waiting.

Equation (7.14) assumes that $N < N^*$, which is a bit problematic because we have not yet solved for N^*. The coefficient $\gamma > 0$ is also unknown, but we will solve for it as well. The coefficient β is given by the positive root of a quadratic and takes the form

$$\beta = \left(1/2 - \mu/\sigma^2\right) + \sqrt{\left(\mu/\sigma^2 - 1/2\right)^2 + 2\delta/\sigma^2} > 1 \qquad (7.15)$$

Although the derivation of equations (7.14) and (7.15) is beyond the mathematical scope of this text, the form of V_W has certain intuitive appeal. First, if $N \to 0$, $V_W \to 0$. In other words, if net benefits fall to 0, the value of the option to construct the irreversible project goes to 0 as well. Note: In equation (7.11), if N falls to 0 it can never become positive again. Conversely, as N increases, the value of the option to invest should increase. With $\gamma > 0$ and $\beta > 1$ (because $\delta > \mu$), V_W will increase with an increase in N.

The unknown trigger value, N^*, and the coefficient γ can be determined via two conditions that must hold at the trigger value. The first condition is called the *value-matching condition* and simply requires $V_W = V_I - K$. This says that at N^* you are indifferent between waiting and the discounted expected net value of the project, less construction cost. Given our forms for V_W and V_I this condition requires

$$\gamma N^\beta = \frac{N}{(\delta - \mu)} - K \qquad (7.16)$$

The second condition is called the *smooth-pasting condition*. It requires equality of the first derivatives of the value functions at N^*, or $V'_W = V'_I$. It says that the value function in the region where waiting is optimal should smoothly meet the value function in the region where construction is optimal. Given our forms for V_W and V_I this condition requires

$$\beta \gamma N^{(\beta-1)} = \frac{1}{(\delta - \mu)} \qquad (7.17)$$

Equations (7.16) and (7.17) constitute a two-equation system in the unknowns γ and N^*. Solving (7.17) for γ yields

$$\gamma = \frac{N^{(1-\beta)}}{\beta(\delta - \mu)} \qquad (7.18)$$

Substituting this result back into (7.16) and solving for $N = N^*$ yield

$$N^* = \frac{\beta(\delta - \mu)K}{(\beta - 1)} \qquad (7.19)$$

This is the trigger value that our stochastically evolving N must reach before we will commit to constructing a project we can never abandon. Conventional cost–benefit analysis would simply say you should construct when $N = \delta K$. In other words, construct when the current net benefit flow covers the interest cost of construction. The critical coefficient with irreversibility and uncertainty becomes $\Delta = \beta(\delta - \mu)/(\beta - 1)$.

If $\Delta > \delta$, then we have a more conservative investment rule. Let's go back to Spreadsheet 7.3, add a few more bells and whistles, and see if the three realizations for N_t in that spreadsheet would ever justify construction when $K = 100$ and $\delta = 0.1$.

In Spreadsheet 7.4 we have inserted the values for K and δ; calculated β, Δ, and N^*; and deleted the *UB* and *LB* values for the 95% confidence interval. In \$H\$12:\$H\$42 we have filled down the values of N^* so we can easily select and plot the three realizations for N_t and N^*. In the figure at the bottom of the spreadsheet we can see that all of the realizations reach N^* before $t = 30$, but they do so at different times. The first realization exceeds N^* for the first time in $t = 14$, the second realization exceeds N^* in $t = 25$, and the third realization reaches N^* in $t = 21$. Note that the third realization falls back below N^* in $t = 22$. This, of course, is one of the risks of irreversibility. Even though you have an expectation that net benefit will be drifting upward ($\mu = 0.04$), the standard deviation rate means that once you invest, it is still possible for the realization to turn "nasty," with an interval where net revenue may not cover the interest payment on K. Also note that $\Delta = 0.11089454 > \delta = 0.1$, which confirms our intuition that with irreversibility and uncertainty we would wait for a larger value of N to be realized before we commit to this project. Finally, when you replicate Spreadsheet 7.3, the ε_{t+1} values that you obtain will be different, but the programming of N_t and N^* will be the same.

The decision to cut a stand of old-growth forest might be viewed as an irreversible and risky decision. Uncertainty can arise because the future price of old-growth timber is uncertain, future amenity value is uncertain, or both. To keep things simple, consider a model in which the net value of old-growth timber in a particular forest parcel is known and unchanging at N dollars. Uncertainty arises because amenity value (the use value of visitors, the option value of potential visitors, and the existence value of nonvisitors) is stochastically evolving according to

$$dA = \mu A dt + \sigma A dz \qquad (7.20)$$

where μ is now the mean or expected drift rate in amenity value, A; $\sigma > 0$ is the standard deviation rate; and $dz = \varepsilon(t)\sqrt{dt}$, where the $\varepsilon(t)$ are generated from a standard normal distribution.

Amenity value is said to evolve according to geometric Brownian motion. With a growing or more affluent population, we might expect that the amenity value attached to the remaining stands of old growth is also growing, and that $\mu > 0$. We will assume that $\delta > \mu$, where δ is the risk-free social rate of discount. If this were not the case, if $\mu > \delta$, then the old-growth forest should be permanently preserved, since it represents a natural asset that is growing in expected value more rapidly than the social rate of discount.

In this model the trigger value, A^*, will be a lower bound or barrier. If A remains above A^*, it will be optimal to continue to preserve the forest. If A is currently below A^*, or if it falls to A^*, it is optimal to cut the forest, sell the timber, and place N in a risk-free portfolio where it will earn a return of δ.

What is the value of the old-growth forest? If amenity value currently exceeds the trigger value $(A > A^*)$, it can be shown that preservation has an expected present value given by

$$V_P = \gamma A^{-\alpha} + \frac{A}{(\delta - \mu)} \tag{7.21}$$

The first term on the RHS is the option value of preservation, where $\gamma > 0$ is an unknown parameter which will be determined simultaneously with A^*, and $-\alpha$ is the negative root of a quadratic given by

$$-\alpha = \left(1/2 - \mu/\sigma^2\right) - \sqrt{\left(\mu/\sigma^2 - 1/2\right)^2 + 2\delta/\sigma^2} < 0 \tag{7.22}$$

The second term on the RHS of (7.21), $A/(\delta - \mu)$, is the expected value of never cutting. Thus V_P is the sum of the option value to cut plus the expected present value of never cutting.

Again, it is not possible with standard calculus to derive the expression for V_P, but the option value of preservation, $\gamma A^{-\alpha}$, also has intuitive appeal. Suppose amenity value drifts to a large value. The option to cut such a valuable old-growth forest will approach 0 (remember $-\alpha < 0$) and one would never wish to exercise such an option. Conversely, if $A \to 0$ the option to cut becomes very valuable and will be exercised when A first reaches A^*.

What is the value of cutting? That's easy; it is simply

$$V_C = N \tag{7.23}$$

As in the previous problem, we will determine γ and A^* by using the value-matching and smooth-pasting conditions. The value-matching condition requires that $V_P = V_C$ at A^*, or

$$\gamma A^{-\alpha} + \frac{A}{(\delta - \mu)} = N \tag{7.24}$$

while the smooth-pasting condition requires $V'_P = V'_C$ at A^*, or

$$-\alpha \gamma A^{-(\alpha+1)} + \frac{1}{(\delta - \mu)} = 0 \tag{7.25}$$

Solving this last expression for γ yields

	A	B	C	D	E	F	G	H
1	NO =	5						
2	µ =	0.04						
3	σ =	0.1						
4	K =	100						
5	δ =	0.1						
6								
7	β =	2.17890835						
8	Δ =	0.11089454						
9	N* =	11.0894542						
10								
11	t	First Epsilon	Second Epsilon	Third Epsilon	First Nt	Second Nt	Third Nt	N*
12	0	0	0	0	5	5	5	11.0894542
13	1	-0.0765726	0.37647396	-0.3016726	5.16171368	5.38823698	5.04916371	11.0894542
14	2	-0.7924234	1.37450115	-0.4212893	4.95915596	6.34438026	5.03841439	11.0894542
15	3	-0.5722904	-1.5061732	0.92424671	4.87371444	5.64258188	5.70562476	11.0894542
16	4	0.59428203	-0.0682508	-0.1690216	5.35829911	5.82977411	5.83741235	11.0894542
17	5	0.5533343	0.18082915	0.01690751	5.86912414	6.16838438	6.08077845	11.0894542
18	6	1.65872734	-0.4464209	-2.3927169	7.07741677	6.13975017	4.86905148	11.0894542
19	7	1.34245511	1.1791235	1.53125711	8.31062487	7.10929255	5.80939051	11.0894542
20	8	-0.200148	0.42204192	-0.31125711	8.47671441	7.6937062	5.9638276	11.0894542
21	9	0.56931867	-0.6545747	-1.1618977	9.29837817	7.4978439	5.50944497	11.0894542
22	10	-0.3011928	-0.2416971	0.91857601	9.39025283	7.61653696	6.23590716	11.0894542
23	11	1.12074076	1.01296791	0.71093154	10.8182669	8.69272919	6.92867376	11.0894542
24	12	-0.2263653	0.38482199	-0.279091	11.0061095	9.37495369	7.01244769	11.0894542
25	13	-0.440175	-2.4204019	0.60572916	10.9618925	7.4808363	7.71771	11.0894542
26	14	0.43575483	-0.5284505	0.79541223	11.878038	7.38474456	8.64029449	11.0894542
27	15	1.07027972	-0.4877154	0.28410568	13.6244418	7.31996898	9.23138195	11.0894542
28	16	-1.109911	-0.4005631	-0.9582004	12.6572278	7.31955682	8.71608582	11.0894542
29	17	-0.6005916	-0.361938	1.56121587	12.4033344	7.34741654	10.4254984	11.0894542
30	18	-0.5785182	0.52221594	-1.9048821	12.1819122	8.02500701	8.85658383	11.0894542
31	19	0.45768957	0.12424607	0.37528366	13.2267421	8.44571485	9.5432203	11.0894542

32	20	1.3533645	-0.4171557	0.6112532	15.5458722	8.43122566	10.5082815	11.0894542
33	21	-0.2461888	-0.1794683	0.61994342	15.784985	8.6171609	11.5800668	11.0894542
34	22	0.59140802	-0.4923731	-1.5647174	17.3499211	8.53756148	10.2313162	11.0894542
35	23	-1.0751751	0.32715207	0.53232498	16.1784977	9.15837202	11.1852074	11.0894542
36	24	-0.9693372	0.09173505	1.09823304	15.2573956	9.60872127	12.8610121	11.0894542
37	25	-0.4619835	1.81204996	0.76573997	15.1628249	11.7342184	14.3602717	11.0894542
38	26	-0.410987	0.22821041	0.1367448	15.1461655	12.471342	15.1310518	11.0894542
39	27	0.49756181	1.56628175	-0.6794676	16.5056275	14.9235978	14.708188	11.0894542
40	28	0.04851927	0.5765753	0.42497049	17.2459367	16.3809995	15.9215701	11.0894542
41	29	-0.033283	0.19831418	0.66904931	17.8783746	17.3610979	17.6236644	11.0894542
42	30	-2.0005427	-0.9363339	-1.357198	15.0168643	16.4299634	15.9367308	11.0894542
43								
44								
45								
46								
47								
48								
49								
50								
51								
52								
53								
54								
55								
56								
57								
58								
59								
60								

Three Realizations for N_t and the Trigger Value N^*

Spreadsheet 7.4

$$\gamma = \frac{A^{(\alpha+1)}}{\alpha(\alpha-\mu)} \tag{7.26}$$

Substituting the expression for γ into (7.24) and solving for $A = A^*$ yield

$$A^* = \frac{\alpha(\delta-\mu)N}{(\alpha+1)} \tag{7.27}$$

This is the critical lower bound which A must initially exceed and never fall below if preservation of the old-growth forest is to remain optimal. The critical coefficient in this model is $\Delta = \alpha(\delta - \mu)/(\alpha + 1)$. We would expect that $\Delta < \delta$. The intuition is, since cutting is an irreversible act, we would allow A to drift below δN before cutting, whereas traditional cost–benefit analysis would say to cut the first time that A reached δN.

7.5   Questions and Exercises

Q7.1 What is the basic question cost–benefit analysis seeks to answer?

Q7.2 What is the definition of option value?

Q7.3 What is a trigger value? How is it used to determine the optimal timing of an irreversible and risky project?

E7.1 Consider a three-period problem where $t = 0,1,2$. If an old-growth forest is cut in $t = 0$, it will yield net revenues of T_0 followed by net agricultural revenues of N_1 in $t = 1$ and N_2 in $t = 2$. If the forest is not cut in $t = 0$, society will receive an amenity flow of A_0. If the forest is uncut at the beginning of $t = 1$, it will be optimal to cut in state 1, when net timber revenue will be T_1, and it will be optimal to preserve in state 2, when amenity value is A_1. The subjective probability of state 1 in $t = 1$ is π_1, and thus the subjective probability of state 2 in $t = 1$ is $(1 - \pi_1)$. If the forest has not been cut at the beginning of $t = 2$, it will be optimal to cut in state 1, when net timber revenues are T_2, and it will be optimal to preserve in state 2, when the amenity value is A_2. The subjective probability of state 1 in $t = 2$ is π_2 and the subjective probability of state 2 is $(1 - \pi_2)$.

(a) What is the expression for the option value of preservation in $t = 0$?

(b) Suppose $T_0 = 100$, $N_1 = 5$, $A_0 = 10$, $N_2 = 5$, $\pi_1 = 0.5$, $T_1 = 120$, $A_1 = 12$, $\pi_2 = 0.6$, $T_2 = 130$, $A_2 = 15$, and $\delta = 0.05$. What is the optimal first-period decision? Why? What is the option value of preservation in $t = 0$?

(c) Suppose δ increases to 0.1 while the other parameters in part (b) are unchanged. What is the optimal first-period decision now? Why?

(d) What is the probability that the forest will not be cut?

E7.2 Consider an old-growth forest where amenity value is evolving according to equation (7.20) with $\mu = 0.02$ and $\sigma = 0.2$. The known and unchanging net value of the timber is $N = \$500$ million. Suppose the risk-free social discount rate is $\delta = 0.05$. What is the trigger value A^* which would cause the forest to be cut?

CHAPTER 8

Sustainable Development

8.0   Introduction and Overview

The term *sustainable development* entered the lexicon of specialists following the release of a report by the UN's World Commission on Environment and Development (WCED). The commission, chaired by Gro
Harlem Brundtland of Norway, defined *sustainable development* as
"development that meets the needs of the present without compromis-
ing the ability of future generations to meet their own needs. . . . At a
minimum, sustainable development must not endanger the natural
systems that support life on Earth." In 1992, at the Earth Summit in Rio
de Janeiro, sustainable development emerged as the common theme
linking conventions to reduce the emissions of greenhouse gases and to
preserve biodiversity. With these conventions being ratified by more than
140 countries, one might conclude that the concept must have broad
international appeal.

The widespread acceptance of sustainable development as a guiding
philosophy is also the result of its vagueness or multiple interpretations.
Sustainable development means different things to different people,
including academics, who often define the term from the perspective of
a particular paradigm within their specialized field. Economists would
tend to think of sustainable development as a steady state within a
natural resource or macroeconomic growth model. Sociologists might
think of sustainable development in terms of a socioeconomic system
that evolves slowly and nondestructively with its supporting ecosystem.

The word *sustainable* implies some sort of time horizon. There are
many harvest and extraction rates which might be sustainable over a
period of 10 or 20 years. This is probably too short an interval for most
people's definition of sustainable. If sustainable means "can be maintained ad infinitum," then even primitive hunting–gathering societies
would probably fail to qualify as sustainable.

We have spent a considerable amount of time and effort in determining the existence and character of steady-state equilibrium in models of
renewable resources and stock pollutants. There are many sustainable
stock levels for an economy based on the harvest of a renewable

166

resource. We will consider sustainable development from this perspective in the next section.

The WCED makes specific reference to the development needs of the present generation, as well as the ability of future generations to meet their own needs. This raises the question of intergenerational equity and the altruistic feelings that the present generation may have for its children and grandchildren. If each generation cares about the welfare of the next generation (and the resources and natural environments they will inherit), how will resources be allocated over time? A model with discounting and altruism will be analyzed in the third section of this chapter.

Suppose the biophysical world is continuously evolving, replete with extinctions and natural events that randomly alter the environment and its ability to support the socioeconomic systems of humans. How can we talk about sustainable development in a world that is stochastically evolving? The concept of coevolution seems appropriate in such a world. It is discussed in Section 8.3.

In a stochastic environment, be it a business or a tropical rainforest, the admonition to "manage adaptively" is gaining widespread acceptance. The trigger value models encountered in Chapter 7 were basically adaptive models in which a decision rule was established indicating the conditions that would justify the taking of an irreversible action. Can such an approach guide incremental development decisions? This prospect is considered in Section 8.4.

Section 8.5 ponders the questions "Is sustainable development feasible or economically desirable? Has the concept outlived its usefulness?" Section 8.6 concludes with some questions and exercises.

8.1   Sustainable Development as a Steady State

If an economy were simply based on the harvest of a renewable resource, then sustainable development might simply mean the adoption of a harvest rate that matched net growth, or $Y = F(X)$ in the notation of Chapter 1. We saw, however, that with a concave net growth function, such as the logistic $Y = F(X) = rX(1 - X/K)$, there were an infinite number of steady-state pairs (X, Y). The "best" sustainable (X, Y) pair depended on the objectives of the "owner" or manager of the resource.

Suppose that net benefit only depends on harvest and is written as $\pi = \pi(Y)$, where $\pi'(\bullet) > 0$ and $\pi''(\bullet) < 0$. (Since we are only considering alternative steady states we can dispense with all time subscripts.) In this case the maximization of the present value of net benefits implies that the optimal stock size must satisfy $F'(X) = \delta$. (This is true for any strictly concave $\pi[Y]$.) This is one equation in the optimal steady-state stock. Suppose that $Y = F(X) = rX(1 - X/K)$. Then $F'(X) = r(1 - 2X/K) = \delta$ implies $X' = K(r - \delta)/(2r)$, which for $\delta > 0$ implies that $X' < MSY = K/2$. Because the practice of discounting reduces the weight assigned to the net benefits of future generations, some have argued that the "equitable" steady-state biomass is the optimal level when $\delta \to 0$ or $X' = X_{MSY} = K/2$.

When net benefit depends on both harvest and biomass, so that $\pi = \pi(X,Y)$, we obtained $F'(X) + \pi_X(\bullet)/\pi_Y(\bullet) = \delta$, where $\pi_X(\bullet)/\pi_Y(\bullet) > 0$ was called the marginal stock effect. (Note: $\pi_X[\bullet] = \partial\pi[\bullet]/\partial X$ and $\pi_Y[\bullet] = \partial\pi[\bullet]/\partial Y$. See equation [1.16].) If the marginal stock effect is greater than the discount rate, then the steady-state optimal biomass would be $X'' > X_{MSY}$: that is, the optimal stock exceeds the stock level that maximizes sustainable yield. If it is again argued on the basis of intergenerational equity that the discount rate should become vanishingly small, then $F'(X) = -\pi_X(\bullet)/\pi_Y(\bullet)$ and this will imply an optimal biomass $X''' > X''$. When $\pi = \ln(XY)$, where $\ln(\bullet)$ is the natural log operator, and when $Y = F(X) = rX(1 - X/K)$, equation (1.16) becomes $r(1 - 2X/K) + Y/X = \delta$. Substituting $Y = rX(1 - X/K)$ into this equation and solving for X yield an explicit solution $X'' = K(2r - \delta)/(3r)$. As $\delta \to 0$ we get $X''' = 2K/3$.

These various steady-state optima are calculated and plotted in Spreadsheet 8.1 for the case when $Y = F(X) = rX(1 - X/K)$ and $\pi = \ln(XY)$ for $r = 0.5$, $K = 1$, and $\delta = 0.05$. These functional forms and parameter values result in the values $X' = 0.45$, $X_{MSY} = 0.5$, $X'' = 0.6333$, and $X''' = 0.6666$. Recall that the marginal stock effect increases the optimal stock $(X'' > X')$ and that the optimal stock increases when the discount rate is reduced. Also recall that the present value of net benefits is undefined when $\delta = 0$, so mathematically we can only let δ go to 0 in the limit. Alternatively, we can regard X_{MSY} and X''' as being the result of two static optimization problems, where X_{MSY} is the solution of the unconstrained maximization of $Y = F(X)$, while X''' is the solution to the maximization of $\pi(X,Y)$ subject to $Y = F(X)$.

8.2   Intergenerational Altruism and the Stock of a Renewable Resource

If a natural resource is the basis of a family's livelihood, and if that family sees itself as part of an ongoing, intergenerational tradition, then one might expect that the behavior of the current generation would be tempered by an altruistic motive to leave an abundant stock for the next generation. To be able to act on such an altruistic motive, it is necessary that the family possess some exclusivity of access to the resource. This

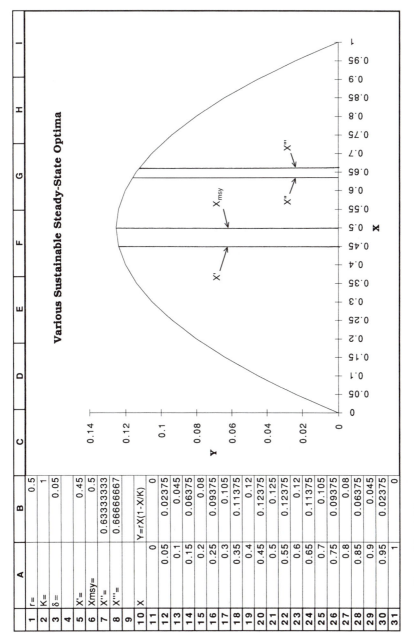

Various Sustainable Steady-State Optima

	A	B
1	r =	0.5
2	K=	1
3	δ=	0.05
4		
5	X'=	0.45
6	Xmsy=	0.5
7	X''=	0.63333333
8	X'''=	0.66666667
9		
10	X	Y=rX(1-X/K)
11	0	0
12	0.05	0.02375
13	0.1	0.045
14	0.15	0.06375
15	0.2	0.08
16	0.25	0.09375
17	0.3	0.105
18	0.35	0.11375
19	0.4	0.12
20	0.45	0.12375
21	0.5	0.125
22	0.55	0.12375
23	0.6	0.12
24	0.65	0.11375
25	0.7	0.105
26	0.75	0.09375
27	0.8	0.08
28	0.85	0.06375
29	0.9	0.045
30	0.95	0.02375
31	1	0

Spreadsheet 8.1

situation is thought to exist in the lobster fishery off the coast of Maine. In that fishery, sons often follow fathers in the harvesting of lobsters from well-defined coastal areas, which, over time, have become the exclusive lobster grounds for that family.

Suppose that the placement and retrieval of the "lobster pots" (traps baited with fish or meat) are a two-person operation. Let the father in period t be the skipper (captain), who determines the number of pots to be placed on the family's grounds. The son is the crew member in period t but will become the skipper in period $t+1$. Assume that there is a high correlation between the number of pots and harvest, Y_t. Let $\pi_t = (p - cY_t/X_t)Y_t$ be the function describing net revenue in period t as a function of harvest and the lobster stock, X_t, where p and c are the per unit price for lobster and a positive cost parameter, respectively. The father's share of net revenue is α $(1 > \alpha > 0)$, while the son receives $(1 - \alpha)$.

Although lobstering has been a family tradition, and the father is certain that the son will continue that tradition in period $t+1$, he is pessimistic about the participation in the fishery by his grandchildren. In fact, the father, in period t, believes that his son will have to share net revenue in period $t+1$ with a nonfamily crew member, and that the family tradition of lobstering will cease in period $t+2$. How will the father's view of the future affect his harvest decision in period t?

We will again resort to the logic of dynamic programming to answer this question. This requires us to determine the son's optimal harvest in period $t+1$ before we can determine the father's optimal harvest in period t.

In period $t+1$ the son, now skipper, receives $\alpha(p - cY_{t+1}/X_{t+1})Y_{t+1}$. If the son maximizes this share by choosing Y_{t+1} we obtain the static first-order condition requiring that price equal marginal cost or $p = 2cY_{t+1}/X_{t+1}$, which can be solved for $Y_{t+1} = pX_{t+1}/(2c)$. This becomes the father's expectation of the son's harvest decision in period $t+1$.

In period t the father wishes to maximize net revenue which he shares with his son but realizes that his harvest decision in period t will affect stock size, and thus the share of net revenue his son receives in period $t+1$. This effect occurs through the dynamics of the lobster population, in which it is assumed that $X_{t+1} = X_t + F(X_t) - Y_t$. Suppose the father seeks to maximize

$$\pi = (p - cY_t/X_t)Y_t + \rho\{\alpha(p - cY_{t+1}/X_{t+1})Y_{t+1}\} \tag{8.1}$$

Substituting the son's optimal decision rule $Y_{t+1} = pX_{t+1}/(2c)$ into (8.1) yields

$$\pi = (p - cY_t/X_t)Y_t + \rho\{[\alpha p^2/(4c)]X_{t+1}\} \tag{8.2}$$

But we also know $X_{t+1} = X_t + F(X_t) - Y_t$, which upon substitution in (8.2) yields the expression that the father can optimize with respect to Y_t

$$\pi = (p - cY_t/X_t)Y_t + \rho\{[\alpha p^2/(4c)][X_t + F(X_t) - Y_t]\} \tag{8.3}$$

In (8.3) X_t is taken as a given. Setting $d\pi/dY_t = 0$ and solving for Y_t will yield

$$Y_t = \frac{p[4c(1+\delta) - \alpha p]X_t}{8c(1+\delta)} \tag{8.4}$$

Equation (8.4) is the father's harvest rule. It is based on his expectations of the future (his son maximizes $\alpha(p - cY_{t+1}/X_{t+1})Y_{t+1}$ in period $t + 1$) and it depends on the stock the father inherits in period t.

Consider the implications if all previous fathers had had the same expectations, and thus the same harvest rule. What would be the steady-state stock that the father of period t would inherit? This can be found by equating the harvest rule to net growth, $F(X)$. Suppose net growth is logistic. Equating $F(X) = rX(1 - X/K)$ with the RHS of (8.4) and solving for X yield

$$X = \frac{K[8cr(1+\delta) - 4cp(1+\delta) + \alpha p^2]}{8cr(1+\delta)} \tag{8.5}$$

How would this stock level compare to the steady-state level that maximizes the present value of net revenue? We know that the bioeconomic optimum is defined by the equations $F'(X) + \pi_X/\pi_Y = \delta$ and $Y = F(X)$. With $\pi = (p - cY/X)Y$ and $F(X) = rX(1 - X/K)$ the optimal level for X must satisfy

$$r(1 - 2X/K) + \frac{cr^2(1 - X/K)^2}{[p - 2cr(1 - X/K)]} = \delta \tag{8.6}$$

Given parameter values for α, c, δ, K, p, and r, Solver can be used to find the value of X which satisfies (8.6). This value can then be compared with the X value from equation (8.5) to see how close the father/son steady state is to the bioeconomic optimum. This done in Spreadsheet 8.2 for $\alpha = 0.7, c = 1, \delta = 0.05, K = 1, p = 0.25, r = 0.5$.

The parameter values are entered in \$B\$1:\$B\$6. Equation (8.5) is programmed in cell \$B\$8, a guess of $X = 0.8$ was initially entered in \$B\$9, and equation (8.6), with δ transposed to the LHS, was programmed in \$B\$10. Solver was summoned and told to drive the value in \$B\$10 to 0 by changing the value in \$B\$9.

The father/son steady-state stock is calculated to be 0.7604 and the

	A	B
1	α =	0.7
2	c=	1
3	δ =	0.05
4	K=	1
5	p=	0.25
6	r=	0.5
7		
8	Father/Son X	0.76041667
9	Optimal X	0.78464641
10	G(X)=0	-7.4357E-08

Spreadsheet 8.2

optimal (present value maximizing) stock level was determined by Solver to be 0.7846. The two steady states are not far apart. One might conclude that if (i) property rights to a renewable resource can be assigned (so exclusivity of harvest in an area is protected) and (ii) altruism between at least two generations (father/son) exists, then the resulting steady-state stock may be close to the present value maximizing optimum.

A couple of qualifiers are in order. First, Solver indicates the existence of several solutions to equation (8.6). By starting from an initial guess of $X = 0.5$, Solver iterates to $X = 0.1487$ as the bioeconomic optimum. The second-order conditions, however, are not satisfied at this solution.

Second, the steady state implied by the static optimization of π_t implies $Y = pX/(2c)$ with an associated steady-state stock of $X = K[2cr - p]/(2cr)$ $= 0.75$. This is also very close to the optimal stock of 0.7846.

In general, an altruistic motive, even for just one period, should result in a steady state closer to the present value maximizing optimum. If the father and son live for more than one period, and if the father optimizes near-term harvests while attaching a positive weight to the net revenue earned when the son is the skipper, then the altruistic and bioeconomic steady states are likely to be even closer. The father's problem becomes analytically and computationally more difficult the longer the horizon for which he must predict the behavior of his offspring. The current model was tractable because of the quadratic net revenue function and because the father only needed to form rational expectations about the son's behavior for one period into the future.

8.3 Coevolution

In resource systems, where the difference equations are changing over time, or where a random variable causes "stochastic evolution," the existence of a steady state may be impossible or at least highly unlikely. The notion of sustainable development as a steady state is also inappropriate. Both ecological and socioeconomic systems often exhibit changes that do not seem consistent with a stationary set of deterministic difference equations.

In ecology, coevolution is concerned with the dynamics of two or more species that interact over time. It is also possible to speak of the coevolution of a socioeconomic system and the underlying natural environment which provides resource and amenity service flows. *Coevolution, in this context, might be defined as the evolution of a socioeconomic system and its natural environment in a way that is nondestructive.* Specifically, agents within the socioeconomic system engage in activities which may involve harvest, extraction, and waste generation, but on a scale which does not drastically or irreversibly alter the natural environment. Variables used to measure or monitor the system may always be changing, but they remain within bounds, which from the perspective of the socioeconomic system are acceptable.

The terms *nondestructive* and *acceptable* are obviously subjective and imply *Homo economicus* is still in the driver's seat, determining what type of changes are acceptable. Such a perspective may be objectionable to some, but there is nothing preventing *Homo economicus* from holding strong environmental values and altruistic motives toward future generations. It also seems appropriate that *Homo economicus* bear responsibility for the environmental consequences of resource development and waste generation. In this section we will construct a model of coevolution and show how acceptability might be given a quantitative dimension.

We will begin with a deterministic, three-species system which converges to a "pristine" steady state. The three species are grass, an herbivore, and a carnivore, which is a predator of the herbivore. This deterministic system is then modified to allow for the intrinsic growth rate of grass to be a normally distributed iid random variable. *Coevolution becomes an exercise in stochastic simulation.* An index of biodiversity is proposed. It depends on the size of each species relative to its size in the pristine steady state. Into this system we introduce a domestic species, cattle, which compete with the herbivore for grass. It is possible to explore the stochastic implications of different stocking rates (number of cattle) and to simulate their impact on biodiversity.

Let $X_{1,t}$ be the biomass of grass available to the herbivore, $X_{2,t}$, in period t. The herbivore is a prey species (food source) for the predator, $X_{3,t}$. When cattle are introduced, $C_t = C$ will denote the stocking rate. It is assumed that the carnivore does not prey on domestic cattle, although the model could be easily modified to allow for that possibility.

The equation describing the dynamics of grass biomass is given by

$$X_{1,t+1} = X_{1,t} + r_{1,t+1} X_{1,t} (1 - X_{1,t}/K) - \alpha_1 C_t - \alpha_2 X_{2,t} \tag{8.7}$$

where the intrinsic growth rate, $r_{1,t+1}$, will subsequently be treated as an iid normal random variable. In order to get a feel for the expected biomass of grass and the number of herbivores and carnivores in the pristine system, we will initially replace $r_{1,t+1}$ with its expected value $r_1 = E\{r_{1,t+1}\}$. Cattle and the wild herbivore consume grass at the positive rates of α_1 and α_2 per head, per period. Their presence will reduce grass biomass below K.

The dynamics of the herbivore are given by

$$X_{2,t+1} = X_{2,t} + r_2 X_{2,t} [1 - X_{2,t}/(\beta X_{1,t})] - \gamma X_{2,t} X_{3,t} \tag{8.8}$$

where r_2 is the intrinsic growth rate, and the carrying capacity of the herbivore depends on the availability of grass according to $\beta X_{1,t}$. The term $\gamma X_{2,t} X_{3,t}$ determines the number of "kills" by the predator, where $\gamma > 0$ reflects the strength of predation.

The dynamics of the predator are given by

$$X_{3,t+1} = X_{3,t} + r_3 X_{3,t} [1 - X_{3,t}/(\eta X_{2,t})] \tag{8.9}$$

where r_3 is the intrinsic growth rate of the predator whose environmental carrying capacity depends on the herbivore population according to $\eta X_{2,t}$.

By temporarily suppressing the stochasticity in r_1, and by setting $C_t = C$ (a constant) it is possible to identify the three equations which will define the steady-state levels for X_1, X_2, and X_3. Knowing the steady state for the pristine system will be useful in defining our index of biodiversity and in evaluating the evolution of the system when $r_{1,t+1}$ is a random variable.

Evaluating (8.7)–(8.9) in steady state results in the following equations: $\alpha_1 C + \alpha_2 X_2 = r_1 X_1 (1 - X_1/K)$, $r_2 (1 - X_2/(\beta X_1)) = \gamma X_3$, and $X_3 = \eta X_2$. The first equation simply says that the amount of grass consumed by cattle and the herbivore must equal net growth. The second equation results from the requirement that the steady-state rate of predation must equal the rate of net growth in the herbivore. The third equation says that the steady-state predator population equals the herbivore population times η, where $1/\eta$ is the number of herbivores needed to support a single predator, per period.

Some algebra will show that

$$X_2 = \frac{\beta X_1}{[(\beta\gamma\eta/r_2)X_1 + 1]} \tag{8.10}$$

and that X_1 must satisfy

$$G(X_1) = \alpha_1 C[(\beta\gamma\eta/r_2)X_1 + 1] + \alpha_2\beta X_1$$
$$-r_1 X_1(1 - X_1/K)[(\beta\gamma\eta/r_2)X_1 + 1] = 0 \tag{8.11}$$

With parameter values for r_1, K, α_1, α_2, r_2, β, γ, r_3, η, and C, equation (8.11) might be solved numerically for X_1. Then X_2 would be given by equation (8.10) and $X_3 = \eta X_2$. If this is done for $C = 0$ (no cattle), and if (8.11) implies a unique positive level for X_1, then we will have numerically solved for the pristine steady state: that is, the equilibrium before *Homo economicus* decides to start grazing cattle.

This is done in Spreadsheet 8.3 for the parameter values $r_1 = 1.5$, $K = 1{,}000{,}000$, $\alpha_1 = 100$, $\alpha_2 = 20$, $r_2 = 0.5$, $\beta = 0.01$, $\gamma = 0.001$, $r_3 = 0.2$, $\eta = 0.02$, and $C = 0$. In cell $\$B\$12$ a guess for X_1 was entered. (In our case it was $X_1 = 1{,}000{,}000$.) Equation (8.11) was programmed in cell $\$B\$13$. Solver was called and asked to drive the value in cell $\$B\$13$ to 0 by changing the guess for X_1 in cell $\$B\$12$ subject to the constraint $\$B\$12 \geq 0$. (Solver was run twice to obtain the value $G(X_1) = 5.8208E - 11$.) Equation (8.10) was programmed in cell $\$B\$14$ and $X_3 = \eta X_2$ in cell $\$B\$15$. This resulted in the values $X_1 = 902{,}018.967$, $X_2 = 6{,}628.55627$, and $X_3 = 132.571125$. These values are in turn used as the initial conditions, $X_{1,0}$, $X_{2,0}$, and $X_{3,0}$ in cells $\$F\$2$, $\$G\$2$, and $\$H\$2$, respectively. They will also be used as reference levels in our index of biodiversity, to be described momentarily.

We now allow $r_{1,t+1}$ to be an iid normal random variable. We will specify a mean or expected value of $r_1 = E\{r_{1,t+1}\} = 1.5$ and a standard deviation of $\sigma = 0.5$, and we will generate a sample of 41 variates in column E by using Excel's random number generator found in the Analysis Tools menu. Select $\$E\$3:\$E\$43$ and Analysis Tools from under the Options Menu. Select Random Number Generation and the Normal Distribution, specifying a mean of 1.5 and a standard deviation of 0.5. Click OK and Excel will generate the desired sample of iid normal random variates.

In cell $\$F\$3$ we program the expression for $X_{1,1}$ using the first of the randomly generated intrinsic growth rates. The equation is entered as =F2+E3*F2*(1−F2/\$B\$2)−\$B\$3*\$B\$10−\$B\$4*G2. In cell $\$G\$3$ we type the equation for $X_{2,1}$ as =G2+\$B\$5*G2*(1−G2/(\$B\$6*F2))−

$B$7*G2*H2, and in cell $H$3 we enter $X_{3,1}$ as =H2+$B$8*H2*(1−H2/($B$9*G2)). We then select the block $F$3:$H$43 and fill down, generating a stochastic simulation for our pristine grass–herbivore–carnivore system. Plots of $X_{1,t}$, $X_{2,t}$, and $X_{3,t}$ show the nonstationary, ragged evolution of all three species induced by the stochastic growth rate for grass.

As a measure of biodiversity we construct the index number

$$B_t = 100 \left(\frac{X_{1,t}}{X_{1,p}} \right) \left(\frac{X_{2,t}}{X_{2,p}} \right) \left(\frac{X_{3,t}}{X_{3,p}} \right) \tag{8.12}$$

where $X_{1,p}$, $X_{2,p}$, and $X_{3,p}$ are the population levels for grass, the herbivore, and the carnivore in the pristine steady state. Since we specified the pristine steady state as the initial condition, $B_0 = 100$. In cell $I$2 we have programmed =100*(F2/$F$2)*(G2/$G$2)*(H2/$H$2) and we fill down to $I$43. The biodiversity index is plotted at the bottom of Spreadsheet 8.3.

Some comments about the biodiversity index are in order. First, there does not appear to be any widely accepted index of biodiversity. The index given by (8.12) has the property that if any species becomes extinct, $B_t = 0$. Although this property may be desirable, equation (8.12) has some shortcomings. The pristine steady state is associated with an index of 100, but an index of 100 would also result if the herbivore were four times its pristine population and grass biomass and the predator were at one-half of their pristine populations. This latter composition would probably be viewed as "less healthy" than the pristine steady state, which one would intuitively regard as a more healthy, natural balance of populations. Thus, the index in (8.12) does have the problem that different and potentially unhealthy population levels can yield the same index number. Plotting the time paths for each species might provide a visual indication of this potential problem. If any deviation from the pristine steady state is viewed as unhealthy, then the index

$$B_t = 100 \left(\frac{1}{\left[1 + (X_{1,t} - X_{1,p})^2 \right]} \right) \left(\frac{1}{\left[1 + (X_{2,t} - X_{2,p})^2 \right]} \right) \left(\frac{1}{\left[1 + (X_{3,t} - X_{3,p})^2 \right]} \right)$$

might be preferred to (8.12).

Spreadsheet 8.3 presumed that $C_t = C = 0$, and it basically showed that with stochastic growth in the forage base (grass), the ecosystem that comprised our three species would appear to perpetually "wander" about the pristine steady state. This may not always be the case. Depending on the stocking rate, C, and other parameters in the model, the pristine steady state calculated using Solver may be "stochastically unstable," and depending on the initial condition, species extinctions could result. If grass biomass goes to 0 then the "ultimate" steady state, (0,0,0), will be the unfortunate dynamic outcome. Identifying the existence of multiple pristine equilibria (when $G(X_1) = 0$ has more than one positive root) and determining the stability of the stochastic system (which will also depend on σ) are formidable problems beyond the scope of this text. Instead we will suggest some modifications to Spreadsheet 8.3 that are numerically interesting.

Let's introduce cattle into the system and explore the stochastic implications. This is done in Spreadsheet 8.4 where $C = 2,000$. The deterministic steady state (when $r_1 = 1.5$) is calculated as $X_1 = 707,670.962$, $X_2 = 5,515.45787$, and $X_3 = 110.309157$, indicating that the introduction of cattle reduces the population levels of all three species. We continue to use the $C = 0$, pristine steady state as our initial condition and as the reference for our biodiversity index (8.12). The same sample of random variates, $r_{1,t+1}$, in \$E\$3:\$E\$43 is also retained.

The consequences of $C = 2,000$ are dramatic, especially within the first 20 periods. Grass biomass declines from 902,018 to 171,094 in $t = 7$, causing a decline in the herbivore population to 1,620 animals in $t = 8$ with the predator population falling to 44 animals in $t = 11$. The biodiversity index declines from $B_0 = 100$ to $B_8 = 2.498$ in $t = 8$ and it takes until $t = 26$ before it climbs back above 50. (The biodiversity index of the deterministic steady state, when $C = 2,000$, is approximately 54.40.) Thus, it would appear that the stocking of 2,000 cattle in every period puts the natural ecosystem under significant stress during the first 20 periods.

If the random growth rates had been smaller, extinction of one or more species might have occurred. To estimate the likelihood of extinction one could run a large number of stochastic simulations, say 1,000, and observe how often extinction results. Such analysis would give the managers of our rangeland ecosystem an indication of whether $C = 2,000$ is a *stochastically sustainable development*.

The introduction of a stochastic growth rate for grass induced stochastic variation in all of the higher trophic level species. In exploring the stochastic sustainability of a particular stocking rate, managers may choose to adopt a lower bound rule for B_t. The rule might be "Allow no stocking rate which results in a $B_t < 30$ in any of 1,000 stochastic simulations." Justification of such a lower bound for B_t would require a risk–benefit analysis of the cost and likelihood of undesirable evolutions of the ecosystem versus the increase in expected present value from higher stocking rates.

The analysis in Spreadsheet 8.4 assumed that $C_t = C$ for all t. An

	A	B	C	D	E	F	G	H	I
1	r1 =	1.5		t	r1,t	X1,t	X2,t	X3,t	Bt
2	K=	1000000		0		902018.967	6628.55627	132.571125	100
3	α1 =	100		1	1.24182458	879201.23	6628.55628	132.571125	97.4703707
4	α2 =	20		2	1.31794872	886604.729	6565.34763	132.571125	97.353855
5	r2=	0.5		3	1.0700216	862874.306	6546.8113	132.315856	94.2986974
6	β =	0.01		4	0.46023382	786393.977	6470.36736	132.037023	84.7581135
7	γ=	0.001		5	0.66359229	768455.861	6189.34771	131.5004	78.9055089
8	r3=	0.2		6	1.27708512	871902.515	5977.5873	129.861583	85.3868497
9	η =	0.02		7	1.46455131	915924.336	6141.06553	127.621797	90.5617122
10	C=	0		8	1.92350962	941226.628	6369.1417	126.624174	95.765302
11				9	2.09159674	929548.965	6592.27314	126.775002	98.0070988
12	X1=	902018.967		10	1.55703839	899670.344	6715.08546	127.750095	97.3671867
13	G(X1)=0	5.8208E-11		11	1.8780417	934887.47	6708.72564	128.996496	102.068969
14	X2=	6628.55627		12	1.91440785	917248.493	6790.60523	129.992134	102.14797
15	X3=	132.571125		13	2.17811925	946763.688	6789.5606	131.106247	106.321988
16				14	0.13217454	817634.364	6859.67604	132.010913	93.4090635
17			Dynamics of X1,t	15	1.59796736	918711.216	6506.44376	133.008279	100.303899
18				16	0.5675542	830967.809	6590.27666	132.419656	91.1464428
19				17	0.49269824	768366.823	6399.40978	132.296259	82.0677505
20				18	1.69804588	942595.557	6087.59471	131.405644	95.1265137
21				19	1.61581335	908273.987	6365.66248	129.321805	94.3297495
22				20	2.2254198	966365.694	6494.57899	128.913756	102.072373
23				21	0.29404641	846031.516	6722.24724	129.107849	92.633934
24				22	2.06130375	980096.512	6544.85396	130.132894	105.31066
25				23	1.45330654	877549.576	6780.33039	130.284839	97.7986453
26				24	1.23396939	874540.775	6667.73199	131.307423	96.5970619
27			Dynamics of X2,t	25	1.89349516	948938.924	6584.24698	131.710581	103.820109
28				26	1.84982463	906885.096	6724.90371	131.705451	101.33478
29				27	1.38119839	889021.655	6708.26099	132.252379	99.5043864
30				28	1.51122714	903957.357	6644.29297	132.629493	100.49704
31				29	0.97382776	855617.718	6643.35673	132.680667	95.1461963
32				30	1.67772606	930010.215	6504.50671	132.717908	101.285682
33				31	1.6741455	908892.245	6618.86421	132.181738	100.319132
34				32	1.5527092	905090.356	6643.36169	132.220789	100.298866

178

33	1.01917175	859771.814	6648.53883	132.349449	95.4438592
34	1.84442223	949172.406	6522.24987	132.473134	103.46341
35	1.71296728	901368.059	6678.46591	132.0612	100.292985
36	1.39056164	891424.789	6661.60976	132.359418	99.1596956
37	1.92950774	944943.154	6621.58023	132.53283	104.618199
38	1.79704893	906004.08	6734.79557	132.512569	102.006557
39	1.66883064	913426.932	6706.58785	132.94216	102.743558
40	1.1174887	867664.138	6706.229	133.177969	97.7639761
41	1.69742515	928443.145	6574.57891	133.365955	102.703366

Dynamics of X3,t

The Biodiversity Index Bt

Spreadsheet 8.3

179

	A	B	C	D	E	F	G	H	I
1	r1 =	1.5		t	r1,t	X1,t	X2,t	X3,t	Bt
2	K=	1000000		0		902018.967	6628.55627	132.57125	100
3	α1 =	100		1	1.24182458	679201.23	6628.5628	132.57125	75.2978879
4	α2 =	20		2	1.31794872	633793.89	5829.56226	132.57125	61.7944366
5	r2=	0.5		3	1.0700216	565553.797	5290.53009	128.937112	48.6706886
6	β=	0.01		4	0.46023382	372823.889	4779.10957	123.30088	27.716177
7	γ=	0.001		5	0.66359229	232406.986	3516.30248	116.149467	11.974822
8	r3=	0.2		6	1.27708512	189905.232	2205.96574	101.013211	5.338636
9	η=	0.02		7	1.46455131	171094.299	1804.8766	74.9609699	2.92034856
10	C=	2000		8	1.92350962	207790.901	1620.03594	58.820027	2.498023
11				9	2.09159674	319695.958	1703.23511	49.2277433	3.38172365
12	X1=	707670.962		10	1.55703839	424272.241	2017.29237	44.8452462	4.84224006
13	G(X1)=0	2.9104E-09		11	1.8780417	642666.826	2455.89035	43.8450112	8.73034652
14	X2=	5515.45787		12	1.91440785	833185.462	3106.90938	44.7863634	14.6262338
15	X3=	110.309157		13	2.17811925	873778.51	3941.94096	47.2876437	20.5482854
16				14	0.13217454	609517.171	4837.32799	51.0725323	18.9974501
17				15	1.59796736	693096.413	5089.4064	55.8947983	24.741711
18			Dynamics of X1,t	16	0.5675542	512034.882	5481.0629	60.9350686	21.5748646
19				17	0.49269824	325516.821	4954.01127	66.3476982	13.481027
20				18	1.69804588	399252.113	3332.59703	70.7314747	11.8729648
21				19	1.61581335	520152.784	3372.30013	69.8655291	15.4609851
22				20	2.2254198	808157.91	3729.66273	69.3643429	26.3765814
23				21	0.29404641	579153.228	4475.16559	70.336817	22.9986182
24				22	2.06130375	792061.305	4668.98048	73.3492424	34.2210183
25				23	1.45330654	738041.565	5284.88765	76.4959941	37.6419155
26				24	1.23396939	670914.781	5630.88635	80.7227965	38.4730629
27				25	1.89349516	776358.323	5628.82973	85.2951637	47.0241737
28			Dynamics of X2,t	26	1.84982463	784959.523	5922.5978	89.429192	52.4511786
29				27	1.38119839	699651.19	6119.91404	93.8115296	50.6756769
30				28	1.51122714	694821.278	5929.1797	98.1935632	51.03489
31				29	0.97382776	582732.669	5781.76266	101.570371	43.1730871
32				30	1.67772606	675045.41	5217.11077	104.041201	46.2258433
33				31	1.6741455	737942.252	5266.84103	104.10123	51.0440222
34				32	1.5527092	732873.747	5472.45217	104.345449	52.796009

33	1.01917175	622947.772	5594.48143	105.318572	46.3055319
34	1.84442223	744283.13	5290.41289	106.555602	52.9322644
35	1.71296728	764496.659	5491.66626	106.405078	56.3583828
36	1.39056164	705022.161	5680.72328	107.069326	54.098835
37	1.92950774	792679.534	5624.22941	108.302943	60.9140355
38	1.79704893	775519.613	5831.96849	109.108181	62.2560715
39	1.66883064	749405.205	5918.79417	110.517164	61.8437927
40	1.1174887	640890.395	5886.73431	111.984563	53.3006861
41	1.69742515	713817.932	5467.3237	113.078421	55.6747683

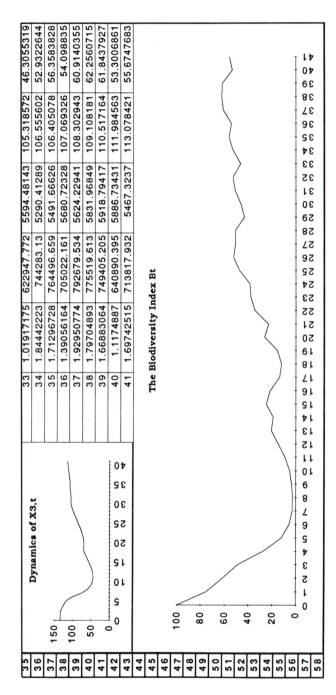

Dynamics of X3,t

The Biodiversity Index Bt

Spreadsheet 8.4

181

obvious modification is to permit adaptive management, where the number of cattle stocked in period t would depend on an assessment of the growth and quality of grass. This moves us from stochastic simulation, as a method to analyze coevolution, to stochastic optimization as a method for adaptive management.

8.4   Adaptive Development

When the future benefits or costs of a development project are uncertain, and if the project can be designed in stages, optimal development is likely to be incremental and adaptive. By observing the outcome of an initial stage or pilot project, one can determine the optimal scale of development in subsequent stages.

Adaptive development will make use of dynamic programming. To determine the value of a pilot project today, we need to know the likelihood and value of the alternative optimal investments in subsequent stages.

Consider a project that can be completed in two stages ($t = 0,1$). In $t = 0$ a decision must be made whether to initiate a small pilot project. Let $d_0 = 1$ denote that the pilot project has been initiated and $d_0 = 0$ that the pilot project has not been undertaken. If $d_0 = 1$, there will be a *signal* in $t = 1$ indicating no environmental costs, $E = 0$, or $E = 1$, indicating significant environmental costs.

If $d_0 = 1$ suppose that the a priori subjective probability that $E = 0$ is π_1, and thus the probability that $E = 1$ is $(1 - \pi_1)$. Let the unit cost of development be $k > 0$. Since the pilot project is a unit-sized project it will cost k if initiated in $t = 0$.

If no environmental costs are signaled, additional development may be optimal. The ultimate scale of the project will be $D = d_0 + d_1 = 1 + d_1$. Beginning in $t = 2$, benefits will flow at a rate of $p(1 + d_1)$ and continue ad infinitum, where $p > 0$. The present value of this benefit stream is given by

$$B = \rho^2 \sum_{\tau=2}^{\infty} \rho^{\tau-2} p(1+d_1) = \rho^2 p(1+d_1) \sum_{\tau=0}^{\infty} \rho^{\tau}$$

$$= \rho^2 p(1+d_1)(1+\delta)/\delta = \rho p(1+d_1)/\delta \qquad (8.13)$$

Even if $E = 0$ for the pilot project, there is a possibility of environmental costs if additional development is undertaken. Suppose the environmental costs, in $t = 2, 3, \ldots, \infty$, are $C_2 = 0$ or $C_2 = \beta(1 + d_1)^2$, where $\beta > 0$. Suppose the probability that $C_2 = 0$, conditional on a signal $E = 0$, is π_2. The probability that $C_2 = \beta(1 + d_1)^2$ is therefore $(1 - \pi_2)$. If $d_1 > 0$ and environmental costs occur, they, like the benefits in (8.13), persist from t

= 2 to infinity, and the present value of net benefits in this situation can be shown to equal

$$N = \rho\left[p(1+d_1) - \beta(1+d_1)^2\right]\Big/\delta \tag{8.14}$$

In $t = 1$ each unit of additional development will also have a cost of $k > 0$. If $E = 0$ after $d_0 = 1$, project managers will choose $d_{1,0}$ to maximize the expected present value of future net benefits as given by

$$V_0(d_{1,0}) = \rho\left[\pi_2[p(1+d_{1,0})/\delta] + (1-\pi_2)\left[p(1+d_{1,0}) - \beta(1+d_{1,0})^2\right]\Big/\delta\right] - kd_{1,0}$$

$$= \rho\left[p(1+d_{1,0}) - (1-\pi_2)\beta(1+d_{1,0})^2\right]\Big/\delta - kd_{1,0} \tag{8.15}$$

where $d_{1,0} \geq 0$ denotes the level of additional development when $d_0 = 1$ and $E = 0$. Note: In (8.15), the present value of benefits, B, are a sure thing (they occur whether $C_2 = 0$ or $C_2 = \beta[1 + d_{1,0}]^2$). There is a probability of $(1 - \pi_2)$ that $C_2 = \beta(1 + d_{1,0})^2$, and the cost of adding $d_{1,0}$ more units is $kd_{1,0}$. The first-order condition for maximizing $V_0(d_{1,0})$ with respect to $d_{1,0}$ requires

$$\rho[p - 2(1-\pi_2)\beta(1+d_{1,0})]\Big/\delta - k = 0 \tag{8.16}$$

Solving (8.16) for the optimal $d_{1,0}$ yields

$$d_{1,0}^* = \frac{[p - (1+\delta)\delta k - 2(1-\pi_2)\beta]}{[2(1-\pi_2)\beta]} \tag{8.17}$$

Now suppose that after $d_0 = 1$ the signal is $E = 1$. We will interpret $E = 1$ to mean that environmental costs in periods $t = 2, 3, \ldots, \infty$, will be $C_2 = \beta(1 + d_{1,1})^2$ *with certainty*, where $d_{1,1} \geq 0$ is the additional level of development taken in light of (or despite) this knowledge. Would additional development take place? Project managers would seek to maximize

$$V_1(d_{1,1}) = \rho\left[p(1+d_{1,1}) - \beta(1+d_{1,1})^2\right]\Big/\delta - kd_{1,1} \tag{8.18}$$

The maximization of $V_1(d_{1,1})$ for $d_{1,1} > 0$ requires

$$\rho[p - 2\beta(1+d_{1,1})]\Big/\delta - k = 0 \tag{8.19}$$

and solving for the optimal level of $d_{1,1}$ yields

$$d_{1,1}^* = \frac{[p - (1+\delta)\delta k - 2\beta]}{2\beta} \tag{8.20}$$

If we undertake the pilot project we now know what the optimal level of development will be if our signal is $E = 0$ or $E = 1$, and by substituting the optimal levels for $d_{1,0}$ and $d_{1,1}$ into their respective value functions we can determine the discounted expected value of the pilot project as

	A	**B**
1	k=	5
2	$\pi 1 =$	0.5
3	p=	1
4	$\delta =$	0.1
5	$\rho =$	0.90909091
6	$\pi 2 =$	0.8
7	$\beta =$	0.225
8		
9	d1,0*=	4
10	d1,1*=	-1.2336E-16
11	V0(d1,0*)=	15.2272727
12	V1(d1,1*)=	7.04545455
13	V(d0=1)=	5.12396694

Spreadsheet 8.5

$$V(d_0 = 1) = \rho[\pi_1 V_0(d_{1,0}^*) + (1 - \pi_1)V_1(d_{1,1}^*)] - k \qquad (8.21)$$

This last expression can be interpreted as the "take-it-or-leave-it" option value of the pilot project in $t = 0$. If it is positive, the pilot project should be undertaken.

A numerical example at this point may be helpful. Suppose we could construct a pilot project in $t = 0$ for $k = \$5$ million. The pilot project may signal no environmental cost ($E = 0$) with probability $\pi_1 = 0.5$, or it may signal significant environmental cost ($E = 1$) with probability $(1 - \pi_1) = 0.5$. If $E = 0$ project managers believe they can add to the project with a probability of $\pi_2 = 0.8$ that there will be no environmental cost in $t = 2, 3, \ldots,$ ∞. If $E = 0$ the probability that environmental costs would be $C_2 = \beta(1 + d_1)^2$ is therefore $(1 - \pi_2) = 0.2$. If $E = 1$ any additional development will result in environmental costs of $C_2 = \beta(1 + d_1)^2$ with certainty. Let $\beta = 0.225$. The completed project yields benefits of $p(1 + d_1)$ in $t = 2, 3, \ldots, \infty$, where $p = \$1$ million. Assume that the discount rate is $\delta = 0.1$. These parameter values are entered in cells \$B\$1:\$B\$7 in Spreadsheet 8.5.

The expression for $d^*_{1,0}$ given in equation (8.17) is programmed in cell \$B\$9 and returns a value of $d^*_{1,0} = 4$. Equation (8.20) for $d^*_{1,1}$ is programmed in cell \$B\$10 and returns the numerical equivalent of $d^*_{1,1} = 0$. These optimal levels for second-stage development, when substituted into their respective value functions, imply $V_0(d^*_{1,0}) = \$15.2273$ million and $V_1(d^*_{1,1}) = \$7.0455$ million, yielding a pilot project value of $V(d_0 = 1) = \$5.1240$ million.

In adaptive development, dynamic programming replaces traditional cost–benefit analysis, and the ultimate scale of development depends on the signals received in earlier stages. To determine the value of an initial pilot project, one needs to know what one can expect to learn and how the project will be optimally modified on the basis of the possible information (signals). Adaptive development requires that projects be designed in stages, with specific protocols for monitoring environmental consequences.

8.5　A Requiem for Sustainable Development?

This chapter has considered development from several perspectives: (1) as a steady-state equilibrium for an economy based on a renewable resource; (2) as an acceptable set of "coevolutionary trajectories" for, say, net revenue and an index of biodiversity; and (3) as an adaptive policy for sequential development in an uncertain environment. The last two perspectives, coevolution and adaptive development, would suggest that the term *sustainable development* may be operationally limited. Our experience since the Earth Summit in 1992 suggests that the concept has had little influence on the domestic and international policies of nation states.

Operationally, if physical and biological systems exhibit natural fluctuation, is sustainable development feasible? In a stochastic socioeconomic system is sustainable development desirable? Is the adjective *sustainable* inconsistent with a dynamic system whose structure is changing with the passage of time? It might be possible to concoct a definition of sustainable development which would encompass development in stochastic and evolving environments, but it may be preferable to coin a new, more descriptive term for what is likely to be a better approach to such problems. Perhaps *adaptive development* is that term.

From a practical perspective, both developed and developing countries seem unable or unwilling to limit the harvest of renewable resources to net growth or to restrict the extraction and burning of fossil fuels to rates which would reduce the emission of greenhouse gases. Many observers believe that major environmental problems have gotten worse since 1992. This would seem to be the case for air quality and water quality (sanitation) in much of the developing world. The lofty rhetoric and signing of international conventions seem to be at best a case of good intent and at worst a case of subterfuge. Using sustainable development as a mantra, and believing that it is feasible and desired on some broad global scale, may have delayed the formulation of policies and projects which could improve the management of a single species, reduce pollution in a particular region, or provide potable water to a rural village.

The orientation of this book has been the microdynamics of resource systems. Our chances of modeling and understanding national or regional resource and environmental problems seem greater than for problems that are global in scale. It is also the case that a region or country may be more effective in formulating and enforcing policies than an international organization such as the United Nations.

Are we simply to throw up our hands at global problems such as climate change? Obviously not, but we should probably proceed from a more micro and perhaps national perspective. For example, the Montreal Protocol focused on the control of chlorofluorocarbons, a single class of pollutants. For other greenhouse gases, especially carbon emissions, the national costs of morbidity and shortened lives may be a more compelling reason for countries to take actions to reduce the burning of carbon-based fuels. For example, the U.S. program of marketable SO_2 permits, which has caused a reduction in acid precipitation in the northeastern United States, has also reduced acid rain in eastern Canada. This program, which was initially applied to U.S. electric utilities, is being expanded to nitrous oxides and extended to other industries. Stiffer air quality standards in the United States will reduce aggregate global emissions.

Another institutional alternative to international organizations are nongovernmental organizations, or NGOs. NGOs often focus on the conservation of a few closely related species or on the solution of a specific development problem. For example, NGOs have brokered agreements between donors, banks, and developing counties which have allowed for the retirement of a portion of a country's international debt in return for the preservation and protection of certain species or ecosystems.

In most instances the success stories in development and conservation have occurred when the problems are micro and well-defined, and incentive-based policies can be employed. Incentive-based policies require an understanding of the motivations of individuals and households as they seek to solve the basic problems of securing water, food, and shelter. Incentive-based policies will try to introduce shadow prices into the optimizing calculus of firms and individuals. For example, sharing safari or tourist revenues with villagers may encourage them to protect wildlife and habitat.

Adaptive models are called for in stochastic environments. Even simple models might suggest appropriate strategies when harvesting a natural resource or developing a natural environment. In resource management, simple "escapement rules," whereby the level of harvest depends on the degree to which a resource population exceeds some critical level, emerge as the best policy when growth is stochastic. This chapter has shown how multistage projects might be adaptively implemented. The disasters with large-scale, take-it-or-leave-it projects have caused funding agencies to think smaller and expand adaptively in light of the information on the costs and benefits generated in the earlier stages of a project.

In the last 15 years resource economics and development economics have converged on many of the same allocation problems. This is not surprising, given the realization that resource management and environmental quality are important to the welfare of the residents of a developing country. In resource economics there has been a move away from deterministic models, with a steady-state optimum, toward stochastic models requiring adaptive management. It seems likely that adaptive development, based on the application of stochastic dynamic programming, may replace sustainable development as a more compelling development philosophy.

8.6   Questions and Exercises

Q8.1 Is sustainable development, based on the harvest of a renewable resource, feasible with a positive discount rate?

Q8.2 How would altruism affect the stocks of natural resources handed down to subsequent generations? Is the ability to act on altruistic motives affected by the assignment of property rights?

Q8.3 What is the definition of coevolution? What numerical method is useful in determining the ecosystem implications of fixed rates of harvest or extraction?

E8.1 You have acquired two neighboring uninhabited islands in the South Pacific and are in the process of planning for their development or preservation. Let $V_1 = v_1 \ln(W_1)$ be the net benefit from preserving W_1 hectares of wilderness on Island #1, $V_2 = v_2 \ln(W_2)$ be the net benefit from preserving W_2 hectares of wilderness on Island #2, and $N = n\ln(D)$ be the net benefit from development of D hectares on either island, where v_1, v_2, and n are positive constants and $\ln(\bullet)$ is the natural log operator. Let $W_{1,0}$ and $W_{2,0}$ denote the size of Islands #1 and #2, respectively, and both are in a pristine, undeveloped state. You wish to maximize the sum of net benefits subject to $W_{1,0} \geq W_1$ and $W_{2,0} \geq W_2$.

(a) Given that D is the optimal total number of hectares developed on both islands, what is the expression defining D in terms of $W_{1,0}$, $W_{2,0}$, and the unknown values for W_1 and W_2?

(b) What are the relevant marginal conditions for determining W_1, W_2 and D?

(c) What are the specific expressions defining W_1, W_2, and D in terms of the parameters v_1, v_2, n, $W_{1,0}$, and $W_{2,0}$?

(d) Suppose that $W_{1,0} = 10$, $W_{2,0} = 5$, $v_1 = 3$, $v_2 = 2$, and $n = 2$. What are the optimal levels for W_1, W_2, and D?

(e) Suppose the expected net benefits of development decline so that $n = 1$, ceteris paribus. What are the revised values for W_1, W_2, and D?

E8.2 A developing country is trying to determine a policy for the preservation of its rain forest. Let X_t denote the number of hectares of rain forest and A_t the number of hectares of agricultural land in period t. The rate of irreversible conversion is denoted by $D_t > 0$. All land is either rain forest or in agriculture and thus $X_{t+1} = X_t - D_t$ and $A_{t+1} = A_t + D_t$. There are net benefits to the stocks of both rain forest and agricultural land and there is a cost to conversion (agricultural development). The country's welfare in period t is given by $W_t = N(A_t) + B(X_t) - cD_t$, where $N(A_t)$ and $B(X_t)$ are strictly concave net benefit functions for agricultural land and rain forest, respectively, and c is the unit cost of clearing and land preparation. The rain forest policy is to permit conversions that will

$$\text{Maximize} \quad \sum_{t=0}^{\infty} \rho^t [N(A_t) + B(X_t) - cD_t]$$

$$\text{Subject to} \quad X_{t+1} = X_t - D_t, \quad A_{t+1} = A_t + D_t, \quad X_0 \text{ and } A_0 \text{ given}$$

where $\rho = 1/(1 + \delta)$ is the usual discount factor. The country is relatively undeveloped and X_0 is significantly larger than A_0.

(a) What is the Lagrangian expression for this problem? Remember each state variable must have a Lagrange multiplier. What are the first-order necessary conditions?

(b) Evaluate the first-order conditions in steady state and identify the two expressions that might be used to solve for the steady-state optimal levels of rain forest, X^*, and agricultural land, A^*. (You may assume $X_0 > X^*$.)

(c) Suppose $N(A_t) = a\ln(A_t)$ and $B(X_t) = b\ln(X_t)$, where a and b are positive constants. Use the two expressions identified in part (b) to solve for the explicit expression for X^*.

Annotated Bibliography

B.0   Texts

Listed in the following are texts pitched at the introductory, intermediate, and graduate levels.

Tietenberg, T. 1996. *Environmental and Natural Resource Economics* (Fourth Edition), Addison-Wesley, Reading, Massachusetts.

A comprehensive introductory text covering both natural resource and environmental economics. The text is aimed at undergraduates with or without introductory economics. Calculus is not required.

Hartwick, J. M. and N. D. Olewiler. 1998. *The Economics of Natural Resource Use* (Second Edition), Addison-Wesley, Reading, Massachusetts.

An intermediate text using graphical analysis and differential calculus. Part I of this text provides two introductory chapters. Part II contains five chapters using static (equilibrium) models to examine the allocation of land, water, and fish; the generation of pollution; and the economics of environmental policy. Part III contains five chapters developing intertemporal (dynamic) models of nonrenewable and renewable resources.

Hanley, N., Shogren, J. F., and B. White. 1997. *Environmental Economics in Theory and Practice*, Oxford University Press, New York.

This is a text for advanced undergraduates or graduate students with two or more semesters of calculus and intermediate or graduate microeconomics. Contrary to its title, it is a comprehensive text covering both environmental and resource economics. The text also contains two chapters (12 and 13) on the theory of nonmarket valuation and methods for estimating environmental costs and benefits (such as contingent valuation, travel cost, and hedonic pricing).

Clark, C. W. 1990. *Mathematical Bioeconomics: The Optimal Management of Renewable Resources* (Second Edition), Wiley-Interscience, New York.

This is a frequently cited classic graduate text for students with a strong background in calculus and differential equations. The second edition focuses exclusively on renewable resources. It contains chapters on optimal control theory and dynamical systems.

Conrad, J. M. and C. W. Clark. 1987. *Natural Resource Economics: Notes and Problems*, Cambridge University Press, New York.

This is a graduate-level text with the premise that numerical examples help in understanding theory, develop economic intuition, and serve as a bridge to the analysis of real-world problems. The first chapter covers the method of Lagrange multipliers, dynamic programming, the maximum principle, and some basic numerical and graphical techniques. This chapter is followed by chapters on renewable and nonrenewable resources, environmental management, and stochastic resource models.

B.1   Basic Concepts

The first section in Chapter 1 of this text discusses the attributes of renewable, nonrenewable, and environmental resources and the role they play in an economy. The second section presented the algebra of discounting; the third section goes through the arduous task of extending the method of Lagrange multipliers to dynamic allocation problems. The following articles are classic references, most written in the 1960s. The texts provide a more contemporary discussion of these topics.

Weisbrod, B. A. 1964. "Collective Consumption Services of Individual Consumption Goods," *Quarterly Journal of Economics*, 78:471–477.

This article introduced the concept of option value for a hospital or park, based on the potential (uncertain) future demand by individuals.

Boulding, K. E. 1966. "The Economics of the Coming Spaceship Earth," in H. Jarrett (ed.), *Environmental Quality in a Growing Economy*, Johns Hopkins University Press, Baltimore.

Another classic, examining the implications of the first and second laws of thermodynamics for an economic system, along with the notion that welfare in a closed economy (spaceship) should be concerned with stock maintenance, as opposed to maximizing throughput (GDP). This article is reprinted in Markandya, A. and J. Richardson, eds. 1992. *Environmental Economics: A Reader*, St. Martin's Press, New York.

Krutilla, J. V. 1967. "Conservation Revisited," *American Economic Review*, 57:777–786.

A third classic, concerned with the ability of markets (1) to efficiently allocate natural resources over time, (2) to signal resource scarcity, and (3) to account for option demand. This article is also reprinted in Markandya and Richardson (1992).

Baumol, W. J. 1968. "On the Social Rate of Discount," *American Economic Review*, 57:788–802.

The fourth classic, it discusses the social rate of discount and the effects of inflation, taxes, and risk on market rates of return.

Kahn, J. R. 1998. *The Economic Approach to Environmental and Natural Resources* (Second Edition), Dryden Press, Fort Worth, Texas.

An introductory text: Chapters 1 and 2 provide a taxonomy of natural resources and examine the role of markets, discounting, and present value.

Tietenberg (1996): Chapters 1 and 2 cover basic concepts. (See B.0 for a complete citation.)

Pearce, D. W. and R. K. Turner. 1990. *Economics of Natural Resources and the Environment*, Johns Hopkins University Press, Baltimore.

This is an intermediate text. Chapters 1, 2, and 3 cover basic concepts, with a particular concern for sustainability. A discussion of the methods of static and dynamic optimization thrusts the reader into more advanced articles and texts.

Dorfman, R. 1969. "An Economic Interpretation of Optimal Control Theory," *American Economic Review*, 59:817–831.

In the 1960s optimal control theory and the maximum principle provided a powerful new way to pose and solve dynamic optimization problems, such as the problem of optimal saving and investment. In this classic, Professor Dorfman tries to bring his colleagues up to speed.

Spence, A. M. and D. A. Starrett. 1975. "Most Rapid Approach Paths in Accumulation Problems," *International Economic Review*, 16:388–403.

This article lays out sufficient conditions for the most rapid approach path (MRAP) to be optimal in both discrete- and continuous-time models.

Conrad and Clark (1987): Chapter 1 covers some of the methods for static and dynamic optimization. (See B.0 for a complete citation.)

Léonard, D. and N. V. Long. 1992. *Optimal Control Theory and Static Optimization in Economics*, Cambridge University Press, New York.

This is a graduate-level text on static and dynamic optimization. Chapter 1 covers static optimization and the method of Lagrange multipliers. Section 4.2 provides a discrete-time derivation of the maximum principle.

B.2   Solving Numerical Allocation Problems

The inclusion of nonlinear programming algorithms in spreadsheet software greatly facilitates the ability to pose and solve simple numerical allocation problems. Prior to the widespread availability of such software, and powerful personal computers (PCs) to run it, resource economists had to resort to analytic approximations or nonlinear programming packages that, in the 1970s, were only available on mainframe computers.

Burt, O. R. 1964. "Optimal Resource Use over Time with an Application to Ground Water," *Management Science*, 11:80–93.

Oscar Burt was perhaps the first economist to apply stochastic dynamic programming to resource management. Burt was initially concerned with the optimal use of groundwater. In this seminal paper, Burt shows how to derive first- and second-order, approximately optimal feedback rules, of the form $x_t = \phi(s_t)$, where x_t is the amount of water to be pumped from a groundwater stock of size s_t. This approach presumes that resource dynamics are linear in the stock and harvest (extraction). Suppose the groundwater stock in $t + 1$ is given by the equation $s_{t+1} = s_t + w_t - x_t$, where w_t is random recharge to the aquifer in period t, with an expected value of $w(s_t)$. Burt shows that a first-order approximation to the optimal feedback rule is implied by the equation $\partial G(x_t,s_t)/\partial x_t = \{1/[\delta - w'(s_t)]\}[\partial G(x_t,s_t)/\partial s_t]$, where $G(x_t,s_t)$ is the net benefit function for the amount x_t pumped from a groundwater stock of size s_t. The feedback policy equation, based on a second-order approximation of the value function, is more complex, but still manageable. The great advantage of these rules, particularly in 1964, was that they spared resource managers the need to approximate numerically the value function itself, a process which, at that time, would have taxed the memory of available computers.

Kolberg, W. C. 1993. "Quick and Easy Optimal Approach Paths for Nonlinear Natural Resource Models," *American Journal of Agricultural Economics*, 75:685–695.

For an autonomous discrete-time problem, Kolberg obtains an approximately optimal current-period decision rule, $U_t = \phi(X_t)$, where U_t is the utilization of the resource in period t and X_t is the resource stock, by (1) identifying an optimal transition equation from the first-order conditions for present value maximization; (2) solving for a steady-state optimum; (3) taking a small perturbation from the steady-state optimum and using the optimal transition equation to iterate backward in time, generating an optimal trajectory, (U_{t-1},X_{t-1}); then (4) econometrically estimating the current period decision rule by regressing U_t on X_t. Kolberg demonstrates his approach for a model of the Northern California anchovy fishery.

Rowse, J. 1995. "Computing Optimal Allocations for Discrete-Time Nonlinear Natural Resource Models," *Natural Resource Modeling*, 9:147–175.

Rowse no longer sees the need for first- or second-order approximations or current period decision rules, such as that derived by Kolberg. With the availability of significant computing power on PCs and workstations, one can use powerful and reasonably friendly nonlinear programming packages to solve for the optimal time path for harvest or extraction. Rowse touts the General Algebraic Modeling System (GAMS) and the optimization subroutine MINOS for solving dynamic allocation problems and presents the code for several problems analyzed in the resource economics literature.

Winston, W. L. and S. C. Albright. 1997. *Practical Management Science: Spreadsheet Modeling and Applications*, Duxbury Press, Belmont, California.

This is a text for advanced undergraduates or M.B.A. students with a familiarity with Microsoft Excel. The book covers a variety of models and methods including linear programming, network models, integer programming, nonlinear programming, goal programming, decision-tree models, inventory models, queueing models, simulation, and forecasting. There are lots of interesting case studies, and although the orientation is on management within a firm, the models and methods have obvious relevance for the management of natural resources.

B.3 The Economics of Fisheries

The are two classic articles on the economics of fishing, both written in the 1950s.

Gordon, H. S. 1954. "The Economic Theory of a Common Property Resource: The Fishery," *Journal of Political Economy*, 62:124–142.

In this paper Gordon lays out the static model of open access as a way of explaining why so many fisheries end up with too many (aging and decaying) vessels chasing too few fish.

Scott, A. D. 1955. "The Fishery: The Objective of Sole Ownership," *Journal of Political Economy*, 63:116–124.

If open access results in excessive effort (E_∞) and a reduction in social welfare, perhaps the optimal level of effort would be E_0, the level adopted by a sole owner with exclusive harvesting rights. The sole owner would set effort so as to maximize static rent, where the vertical difference between the revenue function and cost ray in Figure 3.3 is greatest. If fishery managers could limit the number of vessels and hours fished, they might be able to restrict effort in an open access fishery to E_0. Subsequent analysis in the 1960s and 1970s showed that if the management objective was present value maximization, E_0, when the discount rate was positive, would not be optimal. In 1955, however, Scott's prescriptions made eminent sense.

Smith, V. L. 1968. "Economics of Production from Natural Resources," *American Economic Review*, 58: 409–431.

Vernon Smith wrote two articles in the late 1960s that were the first to model the dynamics of a resource and the capital stock of the exploiting industry as a system. Different models (or cases) were developed to consider renewable or nonrenewable resources with or without stock or crowding externalities. This paper provided the theoretical basis for dynamic open-access models. A familiarity with differential equations and phase-plane analysis is appropriate before attempting this paper.

Plourde, C. G. 1970. "A Simple Model of Replenishable Natural Resource Exploitation," *American Economic Review*, 60:518–522.

A short, compact article using the maximum principle to solve for the rate of harvest which maximizes discounted utility when (1) utility only depends on harvest and (2) growth is logistic.

Burt, O. R. and R. G. Cummings. 1970. "Production and Investment in Natural Resource Industries," *American Economic Review*, 60:576–590.

This paper presents a discrete-time, finite-horizon model of harvest and investment in a natural resource industry. Though only using the method of Lagrange multipliers and differential calculus, this article is not for the algebraically or notationally faint of heart.

Clark, C. W. 1973. "The Economics of Overexploitation," *Science*, 181:630–634.

This paper examines the conditions that would induce the commercial extinction of a plant or animal.

Brown, G. B. Jr. 1974. "An Optimal Program for Managing Common Property Resources with Congestion Externalities," *Journal of Political Economy*, 82:163–174.

Brown examines how a landings tax and a tax on effort might be used to reflect user cost and (static) congestion externalities. Perhaps as a result of this paper, the fishing industry successfully lobbied for a prohibition on the use of landings taxes in the Fishery Management and Conservation Act of 1976.

Wilen, J. 1976. "Common Property Resources and the Dynamics of Overexploitation: The Case of the North Pacific Fur Seal," Department of Economics, Programme in Natural Resource Economics, Paper No. 3, The University of British Columbia, Vancouver.

This is perhaps the first empirical study of a dynamic open-access model based on the earlier work by Vernon Smith. The history of exploitation of the northern fur seal makes for fascinating reading. The seals winter along the California coast and then migrate almost 6,000 miles to breeding grounds on the Pribilof Islands. With the Alaska Purchase in 1867, the United States acquired the Pribilofs and granted exclusive harvest rights for a 20-year period on the islands to the Alaska Commercial Company. When the seals were migrating between breeding and wintering grounds, they were subject to open access, and pressure was put on U.S. officials by the Alaska Commercial Company to prevent Canadian vessels from taking seals in the Bering Sea. Gun-boat diplomacy by the United States and British intervention on behalf of Canada ultimately led to international arbitration. Wilen estimates a dynamic open-access model for different historical periods, checks for stability of the open access equilibrium, and for the period 1882–1900 plots the likely values for the seal population and vessel numbers in "phase space." (This paper needs to be published in a more accessible book of readings!)

Clark, C. W. 1985. *Bioeconomic Modelling and Fisheries Management*, John Wiley & Sons, New York.

In this text Clark takes a more detailed look into models of fishing including search and capture, processing and marketing, age-structured models, regulation, taxes and quotas, multispecies fisheries, fluctuations, and management under uncertainty. As always, Clark combines mathematical rigor with clear and insightful exposition.

Bjørndal, T. and J. M. Conrad. 1987. "The Dynamics of an Open Access Fishery," *Canadian Journal of Economics*, 20:74–85.

This article offers an empirical analysis of the open access forces leading to the decline, and ultimately a moratorium, in the North Sea herring fishery.

Conrad, J. M. 1995. "Bioeconomic Models of the Fishery," in D. W. Bromley (ed.), *The Handbook of Environmental Economics*, Blackwell, Cambridge, Massachusetts.

This is a survey article attempting to review the development of fishery economics, open access models, simple bioeconomic models of optimal fishing, and issues in fisheries management.

Grafton, R. Q. 1996. "Individual Transferable Quotas: Theory and Practice," *Reviews in Fish Biology and Fisheries*, 6:5–20.

This is a well-written paper for a general audience. Grafton first discusses the theory of ITQs and then describes the experience to date with ITQ programs in Canada, Iceland, Australia, and New Zealand. He attempts to determine the effect that ITQs have had on (1) economic efficiency, (2) employment and harvest shares, (3) compliance with management regulations, and (4) cost recovery, management costs, and distribution of resource rents between fishers and the government. The article contains a glossary of terms used by fisheries economists in discussing ITQs and a good set of references.

Homans, F. R. and J. E. Wilen. 1997. "A Model of Regulated Open Access Resource Use," *Journal of Environmental Economics and Management*, 32:1–21.

This paper presents a more plausible model of regulation, in which management authorities set a TAC according to a linear adaptive policy and fishers make decisions on fishing effort that determine season length. The TAC leads to large expenditures of effort during a compressed (shortened) season. The model is applied to the North Pacific halibut fishery.

B.4   The Economics of Forestry

Hyde, W. F. 1980. *Timber Supply, Land Allocation, and Economic Efficiency*, Johns Hopkins University Press, Baltimore.

This text was written at a time when there was a concern about the adequacy of private and public lands to supply sufficient timber to the U.S. economy. At the time, forest plans by the U.S. Forest Service were calling for management to meet "multiple objectives," including recreation, wildlife habitat, and watershed protection. In addition, wilderness groups were calling for an expansion of the system of national parks (like the creation of the North Cascades National Park), where the harvest of timber would be prohibited. The forest industry, and some members of the U.S. Congress, were concerned that the multiple use management doctrines and the expansion of the national park system would severely limit the land available for timber harvest and rotational forestry. Would a "timber famine" ensue? Hyde concludes that the efficient management of private and public lands currently devoted to rotational forestry should provide an adequate supply of timber in the future. In fact, more intensive silvicultural practices may lead to greater timber output from fewer hectares, further reducing the "perceived" conflict between timber supply, on the one hand, and multiple uses or additions to the inventory of wilderness, on the other.

Johansson, P.-O. and K.-G. Löfgren. 1985. *The Economics of Forestry and Natural Resources*, Basil Blackwell, Oxford, England.

Although the emphasis of this book is on the economics of forestry, it contains chapters on the theory of investment, benefit–cost rules for natural resources, and the economics of nonrenewable and renewable resources. The effects of different forest taxes, improved biotechnology, perfect and imperfect markets, and risk are examined in terms of the change in rotation length and other forest practices. There is an econometric analysis of the demand and supply of wood in Sweden.

Samuelson, P. A. 1976. "Economics of Forestry in an Evolving Society," *Economic Inquiry*, 14:466–492.

This is a classic. The Nobel Laureate and a founding father of modern (mathematical) economics surveys 125 years of writings by foresters and economists, warts (mistakes) and all. After posing and solving the infinite-rotation problem, and noting the potentially strong private incentive to invest the net revenue from timber in *other*, higher-yield investments, Samuelson considers the potential externalities and public services that forests might provide in a democratic, developed country. The paper was originally presented at a conference in 1974; that makes Professor Samuelson perceptive if not a prophet when he notes, "Ecologists know that soil erosion and atmospheric quality at one spot on the globe may be importantly affected by whether or not trees are being grown at places some distance away. To the degree this is so, the simple Faustmann calculus and the bouncings of futures contracts for plywood on the organized exchanges need to be altered in the interests of the public."

Hartman, R. 1976. "The Harvesting Decision When a Standing Forest Has Value," *Economic Inquiry*, 14:52–58.

From the same issue of *Economic Inquiry* that contains the Samuelson classic, Hartman extends the Faustmann model so that a stand of trees provides a continuous flow of amenity value that increases with the age of the stand. He derives a first-order condition that can be used to calculate the amenity-inclusive optimal rotation.

Deacon, R. T. 1985. "The Simple Analytics of Forest Economics," in R. T. Deacon and M. B. Johnson (eds.), *Forestlands Public and Private*, Ballinger, San Francisco.

A clear exposition of the Faustmann rotation, pitched at the intermediate level. This paper emphasizes the marginal value of waiting and the marginal cost of waiting and discusses the short-run and long-run comparative statics of timber supply.

Binkley, C. S. 1987. "When Is the Optimal Economic Rotation Longer Than the Rotation of Maximum Sustained Yield?" *Journal of Environmental Economics and Management*, 14:152–158.

This article establishes the condition under which the Faustmann rotation (T^*) may be longer than the rotation that maximizes mean annual increment (T_{MAI}). This might occur with a fast-growing species, for which the cost/price ratio (c/p) is relatively large. A sufficient condition for $T^* > T_{MAI}$ is for $1/T_{MAI} > \delta$. Using an exponential volume function, Binkley shows that this will be the case for the fast-growing pine *Pinus patula* on plantations in Tanzania.

Conrad, J. M. and D. Ludwig. 1994. "Forest Land Policy: The Optimal Stock of Old-Growth Forest," *Natural Resource Modeling*, 8:27–45.

This paper presents a continuous-time version of the old-growth forest model of Section 4.6. Although this paper uses the maximum principle, the stopping (optimal inventory) rule for X^* is the same.

B.5 The Economics of Nonrenewable Resources

There are two texts that provide a foundation for reading the now numerous articles on the economics of nonrenewable resources.

Fisher, A. C. 1981. *Resource and Environmental Economics*, Cambridge University Press, Cambridge, England.

This text is accessible to students with intermediate microeconomics and calculus. Chapters 2 and 4 are excellent introductions to models of optimal depletion, monopoly, uncertainty, exploration, and measures of resource scarcity.

Dasgupta, P. S. and G. M. Heal. 1979. *Economic Theory and Exhaustible Resources*, James Nisbet & Co. Ltd. and Cambridge University Press, Cambridge, England.

This is a graduate-level text which is broader in scope than the title might suggest. There are chapters on static allocation, externalities, intertemporal equilibrium, and renewable resources. These are followed by 10 chapters covering optimal depletion, production with a nonrenewable resource as an input, depletion and capital accumulation, intergenerational welfare, imperfect competition, taxation, uncertainty and information, and price dynamics. This is an extremely thorough and rigorous text.

Gray, L. C. 1914. "Rent under the Assumption of Exhaustibility," *Quarterly Journal of Economics*, 28:466–489.

Perhaps the first article to recognize an additional (user) cost to marginal extraction today. In the context of a simple arithmetic example, Gray showed that the present value of marginal net revenue (rent) must be the same in all periods with positive extraction.

Hotelling, H. 1931. "The Economics of Exhaustible Resources," *Journal of Political Economy*, 39:137–175.

This is the classic paper on nonrenewable resources. Hotelling examines price paths and extraction under competition, monopoly, and welfare maximization. Hotelling's use of the calculus of variations probably made this paper inaccessible to most of the economics profession at the time it was published. Hotelling illustrated the theory and mathematics with numerical examples and graphical analysis. In addition to the core sections on competition, monopoly, and welfare maximization, Hotelling considers discontinuous solutions, valuation of the mine under monopoly, the effects of cumulative production, severance taxes, and duopoly. This paper, along with his work on the economics of depreciation, duopoly, stability analysis, and the travel-cost method for estimating recreational demand, made Hotelling not only the father of resource economics, but one of the brightest minds in economics in the early twentieth century.

Devarajan, S. and A. C. Fisher. 1981. "Hotelling's 'Economics of Exhaustible Resources': Fifty Years Later," *Journal of Economic Literature*, 19:65–73.

This is a retrospective on Hotelling's 1931 paper (which was rediscovered by resource economists in the 1960s), in light of the considerable literature which sought to extend Hotelling's analysis to answer theoretical and policy questions raised by the energy "crisis" of the early and mid-1970s.

Barnett, H. J. and C. Morse. 1963. *Scarcity and Growth: The Economics of Natural Resource Availability*, Johns Hopkins University Press, Baltimore.

An influential study of the adequacy of natural resources and the prospects for continued economic growth in the post–World War II era. Barnett and Morse first consider whether physical measures (abundance), prices, or extraction costs might serve as an index of impending resource scarcity. They reject abundance measures as lacking an appropriate economic dimension and instead assemble relative price and unit cost indices for minerals, fossil fuels, and timber for the period 1870–1957. With the exception of timber, they did not observe any significant increase in real prices or average extraction costs. They conclude that although resource scarcity is ever present, it is a dynamic and "kaleidoscopic" condition, with markets, human ingenuity, and commodity substitution working to mitigate the scarcity of a particular resource.

Smith, V. K. 1980. "The Evaluation of Natural Resource Adequacy: Elusive Quest or Frontier of Economic Analysis?" *Land Economics*, 56:257–298.

Smith provides a nice review of Barnett and Morse and the economic research, based on more sophisticated theory and econometrics, which sought to reassess the adequacy of natural resources in the 1970s. Although reexamination provided continued support for Barnett and Morse's optimistic assessment, Smith notes some important caveats and inherent limitations in empirical economic analysis and calls for continued economic research.

Solow, R. M. 1974. "The Economics of Resources or the Resources of Economics," *American Economic Review*, 64(Proceedings):1–14.

This paper is based on the Richard T. Ely lecture given by Professor Solow at the American Economic Association meetings in December 1973. It is an erudite exposition of the role of nonrenewable resources in an economy and the role that markets might play in their optimal depletion, conservation, and exploration.

Review of Economic Studies. 1974. "Symposium on the Economics of Exhaustible Resources," 41.

This was a special issue containing papers by Robert Solow, Joseph Stiglitz, Milton Weinstein and Richard Zeckhauser, Claude Henry, and Partha Dasgupta and Geoffrey Heal.

Stiglitz, J. E. 1976. "Monopoly and the Rate of Extraction of Exhaustible Resources," *American Economic Review*, 66:655–661.

Stiglitz examines when a monopolist may or may not restrict the initial rate of extraction.

Pindyck, R. A. 1978. "The Optimal Exploration and Production of Nonrenewable Resources," *Journal of Political Economy*, 86:841–861.

This paper develops a deterministic model with two state variables ("proved" reserves and cumulative discoveries) in which competitive producers (or a monopolist) must simultaneously determine the levels of extraction and exploration. One possible outcome is a pattern of extraction and discovery which gives rise to a U-shaped price path. The appendix contains a numerical example in which the model is estimated and solved for extraction (10^6 barrels) and exploration (wells drilled) for the Permian region of Texas.

Pindyck, R. S. 1980. "Uncertainty and Natural Resource Markets," *Journal of Political Economy*, 88:1203–1225.

In this paper Professor Pindyck considers a model with continuous price and reserve uncertainty. With nonlinear reserve-dependent extraction costs, $C(R)$, with $C'(R) < 0$ and $C''(R) > 0$, fluctuations in reserves will raise expected (future) costs and there is an incentive to speed up the rate of production. Price would begin lower and rise more rapidly. The model is extended to include exploration which might be undertaken (a) to reduce uncertainty about the size of future reserves, and/or (b) to improve the allocation of future exploratory effort. The paper employs dynamic programming and Itô's Lemma.

Brown, G. M. and B. C. Field. 1978. "Implications of Alternative Measures of Natural Resource Scarcity," *Journal of Political Economy*, 88:229–243.

Brown and Field review various measures of resource scarcity and find commonly used measures, such as market price and average extraction cost, to be deficient. They propose resource rent as a preferred measure, but note the difficulty in obtaining the time-series data to estimate rent accurately. Marginal discovery costs are suggested as a useful proxy.

Arrow, K. J. and S. Chang. 1982. "Optimal Pricing, Use, and Exploration of Uncertain Natural Resource Stocks," *Journal of Environmental Economics and Management*, 9:1–10.

A model of depletion and exploration is developed in which the probability of discovering a field (mine) over a small increment of time (dt) depends on the size of the area explored. With constant exploration costs (per unit area explored) the model results in optimal exploration's being zero or at its maximum, depending on whether the sum of the unit cost of exploration plus user cost is greater than or less than the expected marginal increase in current value from exploration. This paper uses dynamic programming and a first-order Taylor approximation to the Bellman equation.

Devarajan, S. and A. C. Fisher. 1982. "Exploration and Scarcity," *Journal of Political Economy*, 90:1279–1290.

Resource rent (price less marginal extraction cost) was argued by Brown and Field to be the preferred measure of resource scarcity with marginal discovery cost as an empirically more tractable alternative. In a two-period model Devarajan and Fisher show that resource rent will be equal to marginal exploration costs when optimizing firms face a deterministic discovery process and may bound resource rent when discovery is uncertain.

Halvorsen, R. and T. R. Smith. 1984. "On Measuring Natural Resource Scarcity," *Journal of Political Economy*, 92:954–964.

Halvorsen and Smith note that many resource industries are vertically integrated and that this can further exacerbate the problem of measuring scarcity using rent at the time of extraction. With duality theory they show how to estimate econometrically the shadow price on a nonrenewable resource. An empirical study of Canadian mining shows that the shadow price for ore declined significantly from 1956 through 1974.

Farzin, Y. H. 1984. "The Effect of the Discount Rate on Depletion of Exhaustible Resources," *Journal of Political Economy*, 92:841–851.

Farzin shows that if the production cost of a substitute (backstop) depends on the cost of capital (thus, on the rate of discount), a decrease (increase) in the discount rate might cause the nonrenewable resource to be extracted more (less) rapidly. If a decrease in the discount rate lowers the "choke-off" price this will lower the initial price of the nonrenewable resource and may lead to more rapid depletion. If an increase in the discount rate raises the choke-off price, the initial price of the nonrenewable resource increases and will result in less rapid depletion. This result is opposite the "standard" result, in which the choke-off price was regarded as a constant.

Swierzbinski, J. E. and R. Mendelsohn. 1989. "Information and Exhaustible Resources: A Bayesian Analysis," *Journal of Environmental Economics and Management*, 16:193–208.

In a continuous-time model, in which information gathering allows a mine owner to update her estimate of the size of remaining reserves, Swierzbinski and Mendelsohn show that observed resource prices will be a random variable, even though the expected rate of change in price is consistent with the Hotelling Rule.

Cairns, R. D. 1990. "The Economics of Exploration for Nonrenewable Resources," *Journal of Economic Surveys*, 4:361–395.

This paper provides a detailed survey of the economics literature on the exploration for nonrenewable resources.

Livernois, J. 1992. "A Note on the Effect of Tax Brackets on Nonrenewable Resource Extraction," *Journal of Environmental Economics and Management*, 22:272–280.

This paper shows how progressive tax rates for a severance tax or a profits tax, when imposed on a firm extracting a nonrenewable resource, might lead to constant extraction rates over some interval of time.

Farzin, Y. H. 1995. "Technological Change and the Dynamics of Resource Scarcity Measures," *Journal of Environmental Economics and Management*, 29:105–120.

This paper examines the effect that technological change has on measures of resource scarcity (cost, price, and rent). Depending on the form of technological change, the three measures may move together or they may move inconsistently. The paper provides a theoretical basis for why the different measures may diverge empirically. Rent remains the preferred measure.

Olson L. J. and K. C. Knapp. 1997. "Exhaustible Resource Allocation in an Overlapping Generations Economy," *Journal of Environmental Economics and Management*, 32:277–292.

This paper reveals that overlapping generation (OLG) models can result in atypical behavior. In a finite-horizon model, the rate of extraction may increase and price may decrease over the entire horizon. In an infinite-horizon model, cycles in extraction and prices may occur.

Vincent, J. R., Panayotou, T., and J. M. Hartwick. 1997. "Resource Depletion and Sustainability in Small Open Economies," *Journal of Environmental Economics and Management*, 33:274–286.

A small (price-taking) country, extracting and exporting a nonrenewable resource, may need to invest resource rents in other forms of capital in order to sustain domestic consumption.

B.6   Stock Pollutants

The early literature on stock pollutants built upon the extensive literature dealing with optimal economic growth. Now, however, production or consumption gave rise to a waste flow which might accumulate as a stock pollutant. The first of these articles appeared in the early 1970s.

Keeler, E., Spence, A. M., and R. Zeckhauser. 1972. "The Optimal Control of Pollution," *Journal of Economic Theory*, 4:19–34.

Forster, B. 1972. "A Note on the Optimal Control of Pollution," *Journal of Economic Theory*, 5:537–539

Forster, B. 1972. "Optimal Consumption Planning in a Polluted Environment," *Swedish Journal of Economics*, 74:281–285.

Plourde, C. G. 1972. "A Model of Waste Accumulation and Disposal," *Canadian Journal of Economics*, 5:119–125.

Smith, V. L. 1972. "Dynamics of Waste Accumulation: Disposal versus Recycling," *Quarterly Journal of Economics*, 86:600–616.

D'Arge, R. C. and K. C. Kogiku. 1973. "Economic Growth and the Environment," *Review of Economic Studies*, 40:61–77.

Cropper, M. 1976. "Regulating Activities with Catastrophic Environmental Effects," *Journal of Environmental Economics and Management*, 3:1–15.

Forster, B. A. 1977. "On a One-State Variable Optimal Control Problem," in J. D. Pitchford and S. J. Turnovsky (eds.), *Applications of Control Theory to Economic Analysis*, North Holland, Amsterdam. pp. 35–56.

Conrad and Clark (1987): Chapter 4 has sections on residuals management, static externality, and dynamic externality. The latter section contains three models of a stock pollutant. (See B.0 for complete citation.)

Conrad, J. M., and L. J. Olson. 1992. "The Economics of a Stock Pollutant: Aldicarb on Long Island," *Environmental and Resource Economics*, 2:245–258.

This paper looks at an incident of groundwater contamination by the pesticide aldicarb, the likely time path for concentration following a moratorium on its use in 1979, and whether, given the New York State health standard, it would ever be optimal to use aldicarb again once the standard was reestablished.

Xepapadeas, A. P. 1992. "Environmental Policy Design and Dynamic Nonpoint-Source Pollution," *Journal of Environmental Economics and Management*, 23:22–39.

This paper looks at the role of dynamic taxes (charges) in keeping observed concentrations of a pollutant close to desired levels. This is an advanced paper, employing both deterministic and stochastic models.

Tahvonen, O. and J. Kuuluvainen. 1993. "Economic Growth, Pollution, and Renewable Resources," *Journal of Environmental Economics and Management*, 24:101–118.

This paper contains models in which a stock pollutant reduces human welfare directly and in which the stock pollutant might also adversely affect the growth of a renewable resource, which is a factor of production.

Falk, I. and R. Mendelsohn. 1993. "The Economics of Controlling Stock Pollutants: An Efficient Strategy for Greenhouse Gases," *Journal of Environmental Economics and Management*, 25:76–88.

This paper presents a model to control a stock pollutant wherein increasing marginal damage from an increasing pollution stock leads to higher abatement over time. An example of global warming is presented.

Wirl, F. 1994. "Pigouvian Taxation of Energy for Flow and Stock Externalities and Strategic, Noncompetitive Energy Pricing," *Journal of Environmental Economics and Management*, 26:1–18.

Suppose energy is produced and marketed by a price-making cartel which is subject to taxation by a consumer-oriented government. Further, suppose that the consumption of energy results in a flow externality (acid rain) and a stock externality (global warming). This paper explores the time paths for price and the energy tax which result from a differential game between the taxing government and the price-making cartel.

Karp, L. and J. Livernois. 1994. "Using Automatic Tax Changes to Control Pollution Emissions," *Journal of Environmental Economics and Management*, 27:38–48.

Suppose a regulator, although not knowing the cost of pollution abatement, imposes an emission tax on polluting firms, with the tax rate increasing if emissions continue to exceed a target. This paper looks at the welfare implications of such a tax, depending on whether firms behave strategically.

Kennedy, J.O.S. 1995. "Changes in Optimal Pollution Taxes as Population Increases," *Journal of Environmental Economics and Management*, 28:19–33.

In a two-period model, Kennedy examines the types of taxes that may be needed to compensate for immigration when pollution is "depletable" and when it is "undepletable."

Tahvonen, O. 1996. "Trade with Polluting Nonrenewable Resources," *Journal of Environmental Economics and Management*, 30:1–17.

This paper considers the rate of extraction and an excise tax on the consumption of a nonrenewable resource that generates waste flows which might accumulate as a stock pollutant. Extraction costs may depend on the rate of extraction and remaining reserves. The resource sector might be competitive or a price-making monopoly (cartel). The latter case results in a differential game. Time paths are derived for a numerical example.

Tahvonen, O. and S. Seppo. 1996. "Nonconvexities in Optimal Pollution Accumulation," *Journal of Environmental Economics and Management*, 31:160–177.

This paper shows how bounded damages or a nonmonotonic pollution decay function may result in multiple steady-state optima, thus changing the economic properties of optimal pollution control.

Harford, J. 1997. "Stock Pollution, Child-Bearing Externalities, and the Social Discount Rate," *Journal of Environmental Economics and Management*, 33:94–105.

A stock pollutant results from the production of a good used for consumption, childbearing, and capital bequests. Optimality in this model requires a pollution tax and a tax per child equal to the discounted present value of all the pollution taxes that the child and its descendants would pay.

Harford, J. 1998. "The Ultimate Externality," *American Economic Review*, 88:260–265.

Harford derives similar conclusions in a two-period (two-generation) model as in his multigeneration model (*Journal of Environmental Economics and Management* 1997). The math and exposition in this paper are clearer and cleaner.

B.7   Option Value and Risky Development

The literature on cost–benefit analysis is extensive, with practitioners in the social sciences and engineering. The following texts are useful references:

Mishan, E. J. 1976. *Cost–Benefit Analysis*, Praeger, New York.

Bussey, L. E. 1978. *The Economic Analysis of Industrial Projects*, Prentice-Hall, Englewood Cliffs, New Jersey.

Gittinger, J. P. 1982. *Economic Analysis of Agricultural Projects*, Johns Hopkins University Press, Baltimore.

Park, C. S. 1993. *Contemporary Engineering Economics*, Addison-Wesley, Reading, Massachusetts.

Jackson, P. L. 1997. "Fixing Up the Rate of Return Approach: The Rate of Return on Invested Capital," Technical Report No. 1179, School of Operations Research and Industrial Engineering, Cornell University, Ithaca, New York, 14853-3801.

This report contains a nice exposition on the return on invested capital (the RIC).

Beginning with the classic article by Burton Weisbrod (see the citation in Section B.1), there is now an extensive, contentious, and confusing literature on option value and quasi-option value. The profession finally seems to be moving toward a consensus that option value arises when a decision has uncertain future net benefits and is irreversible or costly to reverse. Stochastic dynamic programming is used to value the options afforded by both financial "derivatives" and "real" investments. The following citations trace this evolution:

Long M. F. 1967. "Collective Consumption Services of Individual Consumption Goods: Comment," *Quarterly Journal of Economics*, 81:351–352.

Lindsay, C. M. 1969. "Option Demand and Consumer Surplus," *Quarterly Journal of Economics*, 83:344–346.

Byerlee, D. R. 1971. "Option Demand and Consumer Surplus: Comment," *Quarterly Journal of Economics*, 85:523–527.

Cicchetti, C. J. and A. M. Freeman III. 1971. "Option Demand and Consumer Surplus: Further Comment," *Quarterly Journal of Economics*, 85:528–539.

Schmalensee, R. 1972. "Option Demand and Consumer's Surplus: Valuing Price Changes under Uncertainty," *American Economic Review*, 62:813–824.

Arrow, K. J. and A. C. Fisher. 1974. "Environmental Preservation, Uncertainty, and Irreversibility," *Quarterly Journal of Economics*, 88:312–319.

Henry, C. 1974. "Option Values in the Economics of Irreplaceable Assets," *Review of Economic Studies* (Symposium on the Economics of Exhaustible Resources), 41:89–104.

Henry, C. 1974. "Investment Decisions under Uncertainty: The Irreversibility Effect," *American Economic Review*, 64:1006–1012.

Conrad, J. M. 1980. "Quasi-Option Value and the Expected Value of Information," *Quarterly Journal of Economics*, 94:813–820.

Graham, D. A. 1981. "Cost–Benefit Analysis under Uncertainty," *American Economic Review*, 71:715–725.

Bishop, R. C. 1982. "Option Value: An Exposition and Extension," *Land Economics*, 58:1–15.

Miller, J. R. and F. Lad. 1984. "Flexibility, Learning, and Irreversibility in Environmental Decisions: A Bayesian Approach," *Journal of Environmental Economics and Management*, 11:161–172.

Fisher, A. C. and W. M. Hanemann. 1987. "Quasi-Option Value: Some Misconceptions Dispelled," *Journal of Environmental Economics and Management*, 14:183–190.

Hanemann, W. M. 1989. "Information and the Concept of Option Value," *Journal of Environmental Economics and Management*, 16:23–37.

Cochrane, H. and H. Cutler. 1990. "The Economics of Sequential Choice Applied to Quasi-Option Value," *Journal of Environmental Economics and Management*, 18:238–246.

Chavas, J.-P. and D. Mullarkey. 1997. "On the Valuation of Risk in Welfare Analysis," Working Paper, Department of Agricultural and Applied Economics, University of Wisconsin, Madison.

Coggins, J. S. and C. A. Ramezani. 1998. "An Arbitrage-Free Approach to Quasi-Option Value," *Journal of Environmental Economics and Management*, 35:103–125.

Merton, R. C. 1998. "Applications of Option-Pricing Theory: Twenty-Five Years Later," *American Economic Review*, 88:323–349.

> This is the lecture Robert C. Merton delivered in Stockholm, Sweden, on December 9, 1997, when he received the Nobel Prize in Economic Science. Section II contains a nice discussion of the application of option-pricing to real investments.

Stopping-rule models are concerned with the optimal timing of a binary (0,1) variable, which may represent the decision to initiate or terminate an investment or project. Stopping-rule models often give rise to "trigger values." These models have a potentially rich set of applications in resource and environmental economics. The following references provide an introduction and a guide to some of the applications to date.

Brennen, M. J. and E. S. Schwartz. 1985. "Evaluating Natural Resource Investments," *Journal of Business*, 58:135–157.

McDonald, R. and D. Siegal. 1986. "The Value of Waiting to Invest," *Quarterly Journal of Economics*, 101:707–728.

Paddock, J. L., D. R. Siegel, and J. L. Smith. 1988. "Option Valuation of Claims on Real Assets: The Case of Offshore Petroleum Leases," *Quarterly Journal of Economics*, 103:479–508.

Dixit, A. K. 1989. "Entry and Exit Decisions under Uncertainty," *Journal of Political Economy*, 97:620–638.

Clarke, H. R. and W. J. Reed. 1990. "Applications of Optimal Stopping Rules in Resource Economics." *Economic Record*, 66:254–265.

Zinkham, F. C. 1991. "Option-Pricing and Timberand's Land-Use Conversion Option," *Land Economics*, 67:317–325.

Reed, W. J. 1993. "The Decision to Conserve or Harvest Old-Growth Forest," *Ecological Economics*, 8:45–69.

Dixit, A. K. and R. S. Pindyck. 1994. *Investment under Uncertainty*, Princeton University Press, Princeton, New Jersey.

Conrad, J. M. 1997. "Global Warming: When to Bite the Bullet," *Land Economics*, 73:164–173.

Conrad, J. M. 1997. "On the Option Value of Old-Growth Forest," *Ecological Economics*, 22:97–102.

B.8 Sustainable Development

Two edited volumes and a special issue of *Land Economics* provide a nice set of articles on the economics of sustainability.

Costanza, R. (ed.). 1991. *Ecological Economics: The Science and Management of Sustainability*, Columbia University Press, New York.

Bromley, D. W. (ed.). 1995. *Handbook of Environmental Economics*, Blackwell Publishers, Cambridge, Massachusetts.

Howarth, R. (ed.). 1997. "Special Issue: Defining Sustainability," *Land Economics*, 73 (November).

Within the special issue of *Land Economics*, see the article by Graciela Chichilnisky, "What Is Sustainable Development?" for an analysis of sustainability in a renewable-resource economy.

The concept of coevolution was developed in a series of articles by Richard Norgaard.

Norgaard, R. B. 1985. "Environmental Economics: An Evolutionary Critique and a Plea for Pluralism," *Journal of Environmental Economics and Management*, 12:382–394.

Norgaard, R. B. and J. A. Dixon. 1986. "Pluralistic Project Design: An Argument for Combining Economic and Coevolutionary Methodologies," *Policy Sciences* 19:297–317.

Norgaard, R. B. 1988. "Sustainable Development: A Coevolutionary View," *Futures* (December):606–620.

Norgaard, R. B. 1989. "The Case for Methodological Pluralism," *Ecological Economics*, 1:37–57.

Norgaard, R. B. 1993. "The Coevolution of Economic and Environmental Systems and the Emergence of Unsustainability," in R. W. England (ed.), *Evolutionary Concepts in Contemporary Economics*, University of Michigan Press, Ann Arbor.

Additional articles of interest include the following:

Howarth, R. B. and R. B. Norgaard, 1990. "Intergenerational Resource Rights, Efficiency, and Social Optimality," *Land Economics*, 66:1–11.

Conrad, J. M. and G. Salas. 1993. "Economic Strategies for Coevolution: Timber and Butterflies in Mexico," *Land Economics*, 69:404–415.

Brander, J. A. and M. S. Taylor. 1998. "The Simple Economics of Easter Island: A Ricardo–Malthus Model of Renewable Resource Use," *American Economic Review*, 88:119–138.

Index